Evolving Instruction

Evolving Instruction

Eugene E. Haddan

Eastern Michigan University

The Macmillan Company

Collier-Macmillan Limited, London

To my wife, Lynn

Preface

Schools and departments of education throughout the United States have been founded on the premise and perpetuated in the hope that the ability to teach can be taught. They have assumed that those who might be poor teachers even despite excellence in their subjects can become better teachers via courses, seminars, and practicums in education. Even those who fortunately possess a certain natural talent for teaching have been subjected to the routines of teacher preparation, with the expectation that they, too, may profit from the formal instruction provided.

To question the need for teacher preparation in anything but subject matter is to imply that the possession of substantive knowledge suffices for sharing it. The lay public, students preparing to teach, and even college and university staff members outside the field of education have hacked away incessantly at the validity of those assumptions implicit in the continued existence of the professional study of education. The attacks have been successfully ignored, repulsed, or derided by those responsible for this professional study. Occasionally, however, some within the ranks have wondered whether teacher preparation is to remain unchanged and unchangeable indefinitely in a kind of limbo, camping on the borderlands of a quasi-scientific realm. Some with a theoretical bent have opined that there may be merit in the suggestion that art, not science, is the proper province for the nurture of teachers.

This opinion gathers strength from the complex-variable argument that has plagued many valiant efforts to establish a body of valid information and a statement of principles of a science of teaching. The argument runs something like this: The processes, activities, or behaviors that characterize human beings are not simple single variables, but are exceedingly complex and cannot be isolated and separately analyzed. Even as they are being studied they change, and their relationships with other factors also shift. Therefore very little can be accomplished by studying them systematically. For example, a new teacher, a failing mark, or an athletic victory may greatly alter the attitudes and motivations of those involved and produce a marked change in teacher behavior.

Those who advocate teaching as an art suggest that there may be an incompatibility between art and science that itself erects an insurmountable barrier between teaching and a scientific approach to its principles. When the emphasis is on teaching as an art, then the function of education may ultimately become one of encouraging the emergence not only of aesthetic appreciations, but also of expressions of developing selfhood in the pupils. The approach would promote abilities to respond to cues provided both by the subject matter and by interactions between it and personality factors. Such combinations of stimulus and response patterns, according to those who emphasize the art of teaching, do not tend to recur; hence teaching must necessarily be a creative effort. Desirable characteristics of instruction are demonstrated by means of brief descriptions of classroom happenings, such as those furnished by Highet (1950) and others, and more systematically, by time-sampling techniques, perhaps similar to the interaction analysis developed by Flanders (1960).*

All this is plausible enough, and may carry an element of truth. But we should make certain that it is not an excuse, an evasion to escape the rigors of more detailed analysis. Teaching may yet reside comfortably within the domain of science. If so, it behooves education to explore more carefully the known facilitating conditions and to posit others already suggested by integrating earlier investigations. With all the many storms that the problem of teaching instructional procedures has weathered, there remains the

---

* To use time sampling, one merely records what is occurring in a classroom at regular intervals, say, every three seconds. To facilitate the recording, behaviors are assigned to categories, such as questions and answers, and are then represented by symbols that may be easily recorded.

nagging suspicion that teaching is somehow related to learning. Still, many who would readily admit to such connections begin a strategic withdrawal when theories of teaching are mentioned. Theories require a bridging of an apparent gap between generalities and practice. *Principles of learning,* suggesting specific applications in teaching, are acceptable, however. But those who urge the use of learning-theory contributions to teaching are divided on whether learning theories ought to be accepted as basic to theories of instruction or ought to serve as suggestive parallels. The feeling that the twain can never meet arises from the paradox that whereas teaching deals with observable variables, learning is concerned with an inferred process or with products of that process.

This book makes no attempt to establish a theory of teaching, or instruction. Instead, it provides selected descriptions of some notable attempts to improve instruction, which may all in good time be built into a theory of teaching. It would not be accurate to call it a book about a theory of teaching, for, as Gage (1963) has pointed out, teaching embraces attributes too numerous to be encompassed at the present time by a single theory or even by a single family of theories. And although there is some occasional analysis here, a description of this book as an analysis of instruction would hardly be adequate. It is intended as a source book, describing various theoretical approaches and innovative practices. As has been the case with so many other books, this one has arisen from a perceived need. When the author first taught a course in principles of teaching, he began a search for a one-volume textbook that would provide information about most of the major systematic attempts to improve instruction. There was no book that met the requirements, so a cumulative folder proliferated into the materials found in this book. The stimulating exchange of ideas among students at Eastern Michigan University gave impetus to the development of this book. The encouragement of colleagues sustained the author in his strivings. The meticulous scanning of William Clark Trow made possible the smoothing out of rough edges. A quite difficult deciphering task was accomplished by Georgette Libby, who diligently typed the manuscript.

E. E. H.

Ypsilanti

Contents

5 Ordering Knowledge

6 Classification of Pupils and Teachers for Effective Instruction

7 The Self and Teaching

8 Teaching as an Art   199

9 Technology and Teaching   223

10 Systems and Simulations   268

11 Some Forward Looks in Education   285

1

The Need for a Theory of Teaching

> The most outstanding men to have studied learning
> and instruction have . . . combined in proper propor-
> tions ways of twentieth-century empiricism with old-
> fashioned habits of induction and conceptualization.
>
> M. C. WITTROCK (1967)

For as long as there have been teachers to teach and pupils to learn, there have been differences in instructional methods. Yet research and theory making has been largely based on learning rather than on teaching. This in spite of the fact that teaching addresses itself to a series of acts or behaviors that are actually observable, whereas learning must be inferred. Theories have been developed around learning, as a process, rather than around teaching, as behavior. The hints and helps that were intended to aid have been those that have survived the pragmatic tests of time—if they seemed to work, they were retained; if not, they were discarded. However, even the most useful generalities have not made teachers feel that the improvements achieved over the centuries have been particularly valuable. Subject-matter experts in particular, tradition-ally place knowledge of content well above method in the value hierarchy, and some have asserted that the contribution of educational training is little more than that of helping teachers acquire a bedside manner. "The great debate" of the fifties, ably reported by C. Winfield Scott and others, would seem to conclude that teacher education has so little to offer that it cannot be justified. And in his *Focus on Change*, J. Lloyd Trump (1966) adds a note for the future, insisting that teachers, as the products of changing systems and as components in changing systems, must be provided with certain built-in provisions for adapting to change. Schools of education can hardly point with pride to their products, as representatives of what teacher training might well be expected to produce.

SIGNS OF NEED

One source of evidence for a need for theories of teaching is found in the absence of published material concerned with these theories.* It may be objected that a scarcity of writings about teaching theories is hardly sufficient evidence that a need for such theories exists. The objection is valid, of course, but when theories are so likely to play a vital role in the development of a strategic pursuit, then their absence is at least one indication that a need has not been met.

If there is a lack of guidelines for applications derived from basic principles and broad generalizations, then the need certainly does exist. If the empirical study of teaching is not to be carried out in a hit-or-miss fashion, then theories of teaching must be established upon the implications of which teachers might act. It is Gage's position that though some implications for teaching have been drawn from theories of learning, these theories have not been adequate for the development of theories of teaching. Students complain that they have learned about learning and about learners, but they have not learned much about teaching. When these students become teachers, the need becomes strikingly evident to their colleagues, supervisors, and principals. School systems sometimes try to fill in some of the gaps seen in beginning

---

* The following sources provide such information as has been assembled: *The Psychological Abstracts; The Annual Review of Psychology; The American Educational Research Association Handbook of Research on Teaching* (1963); *The National Society for the Study of Education* (1964); *The Educational Research Information Center* (ERIC); *Thesaurus of Educational Terms—A Key to the Retrieval of Educational Research Information;* and *The Educational Products Information Exchange* (EPIE)—a plan to relate instructional materials to specific instructional settings. These available sources report data, but they provide little on theory.

teachers by providing pamphlets and opportunities for improvement in discussion groups and so on. The applications of educational psychology may be so vaguely interpreted that teachers are furnished with booklets such as one available to Detroit teachers, *How to Make Your Lions Love You* (1956). The American Educational Research Association publishes a series of booklets, with such titles as *Controlling Classroom Misbehavior* (1965). How-to-do-it books will be in evidence to the extent that teachers have not been (or feel they have not been) taught workable principles to guide their teaching endeavors; they need the recipes that such books provide.

THE TEACHER'S NEED FOR THEORIES

Teachers, as well as teaching theorists, need theories. They ought not to remain content with a psychology of education that leaves them to infer from learning principles what they need to know and do. Ideal theories of teaching would state explicitly how teachers behave, or should behave, under what conditions; why they behave as they do; and what effects their behaviors have on learners. But the detailed statements required by such theories would be quite numerous, though the theories themselves might be quite compact.

N. L. Gage (1963, p. 134) writes of two kinds of theory on teaching. The first one explains why teachers behave as they do in teaching: the *teacher's behavior* is treated as something to be modified. The second kind of theory explains how the behavior of the teacher can influence the learning of the pupil: the *pupil's behavior* is treated as something to be modified. Gage suggests that theories may be used to increase understanding, prediction, and control. He cautions, however, that mere ability to predict an outcome does not imply that the behavior is understood or controlled. Predictions might be based upon correlations that do not explain how the factors are related. When two variables tend to move together consistantly, one is not necessarily the cause of the other, nor do they have any necessary connection. Still, theory is concerned with understanding. Research on teaching should be aimed at building theories that serve as *ends* and should be focused upon behaviors of teachers. Theories that serve as *means* are also needed, so that researchers may use them for facilitating more orderly thinking.

The strength in the old-fashioned formal pedagogy lay in its systematic directives (often in the form of manuals, or cookbooks of teaching) for improving teaching proficiency. Its weaknesses lay in its inflexibility, its inability to meet the demands of broader application, so as to transfer its prescriptions to other situations. The need for the discovery of principles, or of a theory or family of theories of teaching, becomes ever more obvious in an age of rapid change. Many teachers now question the application of so-called substantive knowledge (the well-accepted body of information that has long been taught as content), and they even doubt that a need exists for it. Inability to instruct adequately is a serious weakness in a world that demands an ever-widening range of ability to transfer what has been learned. Adequate instruction must be developed from theoretical bases that were nonexistent when the earlier pedagogues made their pronouncements. Theory refers to an ordering of the phenomena involved in teaching in a systematic way. It is no longer satisfactory to seek facts empirically on suspicion, not knowing where they are, why they might be there, or how to interpret them when found. Instead. they must be deducible from some pattern of interrelationships, in this case the ordering of the phenomena involved in teaching in a systematic way. As Schueler and Lesser wrote in 1967:

> Viewed as the fulfillment of pedagogic goals, teaching must have recognized purposes, partially at least, of the teacher's choosing. He must fashion and guide learning activities appropriate to these purposes, and evaluate the degree of fulfillment.
> A sound command of the range of means possible for reaching desired ends is required, as well as the ability to choose among them, carry them out, and assess their success. (p. 8)

Educators may readily agree with these self-evident statements, yet how frequently are teachers unable to utilize their intent!

TEACHING IS MULTIFACETED

Perhaps the theorists in education are at fault in not establishing a unified theory or any really definable body of principles for teaching. Or, as is sometimes suggested, the term *teaching* may be misleading. If it is too generic, embracing far too extensive a domain of acts by the classroom manager, perhaps the search ought to be narrowed so that a class of more specific acts is sought. It is possible to demonstrate what is meant by *teaching* when it is confined to behaviors exhibited by instructors in classrooms. If it is observed on a sufficient number of occasions, certain evidence of generality may be noted. One is that teaching is not like learning—a series of mental processes. *Classroom teaching* always refers to something that a teacher does to influence learning. He may simply impart information that the learners do not possess. Or, to develop a skill, he may act in ways that others may imitate. He may bring persuasion to bear, spotlighting a particular point of view. Or, he may merely point to sources of information. He may also teach a great deal nonverbally. (Ignoring some behaviors and attending to others; using gestures; remaining silent when a request is made; and the like are examples of nonverbal behavior.) A teacher may require learners to act, so that as they act, they learn, develop further predispositions to learn, and acquire the tools for learning. The teacher will also impose limitations, or obtain common agreement, on the conditions under which the various learnings are to be carried out.

A machine or other device may teach, though it is not ordinarily called a *teacher*. (Some are called *autotutorial devices*.) The device may be referred to as a *teaching aid*, or as an *agent of learning*, which augments teaching. If self-instruction is considered an act of teaching, it may be difficult to determine, and probably not necessary to ascertain, when learning begins and teaching leaves off. Motivation surely has as one of its many roots an origin in *self*-instruction. If it is a desirable aim of teaching to help learners become motivated by intrinsic factors (as well as by extrinsic ones), then self-instruction must be involved. If teaching can be considered only as a process lying at one pole of a continuum with learning at its opposite pole, then theoretical considerations are likely to become burdened and beclouded with unfruitful arguments. Teaching as an externally imposed influence on perceptual inputs may sometimes be so closely associated with teaching as a self-directed way of learning, that important variables may be confounded. At least one facet of teaching, however, may become a focal point for discussion, experimentation, and theory building—the acts of a person other than the learner that induce learning, the stimulus situation provided to induce the desired response. The independent variables must be more clearly defined than heretofore.

WHAT IS THE INDEPENDENT VARIABLE?

General theories of behavior may encompass not only learning, but teaching, which itself is observable behavior. If, however, teaching is treated under a general behavior theory, then it is the observed response —a dependent variable, a function of something else. This viewpoint of teaching may have been responsible for the dearth of reports on theories of teaching. Gage (1964) thinks that it is and suggests that a more fruitful approach is to place the behavior of teachers in the position of *independent* variables, that is, of influencing factors, so that changes in teacher behaviors are seen as producing changes in pupil responses.

According to Ausubel (1967), the teaching theorist in effect uses not only structure and student behavior but also teacher inputs to predict the behavior of the student. However, this may give rise to considerable confusion for the theorist. If teacher inputs are viewed as independent variables, and if student behaviors are seen as dependent variables, the viewing of student behaviors as predictors of other student responses means that dependent variables may also be used to modify other dependent variables.

The Handbook of Research on Teaching (1963) attempted to erect a conceptual framework based on "central (independent) variables," referring to behaviors or characteristics of teachers. Central variables were categorized as (1) teaching methods, (2) instruments and media of teaching, and (3) the teacher's personality and characteristics. However, other variables related to these three, such as social interactions in the classroom and the social background of teaching, have been frequently researched. (Grade level, for example, may reflect the psychological and social maturity of learners, and may therefore affect the objectives and procedures used in teaching. Similarly, subject matter is expected to influence teaching-learning behaviors.)

Feedback has become a popular subject for discussion, but only infrequently has use been made of what appears to be its great promise in teaching. Teachers receive feedback from pupils via tests, oral responses, and various performances (some nonverbal), but to increase teaching effectiveness, the teacher is likely to need an additional kind of feedback, one that reflects *immediately* the effects his teaching has had upon pupils, that indicates without delay the reaction of each student. This kind of feedback is probably necessary in developing a theory of teaching.

The teacher's acts may be called *independent variables* when they affect the pupil's behaviors. These acts are not necessarily the only independent variables, however. As has been stated, pupils themselves may produce behaviors that influence the behaviors of other pupils and of the teacher. Pupil behaviors may then be seen as independent variables, producing change. Thus, the pattern of independent and dependent variables becomes quite complex. If useful teaching theories are to be developed, they will be likely to be derived from observed acts and the consequences of specific acts, not merely from observations of the generalized teacher acting in the presence of the generalized pupil. But here, the personality characteristics of an individual may have tended to obscure some of the necessary generalizations that must be found if theories of teaching are to be built.

It is now generally known what kinds of teachers get along best with most children, adapt well in community functions, work cooperatively with colleagues, and perhaps even share political loads—all important adjuncts to good teaching. But they are not the considerations that apply most *directly* to the ability to stimulate and sustain learning. The teacher is not influencing learning so directly by exercising his community functions, for example, as he is when he tells, questions, and corrects pupils.

Teaching may become increasingly like learning. When the specific behaviors of a classroom teacher are examined closely, the question arises as to how much of a directive function there should be in furthering learning. For example, where do ordering, requesting, cueing, prompting, or hinting come in? How much should be provided? That is, where does teaching leave off in pursuing the problem and where does learning begin? How interrogative should questions be? Questions may be posed so that they are actually statements, or at least hints. A restatement of the pupil's response may be subtly altered to inject the teacher's instruction. The complex variable continues to remain complex.

ARE THE RELEVANT FACTORS TO BE FOUND IN LEARNING, IN TEACHING, OR IN TEACHING-LEARNING?

We have observed that a knowledge of learning theory provides an inadequate base for teaching theory. Scandura (1966) pointed up some difficulties inhering in the view that a theory of *teaching* can be derived from principles determined in a *learning* laboratory. It is difficult to be certain just where the laboratory findings ought to be applied within an educational setting. It is doubtful, however, if a study of teaching alone is adequate. Though a functional analysis of teaching does lead to improving the efficiency of one kind of learning (the kind that can be shaped overtly), still the technique called *shaping* has not been adequately specified for another kind of learning—that of learning symbolic materials. It may be that the necessary techniques will emerge. It becomes increasingly evident that both kinds of learning are necessary. Many teaching-learning situations will eventually be analyzed as systems, in which each part and process is closely related to the functioning of every other part and process. Man himself is a system, and one can erect theories about the functioning of his various subsystems.

SYSTEM DEVELOPMENT IN EDUCATION

A system operation is characterized by mutual reinforcing and interacting processes and their consequences. Chapter 10 of this book deals more fully with systems in education, but at this point they will be briefly described as a convenient way to treat teaching-learning. Task description, task analysis, and job design, carried out in detail, are procedures borrowed from systems engineering, and may be very useful in education. The purposes of a system ought to be explicitly stated (e.g., the objectives of education), and the design of its operating parts should be carefully planned—humans and machines must have their assigned functions carefully researched and designated. Studied selection of job aids, personnel, types of training, and means of evaluation will not then be on a catch-as-catch-can basis. There will be an emphasis on careful planning before the system goes into operation, and on self-regulation and modification while it operates. Self-modification will be instituted early, as need is fed back, and the system will have built into it provisions for continuous self-modification. How well does each person, each part, perform the assigned task and how well does this performance fit into the total functioning of the system? Innovative practices, such as team teaching, are already employing some ideas from systems advantageously, but system development is not tied to any particular method. An example of a systems approach is provided by project ARISTOTLE. This Annual Review and Information Symposium on the Technology of Training, Learning and Education first suggests that the *real* problem be defined; then the many potential solutions should be examined, and one of them selected; finally, the results ought to be measured and the approach modified as many times as necessary to solve the problem. A series of eight steps is considered in carrying out these three general procedures with special reference to personnel training.

1. *Need.* The statement of need should be a report of weaknesses, or failures, of the product in competition with rivals and so on. For example, if better engineering skill is desired, is the need for education or for training, and for what kind of

skill? What sort of people will be used and for what skill areas? And what is the judgment of the people who are at present active in the areas being studied? At this point questions as to how best to meet the need should not be raised, whether of personnel selection or training program. Statements of need tend to be realistic, not based on assumptions so much as on verified facts.

2. *Objectives.* Defining the objectives of the operation or system is an important step, in that all other steps are aimed at building a learning system that will help the learner or trainee to meet these objectives. The question is, what must the learner be able to do or say after he has completed the learning experience? (Because a discussion of writing objectives that are behaviorally defined is included elsewhere in this book, this process of definition will not be detailed at this point.)

3. *Constraints.* The limitations or difficulties expected in making changes or attaining objectives must be listed to facilitate selecting alternatives. Such constraints are identified, then ranked according to their severity and effect on the system design. Facts should not be confused with assumptions; preferred or pet solutions should not result in the listing of unwarranted limitations; and student capabilities should be accurately defined, so that the system will work with that group of learners.

4. *Alternatives.* The alternatives are the potential solutions. The technique of brainstorming is often used for suggesting all possible solutions. It is better if a number of groups participate, and if the atmosphere is one of freedom and of at least temporary acceptance of all suggestions.

5. *Selection.* The best potential solution is presumably selected. First, standards of judgment are set up. Each solution that might be selected is then

rated according to how well it meets the criteria. Solutions might be rated plus if of a high order, zero if only medium, and minus if considered poor. However, the final selection is not made merely on the basis of the solution with the highest score. Objectivity is tempered with common sense—that is, weighing any combination of interrelationships of factors that might have a bearing on the solution.

6. *Implementation.* In the implementation phase, the solution that has been finally selected is tried out in actual practice and preferably over a considerable period of time, so that it is tested fairly.

7. *Evaluation.* Measures are used to evaluate the achievement of the stated objectives, with minimal subjectivity. For example, to say simply, "It seemed to go well with the students," or, "They enjoyed the experience," is too subjective to have much evaluative significance.

8. *Modification.* Because only on rare occasions are all the objectives fully met, the evaluation of the first iteration or first time through will probably indicate that revision is necessary. The first iteration is carefully studied to determine why and how the objectives were not accomplished. Poor design may have been a cause for failure to meet some objectives, or perhaps pressures and changes outside the system may have arisen, making it necessary that the objectives be changed.

Lehmann (1968), in describing the systems approach as applied in ARISTOTLE, says

These are the simple steps of the systems approach. This approach is not the answer to the problem, but it does represent an orderly, scientific way of finding the answer. As was stated at the outset, this process is not new, it is merely the standard logical scientific approach to problem solving. (p. 148)

Thus far, some relatively rude beginnings, in the form of a task description, have posed problems of such magnitude as to stagger the imagination. For example, the cataloguing of only the reinforcement histories of pupils has proved to be an almost insurmountable task. Yet for effective teaching-learning, a necessary adjunct is the availability of an information bank listing these and other details of individual differences. Beyond this, much more is needed, to deal with what Scandura calls "structural relationships between previously acquired knowledge and to-be-learned meaningful material" (p. 142). Any theory of instruction must not be thrown upon the uncertain caprices of procedures established via the basing of inference upon inference.

Even the technologies that might form the bases of subject matter from which to build theories of instruction have themselves been established upon poorly defined bases. For example, references to task analysis and the shaping of behavior (a step-by-step training process) provide illustrations of bases that have not been sufficiently established yet to serve as foundations for theories of instruction. Sequencing and timing, two critical problem areas in teaching, have benefited only a little from what research has revealed.

Distinguishing between grain and chaff is still a knotty problem. An instructional theory might assume that there is no necessity to understand and recognize *all* factors found in the teaching situation that are important to learning.

According to Scandura:

The teaching theorist's foremost problem is not so much how to determine how basic learning principles fit into his theory as it is to integrate precisely those factors with which the learning theorist has not been concerned. He need not be concerned with *how* learning takes place at each stage in the learning sequence—only with *what* learning did take place. The responsibility of the teaching theorist rests largely with being able to predict performance and learning, given structure, stimulus sequence, and student feedback. (p. 143)

THE DEVELOPER OF TEACHING THEORIES: PSYCHOLOGIST? ENGINEER?

Traditionally, the philosopher, then the psychologist, have occupied seats of authority in building educational theories. Many psychologists are still carefully sifting the evidence of the research deluge, or synthesizing accepted concepts in order to erect a logical and a psychological structure upon which teaching may be based. However, some vigorous, new footsteps are being heard in education's hallowed halls. Scandura (1966) contrasts teaching as a technology, based on a science of *learning* and as "technology based on a yet-to-be-discovered theory of *teaching*" (p. 139). In both cases (that of the learning basis and that of the teaching basis), teaching technology is expected to be related to a broad theoretical position. By calling teaching a technology, there is the implication, according to Trow (1963) of

> continuing changes in educational procedures growing out of applied scientific research at the points where theory and practice meet, and resulting in increasing precision in the control of environmental factors through the coordinated action of personnel and instructional media in a man-machine system in the interest of more effective learning. (p. 170)

Technology is this much or it is nothing.

Carpenter and Haddan (1964) sounded the warning that if educators await the development of hardwares and softwares to indicate new directions in instruction, then the influence of the engineer will increase as the influence of the psychologist wanes. Meaning is given to this pronouncement by H. A. Bern (1967), who presented the thesis that ". . . in the heart of the metaphor 'educational engineering' lies a view of a new universe of education now taking shape" (p. 230). Education will need tools that are not presently within its limit of understanding or imagination, but that can be developed. Bern suggested a two-step program: (1) surveying and analyzing areas (largely military and industrial) wherein education and engineering have already effected some cross-fertilization; and (2) developing programs leading to professional degrees in *educational engineering*.

Woodruff and Froyen (1967) spoke of the probability of the means shaping the ends, if education continues merely to find uses for new equipment designed by noneducators. The issue seems clear—the new breed of educationist must not only participate in the shaping of new technologies, he must be sufficiently well versed in the principles of engineering so that he may engage in a meaningful two-way communication.

WILL THERE BE TEACHING LABORATORIES?

The professional education of teachers has been derived almost entirely from the lore of the past, from philosophical and psychological theories, and from psychological laboratories (the latter, since Thorndike) in working on the problem of learning, often with subhuman species as subjects. As a consequence innumerable theories have been propounded, many of which have been quite useful. The practical value of a theory is well known and is well stated by Jahoda, Deutsch, and Cook (1962):

> the intention of a theory in modern science is to summarize existing knowledge, to provide an explanation for observed events and relationships, and to predict the occurrence of as yet unobserved events and relationships on the basis of the explanatory principles embodied in the theory. (p. 481)

A theory is the most efficient way to summarize, explain, and predict events, and a laboratory is the usual place for testing theories. Learning laboratories have produced learning theories from which teaching principles are inferred, but the transfer from the laboratory to the schoolroom has not been notably successful. But peculiarly enough there are no teaching laboratories to develop teaching theories. There are probably many reasons for this—the difficulty in the control of variables, the isolated teacher functions dependent on the teacher's perception of outcomes, and the general emphasis of practically minded people upon how to operate efficiently, rather than upon determining relationships.

The laboratory schools on college campuses were expected to fill the gap between theory and practice, by providing for laboratory investigation of teaching. But their gradual phasing out suggests that they were not sufficiently effective. Of course there have been research and experiments on teaching, sometimes with surprising results. The microteaching concept as developed by Dwight Allen of Stanford and his associates gives promise of an effective laboratory approach to teaching. The work of Hovland and others (1953) on communications and of Galloway (1966) on nonverbal behavior are examples of what is perhaps a movement toward a laboratory investigation of teaching.

CAN EFFECTIVENESS CRITERIA
SUGGEST THEORETICAL DIRECTIONS?

Superficially, it would seem that if teaching simply consists of behaviors that effectively promote learning, then a concomitant result would be the development of scientific theories of teaching. Much of the body of knowledge of the established sciences consists of ideas and facts drawn from practices that furnish more skimpy details and that even deal with more abstract data than does teaching. But the very fact that teaching does furnish so much concrete data makes it difficult to separate the wheat from the chaff. There is too much room for a great variety of interpretations for each of a multitude of behaviors. But it ought to have been possible to catalogue a large number of observed facts along with their consequences, and by noting the common elements to plug into the derived formula the appropriate values represented by each teaching situation.

Mitzel (1957) pointed out the futility of jumping directly from the predictor (independent) variables to the criterion (dependent) variables. It has seemed obvious that "good" teaching ought to be defined by teacher effectiveness—good teachers produce good pupils. However, as Mitzel stated, "these studies have yielded disappointing results: correlations that are non-significant, inconsistent from one study to the next, and usually lacking in psychological and educational meaning" (p. 118). To assign a teacher a level of effectiveness on the basis of pupil behaviors can never be a precise undertaking, because (1) teacher effectiveness criteria will be confounded with insoluble questions of values; (2) the variables are too complex; (3) socially desirable but elusive outcomes of education are extremely difficult to measure; and (4) no variables can be clearly attributed to teaching as compared with the influences of heredity, home, and community. Mitzel therefore described the idea of "microeffectiveness," so that he no longer sought criteria for the *overall* effectiveness of teachers throughout their many and varied functions, but suggested that the specifically defined aspects of each teaching role would produce more fruitful results. Such a microcriterion approach implies the clear specification of effectiveness in terms of subject matter complexity and child development, for example. Mitzel also suggested that his "Type III Variables," concerned with *classroom* behaviors, become the focus of investigation using the criteria of microeffectiveness. *The Handbook of Research on Teaching* (1963) furnishes examples of other similar approaches.

THE TEACHER AS A REPOSITORY OF INFORMATION AND TECHNIQUES

The conventional picture of the teacher as a prestigious figure, standing majestically before an audience and sonorously making important pronouncements (lecturing), is giving way to the concept of the teacher as simply a guide or dispenser of cues. Still, the master teacher acquires an ability to catalogue experiences, information, and procedures. Even though he may have no indelible, computerlike memory, no great cross-indexing capacity, and no really efficient information-retrieval system, he is more than usually competent in these skills for a restricted range of knowledge and applications. For most teachers, however, the ability to arrange data in meaningful, predictable relationships is severely restricted. Hence, teaching aids are needed that will facilitate efficient means for applying the proper formulas to the appropriate occasions. Significant developments will not be likely in this area if only random, unsystematic research efforts continue to prevail. The variables concerned with classroom behaviors become increasingly important, for these are observable.

IS TEACHING READY FOR THEORIES OF TEACHING?

Recent innovations that facilitate learning, involving programmed instruction, computer-assisted instruction, team teaching, and the like have been developed despite the absence of a well-organized body of theory about teaching. B. F. Skinner's ideas, for example, have stimulated the development of various teaching machines and programs, and the applications of the principles involved are numerous. Yet Skinner's principles are primarily concerned with learning, not with teaching. Furthermore, he has insisted that he has merely hit upon a set of workable principles but that these do not constitute a theory. Although he concedes that learning can be studied scientifically, he opines that teaching, at present, is an art. And Skinner criticizes the usual practice of constructing theories, even of learning, because they tend to stimulate an experimentation resulting in inferences not directly related to the observations (1954).

If this is true of a science of learning, it is also true that teaching is far from ready for a highly formalized theory. However, empirically based principles may lead to remarkably useful implications. For example, many automated teaching aids, including computer-assisted instructional stations, have been outgrowths of principles that had made programmed learning effective. And Carpenter and Haddan (1954) suggested ways of systematically applying these principles to different teaching modes, such as the group discussion, the use of films and filmstrips, and even to the field trip. But such suggestions as these do not provide corresponding guidelines for teaching theory. In the absence of a science of teaching, it seems improbable that full-blown theories of teaching will emerge.

ARE TEACHERS READY FOR THEORIES OF TEACHING?

When teaching finally is ready for its theories, will teachers be ready to assume their rightful professional roles? Cookbook procedures are often applied in "methods" courses, and the latter are often taught by experts in subject matter, rather than by experts in teacher preparation. Technicians, not professionals, are therefore the most likely to be produced by adherence to these directive methods, which dispense a recipe for each classroom condition. A teacher who is only a technician will be unable to transfer adequately, to shift appropriately in situations not covered by the furnished prescriptions. Fortunately, some teachers, through accurate evaluations of what are sometimes unpleasant, sometimes gratifying experiences, rise above the technician role. Such teachers are themselves able to develop a great many principles. Discoveries made by self-made professionals may become necessary adjuncts to the development of self as an instrument in teaching, following Combs (1965), who stated that each teacher ought to discover his own best way of teaching, with the prime resource being that of a more fully developed self. One school of thought holds that self-discovery is an inefficient mode, requiring too much retraveling of old, well-established trails to common objectives. Adherents to this view say that the task of discovering principles and theory belongs to those who specialize at such levels, rather than to those engaged in teaching. In the final analysis, however, practicing teachers will be expected to exhibit the behaviors in which the principles are found.

Presumably, a teacher using the self as instrument would be one who also had assumed a *professional* role. Professionalism implies both training and talent in creating operating rules based on known abstractions or general statements, and, as has been stated, in generating some principles of his own. The technician role is assigned to one who typically relies on pre-established techniques and formulas for action. Trump and Baynham (1966) listed six concepts about teachers as professionals:

1. They will differentiate between what they must do and what subprofessional assistants and machines can do.

2. They will have and use professionally designed work rooms and tools.

3. They will recognize differences in teachers' abilities.

4. They will be assigned responsibilities according to their individual skills and will be paid according to the level of those responsibilities.

5. They will be carefully recruited and carefully taught.

6. Above all, they will behave like professional persons, with knowledge, skill, and pride in what they do.

(pp. 52, 53)

Bruner (1966) believed that a theory of instruction must not be based upon *descriptive* theories of learning (i.e., the *status quo*—how teachers now behave in interacting with learners), but on *prescriptive* and normative theories (how learning may be improved). It is so difficult to find the right combination of optimal conditions, implied by the term *prescriptive*, that Travers (1966) was prompted to say, "Optimum conditions of various kinds derive from theories but are not the essence of scientific theories" (p. 50). Travers also stated that the difficulty with studying teacher behavior variables is that hypothetical patterns of teacher behavior can be described, but such patterns may not be the ones acted out by actual teachers.

If there are to be several kinds of theories of instruction, as suggested by Gage (1964), then there would still be room, even under a very systematic treatment of teacher education, for teachers to exercise their own self-directed powers.

IS THE ART OF TEACHING IMPAIRED WHEN SYSTEMATIC TEACHING IS EMPLOYED?

To prefer a less directive approach to teaching, and a more permissive, self-regulating, exploratory one, is not to reject the possibility of a science of teaching—it merely suggests that alternative viewpoints may be embraced within the systematic approach. However, if we are concerned with *acts* of teaching, then a theory of teaching will deal with observables rather than with inferred mental processes. Although inferred processes may be considered helpful, occasionally even necessary, to an explanation of sequential acts, still, it is not until behavior occurs that these processes have any effect on others, and so become a subject of study. Now the acts under consideration comprise *social* behavior, because at least two people are necessary, a teacher and a pupil. Even in daily routines, we try to guess from their actions what others are thinking and what their reactions will be to what we say and do. This sort of guessing is a part of the teaching-learning interaction, whether the behaviors are verbal or nonverbal. The viewpoint that the teacher is a hypothesis maker refers to an if-then kind of sequence that amounts to a series of provisional tries. If the teacher behaves in a certain way, then the learner is expected to behave at least within a predicted category of behaviors. Even those who would prefer to consider teaching as an art would not relinquish *all* ability to predict outcomes, or at least to expect some rather than others. Nor would they abolish every ᵕ ᵕ of influence or even control of the direction of learning efforts.

WHEN WILL EDUCATION DEVELOP INTO MATURITY?

If sophisticated theory building is a mark of a mature discipline, education probably has a long way to go before it even becomes of age. However, there are encouraging signs. First, research techniques have improved and an increasing number of educators are acquiring greater sophistication in research design. Second, the tendency during a discipline's adolescence to jump suddenly from predictor (independent) variables to criterion (dependent) variables, without sufficient evidence to support the consequent generalizations, is becoming more controlled. Third, educators show increasing concern over the stigma of immaturity in their research and theory. Fourth, educators have made vigorous attempts to shed light on possibilities for theories. For example, James MacDonald (1963) suggested four major needs for theory and research on the nature of instruction, i.e., to provide:

1. Adequate instructional models.
2. Empirical analysis.
3. Criterion variables, identified and described.
4. Answers to pertinent questions about instruction.

WILL "THE THEORY MAKER" EMERGE?

Frederick McDonald (1964) believes that education has needed a science of man, perhaps more than it has needed a science of behavior. Philosophy, for example, has aided in charting the course of psychology in the classroom for many years. It is McDonald's belief that education will assimilate a new or a more comprehensive psychological theory when it does appear. The development of education during the fifties and sixties seems to bear this out. McDonald suggested that when such a theory does emerge, it will have at least the following characteristics:

1. It will be based on "good science." This may not be the good science of today—it will be whatever is considered unimpeachable by the scientists of the day.

2. The theory will also embrace social problems. (Thus, to some extent, it will be interdisciplinary.)

3. It will make provisions for the developmental nature of the maturing organism.

4. It will suggest systems that will increase the control (practical applications) of the teacher. (Thus it will increase in effectiveness.)

5. It will make more adequate provisions for treating individual differences than now exist.

6. It will provide for more comprehensive understanding of content's influences upon teaching learning, and for the utilization of attitudes toward content.

In the pages that follow are ideas dealing with some of McDonald's suggestions, but no one man espouses them all. Because a great many preferences for particular learning theories are made on bases other than rational, many educators will be likely to follow *the* man who makes his ideas fit into the spirit of the times, with the emotional component assuming a larger significance. The man may have to be presented through an interpreter, a public relations expert, who will clearly show that the man's ideas fit into the needs (cognitive and emotional) of the times. McDonald said "Educators depend on middlemen for their psychology . . ." (1964, p. 16). If it is true that most of science's great contributions are now made by teams, rather than by the efforts of a single individual, we may speculate that emerging technologies, as intercommunication aids, may also assist in producing *the* men as theory makers.

In many scientific fields, it becomes increasingly difficult to single out the individual who makes *the* significant contribution. Team efforts are often demanded by the nature of the problem. It has been said that education may be approaching a stage in which the problems require team efforts. Perhaps a John Dewey, a William H. Kilpatrick, or a John B. Watson, as a spokesman for a new theory or system of theories, will never emerge. Regional research centers, clearinghouses for innovative contributions, will be furnishing their findings for widespread dissemination. Computer and other networks will make available multiple consultations on a scale never before possible.

Just as no one man invented the rocket that carried the first astronauts to the moon, so it may be that the genius of many men will combine to produce a smoothly operating educational system that makes possible a performance never heretofore achieved.

References

1. Allen, Dwight, "Micro-Teaching: A New Framework for In-service Education," paper presented at American Association of Colleges for Teacher Education Workshop, University of Maryland, 1966.
2. American Educational Research Association, *Controlling Classroom Misbehavior*, Washington, D.C., National Education Association, 1965.
3. Ausubel, David P., "A Cognitive-Structure Theory of School Learning," *Instruction: Some Contemporary Viewpoints*, Laurence Siegel (ed.). San Francisco, Chandler Publishing Company, 1967.
4. Bern, H. A., "Wanted: Educational Engineers," *Phi Delta Kappan* (January 1967), Vol. XLVIII, 230–236.
5. Bruner, Jerome S., "Needed: A Theory of Instruction," *Educational Leadership* (May 1963), Vol. 20, 523–527.
6. ——, *Toward a Theory of Instruction*. Cambridge, Mass., Harvard University Press, 1966.
7. Carpenter, Finley, and Eugene E. Haddan, *Systematic Application of Psychology to Education*. New York, The Macmillan Company, 1964.
8. Combs, Arthur, *The Professional Education of Teachers: A Perceptual View of Teacher Preparation*, Boston, Allyn and Bacon, Inc., 1965.
9. Detroit Federation of Teachers, *How to Make Your Lions Love You*. Detroit, 1956.
10. Flanders, Ned, *Teacher Influence, Pupil Attitudes and Achievement*. Minneapolis, University of Minnesota (U.S. Office of Education Cooperative Research Project No. 397), 1960.
11. Gage, N. L., "Paradigms for Research on Teaching," *Handbook of Research on Teaching*, N. L. Gage (ed.). Chicago, Rand McNally & Company, 1963.

12. ——, and W. R. Unruh, "Theoretical Formulations for Research on Teaching," *Rev. of Educ. Res.* (June 1967), Vol. XXXVII, 338–370.

13. ——, "Theories of Teaching," *Theories of Learning and Instruction.* The Sixty-third Yearbook of the National Society for the Study of Education, Ernest Hilgard and Herman Richey (eds.). Chicago, The University of Chicago Press, 1964.

14. Galloway, Charles, "Teacher Non-Verbal Communication," *Education Leadership Journal* (October 1966), XXIV, 55–63.

15. Haskew, Lawrence D., and Jonathon C. McLendon, *This Is Teaching.* Chicago, Scott, Foresman and Company, 1962.

16. Hovland, C. I., I. L. Janis, and H. H. Kelley, *Communication and Persuasion.* New Haven, Conn., Yale University Press, 1953.

17. Jahoda, Marie, Morton Deutsch, and Stuart Cook, *Research Methods in Social Relations.* New York, Holt, Rinehart and Winston, Inc., 1962.

18. Lehmann, Henry, "The Systems Approach to Education," *Audiovisual Instruction* (February 1968), 144–148.

19. Maccia, Elizabeth S., "Theories of Instruction," *Conceptual Models in Teacher Education*, John R. Verduin, Jr. (ed.). Washington, D.C., American Association of Colleges for Teacher Education, 1967.

20. MacDonald, James B., "The Nature of Instruction: Needed Theory and Research," *Educational Leadership* (October 1963), Vol. 21, 5–7.

21. McDonald, Frederick, "The Influence of Learning Theories on Education," *Theories of Learning and Instruction.* The Sixty-third Yearbook of the National Society for the Study of Education. Chicago, The University of Chicago Press, 1964.

22. Mitzel, H. E., *A Behavioral Approach to the Assessment of Teacher Effectiveness.* Division of Teacher Education, College of the City of New York, 1957.

23. Putnam, Daniel, *A Primer of Pedagogy.* Lansing, Mich., H. R. Patengill, 1894.

24. Scandura, Joseph. "Teaching—Technology or Theory," *American Educational Research Journal* (March 1966), Vol. 3, 139–146.

25. Schueler, Herbert, and Gerald S. Lesser, assisted by Allen L. Dobbins, *Teacher Education and the New Media.* Washington, D.C., American Association of Colleges for Teacher Education, 1967.

26. Scott, C. Winfield, and Clyde M. Hill, *Public Education Under Criticism.* New York, Prentice-Hall, 1954.

27. ——, Clyde M. Hill, and Hobert W. Burns, *The Great Debate.* Englewood Cliffs, N.J., Prentice-Hall, 1959.

28. Skinner, B. F., "The Science of Learning and the Art of Teaching," *Harvard Educational Review*, Vol. XXIV (1954), 86–97.

29. Travers, Robert M. W., "Towards Taking the Fun Out of Building a Theory of Instruction," *Teachers College Record*, Oct., 1966.

30. Trow, William Clark, *Teacher and Technology: New Designs for Learning.* New York, Appleton-Century-Crofts, 1963.

31. Trump, J. Lloyd, and Dorsey Baynham, *Focus on Change: Guide to Better Schools.* Chicago, Rand McNally & Company, 1966.

32. Verduin, John R., Jr., *Conceptual Models in Teacher Education: An Approach to Teaching and Learning.* Washington, D.C., American Association of Colleges for Teacher Education, 1967.
33. Wittrock, M. C., "Paradigms in Research on Teaching," *Educational Psychologist*, Vol. 5, No. 1 (December 1967).
34. Woodruff, Asahel, and Len Froyen, "Implications of Technology for Teaching and Learning," address at Central States Colleges and Universities Professional Education Seminar, University of Northern Iowa, Cedar Falls, 1967.

2

Techniques, Methods, and Principles of Teaching

Techniques are of many kinds. They are ways of implementing a method. Different techniques may therefore be employed within the same method. The lecture method, for example, provides many good and poor illustrations of vocal techniques. Other methods utilize skill in using the voice, such as monologues and musical presentations. There are also techniques designed to increase the amount of two-way communication exchanged and to reduce the number of factors that would interfere with accurate exchange. Inflections and changes in pitch can modulate the voice; and altering the accent on syllables, words, and phrases can influence the listener's thinking. The use of affect-arousing speech; the ability to sound flat, yet scientifically objective; and convincing, persuasive speech, or the ability to reflect indifference—all are techniques that are used quite effectively by experts.

Techniques in manipulating apparatus are also widely utilized by effective instructors. Many procedural manuals are included along with the purchase of new pieces of hardware, for example. Acquiring the many techniques—in the management of instructional media and developing orderly, effective skills in managing learning activities—comprise a great deal of the direct experience of the instructor. Many techniques are specific skills to be exercised in classroom instruction and may be acquired without the presence of pupils, because they involve primarily mechanical skills. What is frequently intended, when the term *creative teaching* is used, is the discovery and use of refined techniques in connection with an accepted objective. It may, however, be applied to the innovative use of methods. There are various techniques in using the panel method of telling—questioning primarily among the panel members themselves; questioning that is directed by the moderator; questioning from the listeners (pupils); posing new subject matter determined by the interests of the listeners; fielding questions as they are thrown; or delaying the questioning until the last member of the panel has spoken. Thus, *method* is broader in meaning than is *technique*, though indiscriminate usage sometimes employs the two terms synonymously.

SOME DISTINCTIONS BETWEEN METHODS AND TECHNIQUES

It will not suffice to say that technique is specific, whereas method is more general, in the sense that one cuts across subject matters, whereas the other does not. Both techniques and methods may be general, in that sense. For instance, the various voice inflections may be used to great advantage in both speech classes and in foreign language instruction, as well as in the dramatic arts using this mode of expression. And some of the methods may be specific to the subject matter, as well as applicable to many content areas.

Ralph S. Ascher (1966) provides some guidelines for differentiating between methods and techniques. The common types of method are listed as *telling, showing,* and *doing*. Because the procedures and processes have been well established, the similarity to the pedagogy of an earlier time is apparent. However, techniques of applying these methods differ from person to person and from age to age. Ascher's categories of method are in the following table:

"Telling" Methods	"Showing" Methods	"Doing" Methods
Lecture	Written words	Role playing
Lecture with questions	Pictures	Project, committee work
Panel	Motion pictures	Written, performance tests
Training Conference	Charts, diagrams	Practical exercises
Debate	Physical objects	On-job training
Case study	Demonstrations	Understudy
Incident process	Observing skits	Supervised practice
Recording	Viewing on-site operations	Guided experiences
Oral quiz		Rotating assignments

(p. 2)

Ascher makes the point that effective use of methods may be readily taught as a proper subject matter for teacher education, whereas techniques, being the actual performances of teachers, present a much more difficult area to influence. One attempt to deal with the techniques used in teaching performance is called *microteaching,* and is described later in this book. Interaction analysis is another aid to teaching techniques, and it will also be described later. It is sometimes said that one of the most troublesome aspects of research in human behavior is that the variables dealt with are quite complex. Techniques are a function of the many complex variables resident in the personality of the teacher. Mannerisms, temperament, attitudes, enthusiasm, appearance, needs, and desires all influence the application of techniques. However, behaviors appropriate to techniques can be taught, despite the difficulty posed by Ascher, that methods are appropriate to the usual modes of classroom instruction, whereas techniques are observed in on-the-job performances.

TEACHING METHODS

There are narrow concepts of method, and broader ones. Kilpatrick (1925) rejected method as dictated by the subject being taught as too narrow, and preferred a project-centered approach. Beauchamp (1965) also discussed narrow and broad concepts of method, pointing out that there is still some confusion between *methods* and *techniques.* "Specific techniques of teaching, such as the administration of tests, the use of workbooks, the class discussion, the use of bulletin boards, and so forth, become important in method, but they are not broad enough to be considered method itself" (pp. 49, 50). The broader concept of method includes both the philosophical base, concerned with ends or objectives, and a psychological base, concerned with the learner, the learning process, and the psychology of subject matter. Broudy (1963) stated that "*method* refers to the formal structure of the sequence of acts commonly denoted by instruction. The term covers both the strategy and tactics of teaching and involves the choice of what is to be taught, and the order in which it is to be taught" (p. 3).

METHOD AND PEDAGOGY

Friedrich Froebel was a philosopher who was also a "psychologizer," to use Beauchamp's term. He not only put into practice many ideas of such predecessors as Comenius, Rousseau, and Pestalozzi, but he was the founder of the kindergarten movement. Froebel also stressed the positive use of the *interests* of the learner. He said that an effective teacher ought to build learning experiences around the manifest interests of children. Their interests ought to be enlarged and enriched, and should lead to other interests. Froebel believed that the child could be readily engaged in *activities*, so that cognitive learning alone, as sheer mental exercises, would not be regarded as the most important aspect of learning. Indeed the name which Froebel first hit upon for his school was not *Kindergarten*, meaning infant school, but *Kleinkinderbeschäftigungsanstalt*, meaning "little children's activity institution."

Broudy and Palmer (1965) called Froebel's approach a form of "dialectical gardening." Not only did he stress the enrichment of the child's experiences through the building or contriving of experiences, but he held the viewpoint that anything is not only a whole itself but is a part of a larger whole. Thus, he would lead pupils from one level of learning to a more inclusive level (the essence of a subsumption theory). His notions about learners were developmental, and development occurs according to a recapitulation, according to Froebel. For each individual, there is a developmental sequence in which cultural epochs are relived, from infancy to childhood. Each man progresses to ever higher levels of development, and Man, as a race, moves upward also. Further, he believed in opposition as necessary to all developmental processes. For example, necessity should call forth freedom; law should call forth self-determination; external compulsion should call forth inner freedom; and external hate should call forth internal love (1911, pp. 13–14).

This double-sided view of education, its give and take, its uniting and dividing, its prescribing and following, its active and passive natures, its being positive yet flexible, its being firm yet yielding, applies to both instructor and instructed. Along with the action-reaction, the swing between opposites, went the understanding that:

> The child, the pupil, has a very keen feeling, a very clear apprehension, and rarely fails to distinguish, whether what the educator, the teacher, or the father says or requests is personal, arbitrary, or whether it is expressed by him as a general law and necessity. (pp. 14–15)

Using this dialectical teaching, the instructor tended to promote in pupils an attitude of always looking for alternatives, not becoming too quickly satisfied with what readily comes to mind.

Froebel also sought *unity*, which meant the development of relationships, within any subject area, even where there appeared to be mostly diversity. Such a seeker of unity is likely to deal with teaching as an enterprise concerned with intellectual, moral, and aesthetic aspects, all in one. He paralleled his teaching methods with his theoretical leanings, and always insisted that intellectual and creative efforts must be made within the rule of what is morally right.

The interrelatedness that Froebel sought was also carried out in connection with another facet of his method—the *symbolic object lesson*. When an object was chosen for study, it was selected because its form suggested something that Nature had developed via opposites. He attempted to endow the activities of the very young child with such a character as to lead the child to closer identification with the Divine Spirit. Speech, modeling, music, and painting, in elementary education, and manual training in high school, were outgrowths of Froebel's influence. However, they soon lost their metaphysical justifications and gave way to a more psychological rationale.

Thus, this "father of the kindergarten" gave to America from Germany a systematic approach that synthesized the teachings of Comenius and Pestalozzi, and made "practical" a dialectic method that had been espoused by the philosopher Hegel.

MOVEMENT AWAY FROM INNER DEVELOPMENT TO EXTERNAL INFLUENCES

Another extremely systematic German was Johann Friedrich Herbart, who for a number of years was professor of philosophy at Königsberg, the position formerly held by Kant. However, he was perhaps less a philosopher than a pedagogue. He did not seek the unification that characterized

Froebel, but rather emphasized the importance of *cognition*. He did not deal with innate powers and capacities, but believed that human experience might be *constructed* from presentations, conveyed via the sense impressions. Herbart's methods could therefore be analyzed into phases, because teaching could be rationalized and systematized according to specific inputs of ideational material.

The first phase of teaching, according to Herbart, was *preparation*, i.e., preparing the learner for the ensuing instruction, and relating motivation, both intrinsic and extrinsic, to the learning task. Motivational preparation involved initial arousal, whereas sustained attention could be induced by exploiting interests that were to be expected according to the stage of development of the child.

The cognitive aspect of preparation was a planning stage. The teacher could make outlines before class time of what he could expect his pupils to have experienced. In class, pupils would be encouraged to discuss whatever they wished that was related to topics with which they were familiar. The teacher then used his skill in summarizing and stressing the most essential ideas, which would then be active in the acceptance of new materials, a process called by Herbart "apperception" and sharply distinguished from the passive associative processes as taught by the British philosopher-psychologists.

The second phase of teaching, *presentation*, dealt with vividness of sense perception, but verbalizing was also quite important. Herbart realized that, for effective learning, the logical and psychological order in teaching must be carefully established. The kind of intermingling of new materials with what had been already learned, a little at a time, as now found in programmed instruction, was espoused by Herbart.

Association, the third phase, concentrated upon the acquisition of concepts. Comparisons and contrasts were made between known instances and those to be learned. *Systematization* was concerned with pulling together the data and principles brought out by the lesson. In a sense, Herbart was the B. F. Skinner of the nineteenth century. Insisting that teaching is a systematic probing of the effective guidance of experiences, both as to inputs and retrievals, Herbart was criticized for assigning too much control to the teacher, producing learning experiences mechanically. Skinner has also been accused of advocating the systematic control of human behavior to the point of mechanization.

Application, the fifth phase of teaching, amounted to providing exercises for the pupil that would test how well he had responded in the previous phases. For example, the ideas learned might be repeated forwards or backwards, from beginning to end, from end to beginning, or even from the middle in either direction. Pupils might be asked to give instances of the application of a generalization, or this requirement might be reversed, so that the pupil was asked to state the generalization illustrated by a specific application. Problem solving was also a means for teaching applications. Exercises sometimes were provided to evaluate what pupils had learned, rather specifically, with the teacher's corrective help, whereas other exercises required that the pupil show the ability to perform in the absence of teacher assistance.

Herbart believed that pupils could become interested in the same sense that they could become attentive—interest was an intellectual process. Thus, although he would not have agreed with Dewey that action is a necessary condition for interest arousal, he would have agreed that interest is highly important.

Herbart's methods were eagerly accepted in this country, as they were in Germany. The importance to teacher education of a more "scientific" set of procedures than had been practiced in the past is obvious. The approach does not focus upon the personality characteristics of the instructor; it emphasizes professional education, as offering at least a minimal level of proficiency. Beyond that, individual differences would be expected to result in individual increases in superiority.

Among those strongly influenced in this country by Herbartian pedagogy was Charles DeGarmo. In his *Essentials of Method* (1893), DeGarmo spoke of education in terms of "analogical theories of mind." In the absence of the plethora of learning theories that currently abound, he readily erected a formal pedagogy based on what was then agreed upon about learning. He mentioned two broad theories of education: (1) the *germ* theory and (2) the *architectural* theory. The germ theory of education held that the mind is a self-producer, producing something predetermined. According to this theory, a gardener who helps a seed to develop into a plant, though the nature and form of the plant is predetermined, is analogous to the teacher. The teacher helps the self-active power of the pupil to emerge, to seize upon its surroundings, using what it will for the development of the self's predetermined form and content. One need not search far to find adherents to this theory today. Abraham Maslow, Arthur Coombs, Gordon Allport, Earl Kelley, and Carl Rogers are among those who feel that this positive, forward-looking outlook is the most applicable of theories in human behavior and development. Today, just as in the time of DeGarmo, there are those who insist that the function of the teacher is not to direct, but to clear the way for learning and development in the individual.

The second of DeGarmo's theories, the architectural theory, stated that the mind is built up by an educational architect, the teacher. Advocates of this viewpoint would assign to the teacher a much more directive, structuring function. DeGarmo felt that the first theory, from the viewpoint of a *science* of education, had little to offer, but he did not suggest that it relegated teaching altogether to the province of art. Still, within the second theory, he saw the possibility of a science of instruction that would give rise to concepts, coordinating and properly relating them.

Herbart expounded a method. DeGarmo distinguished between method and techniques. Method was more than a set of techniques for presenting a subject. Method includes techniques, but it also takes into consideration each child's stage of development. "The method in the subject [matter] at any stage exactly fits a corresponding stage of development . . . in the child" (1893, p. 5). In thinking of method as existent both in the subject under study and in the child's own thought processes, DeGarmo foreshadowed Piaget's stages of conceptual development, as well as the thinking of a host of psychologists who place great faith in readiness. But because of his conception of method, he saw the germ theory and the architectural theory of education not as opposites, but as complementary.

DeGarmo's theories were a means of relating the way pupils learn to the ways teachers must instruct. Laudable efforts to clarify this relationship have been repeated many times over by later investigators; but the weakness of the DeGarmo approach lay in a lack of experimental evidence. Lack of sophistication in the use of controls and in statistical analysis, for example, limited investigations, and the data available were far from adequate. Nowadays, it is not popular to use the terms *mind, apperceptions, notions,* and the *golden mean* (Pestalozzi's statement that the mind must select a moderate course between specific and general notions), because the referents are so vague, so poorly defined. However, DeGarmo had seen that the application of more than the golden mean was necessary. In addition to moving from individual to general notions, after the apperception or assimilation of the individual notions, he insisted that the *application* of universals to particulars must follow.* The logic of the time made evident the need for such an argument, though experimental evidence may have been rather meager and often unsought.

Methods were treated according to their impact upon the learner, upon the thing being learned, and upon the teacher. It was expected that the learner would have knowledge imparted to him, in the form of *explication, predication,* or *demonstration.* Explication dealt with the apprehension of

---

* Among the many today who stress the importance of application, as a testing of the worth of decisions, is Woodruff, whose model will be discussed, and Bloom et al., whose taxonomy of objectives also appears in this volume.

the individual notion and with the transition to the general notion. Predication consisted of the presentation of static information, or description, as well as with genetic forms of instruction, i.e., with information that develops with time. Demonstration had to do with ways of presenting proofs, either deductive or inductive. It was expected that each thing to be learned would consist of a whole and its parts, and therefore one could begin with the whole and proceed to its parts or begin with the parts and proceed to the whole. The whole-to-part sequence was called *analytical method* and the separate-facts-to-total was called *synthetical method*. Either method was considered right, and they could be combined. The teacher was to communicate knowledge, either quite directively, as in a monologue, or with some learner participation, as in a dialogue. Even the dialogue consisted largely of questions, directly by the teacher.

DeGarmo stated that for the essentials of a correct method there should be a conformity to the essential stages:

1. The apperception of new facts, in *preparation* and *presentation*.

2. The *transition* from individual to general notions, whether the general notions appear as definitions, rules, principles, or as moral maxims.

3. The *application* of these general truths to concrete facts, i.e., the return from universals to particulars.

He then went on to illustrate in detail how each of these stages should be applied to various subject matters, showing for each how the teacher might make his preparation and his presentation.

Whether or not DeGarmo's attempt at systematizing teaching represented the tenor of his time, it does illustrate a tendency to support Herbart. Enlightened educators went about establishing a "right method," hoping that if the method were learned well, there might be many more masterful teachers.

DeGarmo's contemporary was Daniel Putnam, who published what he called a *Primer of Pedagogy*, a systematic treatise that defined teaching methods somewhat differently from the way DeGarmo did. "Methods in teaching are ways by which the teacher seeks to reach desired results" (1891, p. 40). He, too, considered the importance of the stage of a child's development, but he did not feel that the laws of development indicated in what way subjects should be presented; these laws did not determine methods of teaching. Even though Putnam recognized that there are parallels between mental activity and different stages of development as set forth, for example, by the culture-epoch theory, he did not believe they were specific enough to provide a basis for telling the teacher how to teach. However, it must be added that development was not considered according to the stages so generally accepted today. For Putnam, the laws of development were

1. The law of the *order* of development. The mental powers and activities of the child are developed and matured in a regular and unvarying order. This order is (a) the perceptive activities; (b) the conceptive or representative activities; and (c) the thinking activities.
2. The law of the *condition* of development. The powers of the child are developed and matured only on condition of being properly exercised.
3. The law of the *means* of development. Appropriate matter for study properly presented to the mind of the child produces this necessary activity.

Theories about learning heavily influenced his laws of development. He advocated observing each child and, by long and patient searching, seeking to discover the methods the child uses when left to himself.

Putnam also believed that by setting forth laws of the mind, one could derive laws of teaching:

1. Teaching wholes, rather than parts.
2. Analysis from wholes to parts.
3. Synthesis, teaching how parts may be put together to form wholes.

He then illustrated how these laws ought to be applied in different subjects.

MOVEMENT AWAY FROM ARMCHAIR LOGIC

More than thirty years after DeGarmo and Putnam had written on method, William H. Kilpatrick, "the million-dollar professor,"* decided

---

* It has been computed that his students paid over one million dollars in fees at Columbia University.

that the narrow applications of methods ought to be supplanted by a wider concept of method. He himself had been taught by applications of narrower concepts, such as the word method, the phonic method, the Grube method, and the Speer method. But by this time, numerous methods and devices began to look more like sales devices, and Kilpatrick was prompted to write that he noticed a superior sort of smile on the faces of educators when methods and devices were mentioned. (The terms *hardware* and *software* sometimes evoke similar responses, nowadays.) These narrow applications of the concept, like the earlier efforts at broader formulations, were rational deductions from experience, and though they did have an empirical base, they lacked the support of scientific evidence. It was natural, therefore, that a tendency to move away from such armchair logic in developing directions for teaching should make itself felt. Even the early Thorndikean psychology that furnished some of the basis for establishing methods was deemed insufficient, with its ideas pertaining to *set, readiness, exercise,* and *satisfyingness.* The needed philosophical influence in bringing many concepts to bear on a central project or problem and in insisting upon the learner's active participation in learning was furnished by John Dewey, and Kilpatrick was the intermediary—the St. Paul of the new dispensation. He had been influenced by Francis Parker and his Quincy method and by DeGarmo, who was still teaching, while studying Dewey's *Interest and Effort in Education* (1913). Kilpatrick had been disappointed with his first course under Dewey, but a decade later he became a Dewey disciple, crediting Dewey and Edward L. Thorndike with providing bases for his book *Foundations of Method* (1925).

Kilpatrick also wrote on method and explained the differences between two major viewpoints. The first view, a narrow one, attached each subject to its own style of method. This preference is shown in some colleges today, where methods courses are taught in the history department, the mathematics department, and so on. The second view, the broad outlook, was brought about by a consideration of what was called *simultaneous learning,* the learning of a number of skills, activities, and concepts all at about the same time. Several things at once were taught by using some learnings as instrumental to or as correlates of some central task or project. Morality, patriotism, political philosophy, and other issues might be associated with and used for learning a spelling lesson, for example. Thus the learning project relating the most learnings could be used for the most effective teaching.

In these two conflicting views Kilpatrick saw two primary teaching problems: (1) managing each of these things singly, in isolation, if possible, and (2) seeing and adjusting many things at the same time. The narrower problem lay in the domain of psychology and had its own applications, but it should be augmented by the wider one, that of philosophy. A broader meaning of method did not refer to principles of teaching, as compared with methods, it merely considered areas that were of large scope. He had moved away from the teachings of DeGarmo and Putnam, and away from instruction whose main purpose was to impart knowledge. The objectives as he now saw them were the development of desirable character and personality traits as outcomes of involvement in projects, or purposeful acts.

Four types of projects were stated to be tasks suitable to the interests of pupils:

1. Where the purpose is to embody some idea in external form, e.g., to present a play or to build a boat.
2. Where the purpose is to enjoy some esthetic experience, e.g., listening to a story or a symphony.
3. Where the purpose is to straighten out some intellectual difficulty, i.e., to solve a problem.
4. Where the purpose is to obtain some item or degree of skill or knowledge.

(Broudy, 1965, pp. 333–334)

Purposing, planning, executing, and judging, eliciting the trial response, correcting the trial response, and eliciting the test response are included in Kilpatrick's learning as a wholehearted effort. But the task of the teacher is seen not as that of imparting task-related cues or directing, but as that of helping each pupil to define his own task to fulfill needs or desires, or to alleviate a difficulty. Reading, telling, and reciting played less of a part than did discussion, planning, and activities.

Thus Kilpatrick viewed the teacher as someone to help:

1. initiate the activity;
2. plan for carrying the activity forward;
3. execute the plan;
4. evaluate progress;
5. think up new leads;
6. formulate the new leads by writing them down for later recall;
7. keep the pupils critical of their own thinking en route to the solution;
8. look back over the whole process to pick up and fix important kinds of learning as well as to draw lessons for the future.

(Broudy, 1965, p. 307)

Many have discussed John Dewey's ideas about permissiveness in learning settings. More to the point are his viewpoints on what the learner ought to be doing, and the teacher's role in promoting that activity. Although much of what Dewey offered may be considered method, he also furnished broader concepts that may be considered principles. Because he insisted that the teacher should know a great deal about both the learner's environment and the learner himself, two principles evolved. The first was that the learner should learn by being actively involved. The second principle was that the learner should be provided with learning experiences related to his previous experiences. Although Dewey did not insist that activity be centered on a project, he and Kilpatrick agreed that active learning, rather than passive, was preferable. Dewey also stressed the value of instrumental learning, wherein one learns behaviors that are instrumental in achieving not only the goals originally intended, but in generalizing to others as well.

Dewey described an ideal home in which such educational processes might operate:

1. The child would learn through being socially conversant with the family, and through his being a part of it. As a family member, he would state his experiences and examine his own misconceptions as they were corrected by other members.

2. The child would participate in the household occupations, so that he might acquire thereby habits of industriousness, order, and a regard for the rights and ideas of others. Here he would also learn to subordinate his own activities to the general interests of the household.

3. There would be a workshop wherein the child could work out his constructive instincts (impulses). A miniature laboratory would be provided.

4. Encouragement would be provided for the child to extend his life into the out-of-doors.

Dewey is often given the credit for espousing a child-centered approach to teaching. Thayer (1965) pointed out that Dewey attempted to synthesize two antithetical positions, that of the child-centered approach and that of the subject-centered approach. He actually insisted that teacher, child, and subject matter were all vitally important to education, but that the child should not be forgotten! The subject matter must be systematically organized; the teacher must have achieved the maturity, the experience, and the background for assisting the child to master the subject matter; and the subject matter ought to be definitely related to the interests of the child. Dewey linked child and subject matter by saying:

> we realize that the child and the curriculum are simply two limits which define a single process. . . . It is continuous reconstruction, moving from the child's present experience out into that represented by the organized bodies of truth that we call studies. (1902, p. 16)

Dewey also wished to soften the conflict between those who would focus upon *interests* as central to learning, and those who stressed *will* to learn. It was his contention that:

> The genuine principle of interest is the principle of the recognized identity of the fact to be learned or the action proposed with the growing self; that it lies in the direction of the agent's own growth, and is, therefore, imperiously demanded, if the agent is to be himself. (1913, p. 7)

He has been generally accepted as a leader in progressive education, but actually he sought to pull together some of the opposing views inherent in traditional practices and in progressive movements. Traditionally, the subject matters worked out by past generations were to be transmitted to new generations, and this was viewed as the chief business of the school. This was to be done directly, rigorously, and with no monkey business. Knowledge of subject matter as determined by proper authority was the objective. Moral training was to be based on what the past had decided upon. Imposition was from above upon those below. By contrast, though they had no quarrel with knowledge, the progressives advocated self-expression, free activity, the cultivation of individuality, learning through experience, and, in general, social and aesthetic as well as more narrowly intellectual values. They also felt that acquiring skills and techniques as instrumental to other ends, rather than as objects of drill, should be a part of educational aims. Preparation ought to be for the future rather than for the immediate present, and there should be developed an acquaintance with a changing world, rather than with static aims and capacities. Dewey found both factions wanting. He emerged with the position that experiences were expected to include the planning of subject matter learnings via activities, which took into consideration individual needs, desires, aims, and capacities.

Reflective Thinking

Disconnected flights of the imagination or randomly disorganized thinking did not qualify as reflective thinking. What was intended was an orderly process, what might now be called problem solving. This systematic method of thinking moved many educators toward reform in methods, in the selection of subject matter, and in the organization of curricula. Reflective thinking was not to be speculation of the armchair variety only —mere guessing and jumping at conclusions. Ideally it would be carried on in support of on-going activities in order to determine the best procedure or cause of action.

Dewey organized problem-solving behavior (1910) into five stages:*

1. A state of perplexity, doubt, frustration, or the like.
2. The identification of what is believed to be the problem.
3. A search for facts and a formulation of possible solutions.
4. The testing of successive solutions, and, when necessary, the reformulation of the problem.
5. The application of the correct solution.

Thus, despite the misapplied criticism that Dewey advocated only a permissive atmosphere in which children learned very little, substantively, he actually did suggest *systematic* procedures designed to increase effective learning.

Martin S. Dworkin includes in his *Dewey on Education: Selections* (1965) a series of declarations comprising Dewey's pedagogic creed:

Article I—What Education Is
Article II—What the School Is
Article III—The Subject Matter of Education
Article IV—The Nature of Method
Article V—The School and Social Progress

---

* This prescientific theory of problem solving has been subjected to the criticism that the stages are not necessarily in this sequence nor is stage 4 always adequate. Also, it sometimes happens that the learner simply rests from his labors, consciously, and the solution appears later, as though the individual had continued working on it. However, this solution may not be the correct one.

Of primary interest at present is Article IV—The Nature of Method.

The essence of method, according to John Dewey, lies in the *powers* of the learners and their *interests*. Thus one would construct guidelines for presenting materials that have been based on the child's own nature.

1. Dewey assumed that *the child is predisposed to act before he is required to remain passive.* Thus, expression will precede conscious impression. Muscular development precedes sensory development, so movements precede conscious sensations. However, because consciousness is essentially motor or impulsive, conscious states tend to be projected into action. Reasoning is the operation of a law of orderly, effective action. Symbols are useful as tools for making learning efforts more efficient.

2. Dewey also believed that the child's power of imagery should be promoted. *The preparation and presentation of lessons should largely give way to training the child's imagery.*

3. A third belief was that interests are good indicators of a child's state of development and can be used as predictors of the stage he is about to enter. If an adult is to move inside the child's frame of reference, he must do so via the child's interests. Dewey believed that a child's interests should not be humored, meaning that the adult should not merely encourage the immediate activity around which the interest revolves. Because the expression of interest is a sign of some deeper impulse or power, it is important to determine what lies back of the whim of the moment. On the other hand, interests ought not to be repressed, because repression might result in the deadening of further interest, the suppressing of initiative, and the weakening of intellectual curiosity and alertness.

4. Dewey did not believe in separating the emotional from the cognitive domain or from psychomotor functioning. An unhealthy, morbid state of mind can be introduced, if emotions are simply

aroused as experiences apart from the activities to which they ought to correspond in learning. He believed that sentimentalism was an example of the improper use of emotions, because feeling divorced it from action. "I believe that if we can only secure right habits of action and thought, with reference to the good, the true, and the beautiful, the emotions will for the most part take care of themselves" (Dewey 1897).

By the nineteen-sixties, writers on method were still recommending the close study of each child, not merely for the purpose of detecting his capacities, interests and needs, but to detect readiness to learn. Hence readiness, according to developmental norms, came to be underlined as a prerequisite, if not for learning, at least for increased efficiency in learning. Readiness was to be determined from a background of observations that had not existed a few decades before. The idea of gearing teaching efforts to a timetable set by the readiness of each child to learn was not new. Froebel, for example, was committed to the recapitulation or culture-epoch theory, according to which stages in the development of the human race are viewed as analogous to the changing natural activities and interests of a child. Materials could be selected on the basis of their appropriateness for certain stages of development. Schools could utilize each stage in development as a preparation for the next one.

Readiness is now generally accepted as a criterion, and is an especially palatable concept for those who follow developmental psychology. Robert Havighurst's (1966) "developmental tasks" for infancy and early childhood, for middle childhood, for adolescence, early adulthood, and even for middle age and later maturity are based on the notion of readiness. His description of "the teachable moment" is widely quoted:

When the body is ripe, and society requires, and the self is ready to achieve a certain task, the teachable moment has come. Efforts at teaching which would have been largely wasted if they had come earlier, give gratifying results when they come at the *teachable moment*, when the task should be learned. (1966, p. 5)

SUBJECT MATTER FUSION

The separate-subjects approach had been attacked by Kilpatrick and Dewey, among others. An organization pattern sometimes called *fusion* incorporates the basic theme that those critics might use to supplant separate-subjects treatments. The separate-subjects effort is still commonly found, though it has gradually been relaxed in some quarters so that content may be arranged around units or themes. The basic assumption behind the separate-subjects approach is that the subject to be taught constitutes a kind of organized cultural package to be transmitted to all pupils. Thus, it becomes the duty of the teacher to transmit this package whether all learners assimilate it well or not. A second assumption is that by teaching subject matter separately, it is possible to make more homogeneous groupings of content. Furthermore, if the subject matter is arranged more homogeneously, pupils are likely to learn it more readily. The third assumption is that an isolated package of subject-matter may be vertically organized in a logical and sequential manner—the work of each grade builds on what has been taught in the grade below. A fourth assumption is that there will be transfer from one subject-matter area to another. These four assumptions have been seriously questioned, giving rise to a different approach.

The different approach, based on a fusion of subject matter, and sometimes called the *experience approach*, boasts some powerful adherents, one of the foremost of whom was Dewey. He insisted that education ought to provide more than simply the transmission of facts to children. Foresight and the recognition of consequences of actions on the part of the learner require an active involvement. Experiences undergone by the learner should be continuous with, and related to, the experiences that are unique to that learner. Packaged education is ill-equipped to cope with the requirements of unique experiences. Some kind of a fusion of subject matters is expected to provide experiences in which the ability to think critically and reflectively is nurtured. The importance of organization of subject matter is no longer stressed, and the accent is upon the importance of the learner himself—his background experiences, his present interests, his goals, and his abilities.

Fusion efforts have ranged all the way from the very simple teaching of similar subject matters at the same time in the school year, focusing upon major areas, or correlations of topics, to limited fusion and to a problems-of-living approach. In this, the curriculum follows Stratemeyer's *Developing a Curriculum for Modern Living* (1957). Here, *persistent life situations* are assigned to major categories, including intellectual power, moral choices, aesthetic expression and appreciation, person-to-person relationships, natural phenomena, technological resources, and economic-social-political structures and forces. The *emergent curriculum* is therefore unplanned, with the idea that it will arise out of the classroom experiences as they occur. Thus, content is determined by the course of events. In the fusion of subject matters and experiences, the skills and knowledge acquired are thus made experimental in solving larger problems.

HAVE PRINCIPLES OF TEACHING BEEN DISCOVERED?

The idea of breadth of application, according to a discovered uniformity not fundamental enough to be called a law, seems to be what is usually meant when principles are mentioned. In education, it would be expected that principles would be stated in the form of generalized directives, which are tentative and flexible, yet form some sort of a stable basis for operation. To be useful as tools, many of these principles ought to be in the form of what Carpenter and Haddan (1964) called power principles, which deal with a descriptive relation between at least two key terms that should be used to name things in the specified situation. *Power* principles include a key term, which is *manipulable*, that is, coming under the control of the teacher.

No sets of principles have emerged that may truly be called principles of teaching-learning; in fact, no principles of *learning* have been unanimously agreed upon by theorizers about teaching although Hilgard (1956) does list some generalizations that are acceptable to most learning theorists. Sometimes confusion has arisen about the relationship between principles of teaching and methods of teaching. Older methods have fallen into disuse, if they were ever really adopted, and newer ones often come under suspicion. Something more is needed than techniques and directives for specific subject matters under prescribed conditions at given grade levels. Educators rightly abhor furnishing teachers with cookbooks filled with instructional recipes. The necessity for the teacher's becoming more than a technician, following rules established by others, is becoming evident as certification requirements are upgraded and teachers are strongly urged to become professionals. The professional, fully aware of principles, ought to be able to develop his own techniques, methods, and operating rules. The area in which answers might be found has often been described as one that deals in open-minded, tentative, and generally inadequate solutions.

William H. Burton (1958), however, and a few others have worked diligently on the problem of discovering and stating principles of teaching. Although it must be admitted that Burton's principles may also be tentative, the ideas involved may be profitably examined. Burton is in agreement with N. L. Gage that no theory of learning, satisfactory in all respects, has been formulated. "We can, however, get on with a more limited job of setting up a reasonably consistent statement of principles useful in everyday teaching" (p. 242).

Burton first suggested that a number of theories of learning be examined in order to determine those principles upon which theorists agree. He found only two ready-made summaries that present the agreements among theorists. The first of these came from Hilgard (1956). (Classification titles and italics are added.)

Intelligence

1. In deciding who should learn what, the *capacities of the learner* are important. Brighter people can learn things less bright ones cannot learn; in general, older children can learn more readily than younger ones; the decline of ability with age, in the adult years, depends upon what it is that is being learned.

Motivation

2. A motivated learner acquires what he learns more readily than one who is not motivated. The relevant motives include both general and specific ones, for example, desire to learn, need for achievement (general), desire for a certain reward or to avoid a threatened punishment (specific).

3. Motivation that is too *intense* (especially pain, fear, anxiety) may be accompanied by distracting emotional states, so that excessive motivation may be less effective than moderate motivation for learning some kinds of tasks, especially those involving difficult discriminations.

4. Learning under the control of *reward* is usually preferable to learning under the control of punishment. Correspondingly, learning motivated by success is preferable to learning motivated by failure. Even though the theoretical issue is still unresolved, the practical outcome

must take into account the social by-products, which tend to be more favorable under reward than under punishment.

5. Learning under *intrinsic* motivation is preferable to learning under extrinsic motivation.

Aspiration level

6. *Tolerance for failure* is best taught through providing a backlog of success that compensates for experienced failure.

7. Individuals need practice in setting *realistic goals* for themselves, goals neither so low as to elicit little effort nor so high as to foreordain to failure.

Learner attitude

8. The *personal history* of the individual, for example, his reaction to authority, may hamper or enhance his ability to learn from a given teacher.

9. Active *participation* by a learner is preferable to passive reception when learning, for example, from a lecture or motion picture.

Learning conditions

10. *Meaningful materials* and meaningful tasks are learned more readily than nonsense materials and more readily than tasks not understood by the learner.

11. There is no substitute for *repetitive practice* in the overlearning of skills (for instance, the performance of a concert pianist), or in the memorization of unrelated facts that have to be automatized.

12. *Information* (feedback) about the nature of a good performance, knowledge of his own mistakes, and knowledge of successful results, aid learning.

13. Transfer to new tasks will be better if, in learning, the learner can *discover relationships* for

himself, and if he has experience during learning of applying the principles within a variety of tasks.

14. Spaced or *distributed recalls* are advantageous in fixing material that is to be long retained.
(Hilgard, 1956, pp. 486–487)

A second summary of learning principles was provided by T. R. McConnell, in "Reconciliation of Learning Theories," in the Forty-first Yearbook of the National Society for the Study of Education (1942). Burton then used these summaries and other research to develop his own position in his "Basic Principles in a Good Teaching-Learning Situation" (1958), in which he included relearning, group process and learning, preserving the learner's security, the motivation of learning, and the principle of readiness. Summaries were made of such processes as the learning of problem-solving skills; the acquisition of meanings, generalizations, and concepts; the achievement of attitudes and appreciations; and the development of skills and abilities.

From all the above considerations, Burton arrived at a listing of characteristics of the learner. Assuming that these comprise most of the major considerations of the nature of the learner, one might therefore see Burton's parallel listings of settings for learnings as possible directives or principles of teaching (italicized identifying terms are added):

The Learner	The Setting for Learning
1. *Organism.* The learner, like all living organisms, is a unitary, integrating whole.	1. The desirable setting for functional learning experiences will provide for natural integration of feeling-doing-thinking.
2. *Needs.* The learner, like any other living organism, seeks always to maintain equilibrium or balance.	2. Desirable learning experiences will provide opportunity for success in meeting needs and solving problems, but will also give constant challenge to go beyond immediate situations.
3. *Goals.* The learner is a goal-seeking organism, pursuing aims to satisfy needs, thus to maintain equilibrium.	3. The desirable setting for learning will be dominated by purposes and goals set up by the learner or learners, either by themselves or with appropriate guidance from the total group, including consultants.

The Learner	*The Setting for Learning*
4. *Exploration.* The learner is an active, behaving, exploring individual.	4. The setting must provide freedom to explore, to construct, to question, to differ, to make mistakes: freedom to develop creative contributions. The limits of freedom are democratic controls, rights of others, and good taste.
5. *Individual Differences.* The learner has a pattern and rhythm of growth peculiar to the individual. Notable differences exist between individuals, in speed of learning, energy output, depth of feeling, facility of insight.	5. Widely varied types of learning experiences should be provided, adaptable to levels of maturity to different rates, interests, abilities, and so forth.
6. *Social environment.* The learner brings with him a personality, a set of aims, values, social habits.	6. The purposes and experiences established should arise out of and be continuous with the life of the learner. The family background and social-class status, as well as the individuality of the learner, must be taken into account.
7. *Guidance.* A learner may be quite immature in relation to one set of standards and experiences, and quite mature in relation to another.	7. Learners need sympathetic guidance while building an awareness and personality within their own experiences. They need protection from situations in which they cannot yet act intelligently; protection from fears and anxieties; protection sufficient to insure security and status on various levels; plus challenge to grow, to conquer problems, to develop self-reliance. The learner needs guidance from consultants who know and understand the problems of a growing personality; who see learning as a developmental process. Guidance must be free from domination or coercion.
8. *Groups.* The learner is a social animal, if normal, and naturally seeks activities involving other persons.	8. The setting must provide many varied opportunities to work in "we" relationships, developing eventually into self-directed group activity. The whole range of interactive human relationships, the cooperative group process, is essential to the development of mature, socialized personality.
	(Burton, p. 248)

TWO OPPOSING CAMPS IN THE
DEVELOPMENT OF THEORETICAL POSITIONS

The two categories are not necessarily mutually inclusive, insofar as the aim of discovering principles of teaching are concerned. One of these insists that a *science* of teaching is possible, if not immanent. Its proponents suggest various ways of structuring the many facets of the teaching-learning situation in an orderly, systematic fashion. It is felt that at least a minimal common base for teaching may be provided for all teachers. The other camp claims that teaching cannot ever become a science, but is, instead, an *art*, subject to individual expressions and techniques. Further, these expressions and techniques are not to be subjected to impositions from other frameworks. Both positions, however, have worked toward the formulation of guidelines that are expected to be useful in what each defines as teaching. The chapters that follow treat first on some possibilities and limitations concerning the building of theories about teaching. The views of some who see teaching as an art will be aired, because their contributions have enriched the pursuit of education in so many ways. Recent innovations will also be described.

Some chapters will be primarily concerned with elements that might contribute to the building of theories. Some will speak of methods, of techniques, and perhaps of principles. In some instances, one man's method may be another man's principles. Those who see teaching as comprised of a transmitter (teacher), a channel for transmission (medium), and a receiver (pupil) will not be displeased to find a discussion on the new media. Those who see teaching-learning as a system may find some pleasure in the systems approaches discussed. Those who see the learning environment primarily as a social one will appreciate the chapter on interacting selves.

References

1. Ascher, Ralph S., "Methods and Techniques in Teacher Development," *Educational Technology* (November 15, 1966), 1–2.
2. Beauchamp, George A., *Basic Dimensions in Elementary Method.* Boston, Allyn and Bacon, Inc., 1965.
3. Broudy, Harry S., "Historic Examples of Teaching Method," *Handbook*

of *Research on Teaching*, H. L. Gage (ed.). Chicago, Rand, McNally & Company, 1963.

4. ——, and John R. Palmer, *Exemplars of Teaching Method*. Chicago, Rand, McNally & Company, 1965.

5. Bugelski, B. R., "Suggestions for Teachers," *The Psychology of Learning Applied to Teaching*. New York, The Bobbs-Merrill Company, Inc., 1964.

6. Burton, William H., "Basic Principles in a Good Teacher-Learning Situation," *Phi Delta Kappan* (March 1958), Vol. 39, 242–248.

7. Carpenter, Finley F., and Eugene E. Haddan, *Systematic Application of Psychology to Education*. New York, The Macmillan Company, 1964.

8. DeGarmo, Charles, *The Essentials of Method*. Boston, D. C. Heath and Company, 1893.

9. Dewey, John, *The Child and the Curriculum*. Chicago, The University of Chicago Press, 1902.

10. ——, *Democracy and Education*. New York, The Macmillan Company, 1916.

11. ——, *How We Think*. Boston, D. C. Heath and Company, 1910.

12. ——, *Interest and Effort in Education*. Boston, Houghton Mifflin Company, 1913.

13. Dewey, John, "My Pedagogic Creed," *The School Journal*, Vol. LIV, No. 3, January 16, 1897, pp. 77–80. Reprinted in Martin S. Dworkin, *Dewey on Education: Selections*. New York, Teachers College Press, Columbia University, 1965.

14. Dworkin, Martin S., *Dewey on Education: Selections*. New York, Teachers College Press, Columbia University, 1965.

15. English, Horace B., and Ava C. English, *A Comprehensive Dictionary of Psychological and Psychoanalytical Terms*. New York, David McKay Company, Inc., 1958.

16. Froebel, F. W., *The Education of Man*, trans. by W. N. Hailmann, International Education Series, Vol. 5. New York, Appleton-Century-Crofts, 1911.

17. Havighurst, Robert J., *Developmental Tasks and Education*. New York, David McKay Company, Inc., 1966.

18. Herbart, Johann Friedrich, *Outlines of Educational Doctrine*, trans. by Alexis F. Large and Charles DeGarmo. New York, The Macmillan Company, 1904.

19. Hilgard, Ernest R., *Theories of Learning*, 2nd ed. New York, Appleton-Century-Crofts, 1956.

20. Kilpatrick, William H., *Foundations of Method*. New York, The Macmillan Company, 1925.

21. ——, *Philosophy of Education*. New York, The Macmillan Company, 1951.

22. ——, "The Project Method," *Teachers College Record*, 1918.

23. McConnell, T. R., "Reconciliation of Learning Theories," *The Psychology of Learning*. Forty-first Yearbook, Part II, National Society for the Study of Education, Bloomington, Ill., Public School Publishing Company, 1942.

24. Putnam, Daniel, *A Primer of Pedagogy*. Lansing, Mich., H. R. Pattengill, 1891.
25. Stratemeyer, Florence B., and Hamden L. Forkner, Margaret G. McKim, and A. Harry Passow, *Developing a Curriculum for Modern Living*. New York, Bureau of Publication, Teachers College, Columbia University, 1957.
26. Thayer, V. T., *Formative Ideas in American Education: From the Colonial Period to the Present*. New York, Dodd, Mead & Company, 1965.

Possibilities for Theory Building

In seeking to establish a number of related concepts that may be useful in building a theory, the theorizer is sometimes concerned equally with the questions that it will pose and with the generalities it may provide as guidelines for application. It may be that a close analysis of the supposed bases for the theory will cause traditional foundations to crumble, or that long-assumed foundations do not in fact exist. The theory builder may have been dealing with abstractions that should be more specifically defined. Educators are familiar with the ready criticism voiced when they speak hypothetically of "the child," when they ought to have spoken of a specific individual. Similarly, there may be tendencies to speak of "the teacher," as a composite of averages, or of "the psychology of learning" as a unified body that actually does not exist as such.

MODELS, PARADIGMS, AND THEORIES

The nature of the general must somehow be conveyed by the specific, and a model is a useful means for bringing this about. Gage (1963) has said that paradigms are models, patterns, or schemata, useful as ways of thinking that can lead to theory development. Silverman (1967) implied as much when he said that:

the best way to proceed in developing a theory of teaching is to begin with what is known about learning in the laboratory and in the classroom by adopting a model derived from a theory of learning and/or from systematic approaches to the study of learning in the laboratory. (p. 4)

First, derive a *model*, based on a theory (learning), and then use that model to develop another theory (teaching). Silverman then went on to differentiate between some of the functions of theories and models. A theory is a system in which the interaction among actual variables is described, whereas a model is an analogy and is judged by its utility. Reification, the treating of an analogy or abstraction as though it is the real thing, poses a danger in the use of models. It is easy to overgeneralize in the use of analogies.

Silverman averred that one builds a theory (1) by making systematic observations or making use of the systematic observations that others have provided; (2) by inventing or locating constructs, which are concepts used in representing the relationships among things or events; and (3) by deriving hypotheses on the basis of the constructs and their relationships. Gage, however, pointed out that a logical and orderly process is not always found leading to a theory—instead, the research may be rather informal, illogical, and messy-looking, though the end product, the theory, may emerge as a logical structure. Lee J. Cronbach (1963) failed to find a single learning theory to account for all learning, and he added that the theorizing of G. A. Miller resembles his own, in that the emphasis is upon the regulation of behavior by its consequences—a reinforcement theory. B. F. Skinner elaborated on this learning approach, in *Science and Human Behavior* (1953), as did Keller and Schoenfeld, in *Principles of Psychology* (1950).

THEORIES OF TEACHING CAN BE BASED ON THEORIES OF LEARNING —CRONBACH'S SEVEN ELEMENTS

Cronbach (1963), in examining what theories have proposed for teaching and learning, concluded that the raising of questions is still important to the present state of the "science" of teaching. One question asked was whether the technical theories of learning suffice for "a description that will apply to all forms of learning, especially to those complex responses for which no technical learning theory has been completely worked out" (1963, p. 73). Strictly speaking, Cronbach's ideas are not theories, but theorizings, in the form of statements of the elements of learning. He presented seven elements of learning, which express in miniature a theory of behavior. These seven elements may then be used as the base for a theory of learning. According to Cronbach, once the aspects of behavior that are called *learning* are more adequately described, it becomes possible to describe the problems of teachers. These problems must necessarily be solved if teachers are to facilitate learning.

The first element of learning is called the *situation*, and it consists of all the objects, persons, and symbols in the learner's environment. The subject matter, the teacher, the pupils, and all the learning aids are parts of the situation. The degree of transfer of learning from one situation to another is a function of the adequacy of earlier learning. Thus, when the curriculum is planned, a variety of situations are selected and arranged in sequence, so that pupils may learn responses that are appropriate to both immediate and extended objectives.

The second element of learning consists of the *personal characteristics* of pupils. In any learning situation, a pupil possesses abilities and response patterns that are typical of his behavior, that is, there is some degree of predictability in his behavior, if the situation is known and the pupil has been carefully studied. The personal characteristics of the learner may establish probabilities upon which a teacher may base his expectations for that particular pupil. If the pupil is not ready for an activity he must be involved in another task (situation) for which his readiness has been predicted. Thus, an understanding of individual differences and an accurate prediction of individual development stages is essential. Suiting the situation to pupil characteristics has been strongly advocated by many experts in developmental psychology.

The third element is called *goal*. The learner wishes to bring about some state of affairs as a consequence of his efforts, and that state of affairs constitutes his goal. It may be the acquisition of material objects, it may be arriving at a geographical location, it may be directing the activity of someone else, or it may be the solving of a problem. The specific goals possible are too numerous to list, of course, and may be immediate and long-range objectives. What complicates the task of the teacher is that a pupil is likely to have several goals, either immediate or long range, influencing his reactions simultaneously. Furthermore, if these goals are to direct the pupil's efforts maximally, they must be his own goals. At the very least, he must have accepted them as his own, even if he may have had little or no part in their selection.* If a pupil is not

* How directive a teacher ought to be in setting up goals is often considered a debatable issue. Discussants may meet on the common ground where it is agreed that the degree of directivity is often a function of the personality of the learner, as well

willing to accept goals that others have helped him to establish, a skilled teacher will learn how to make his goals those of the pupil, in various ways ranging from rather direct to very subtle. One of the teacher's major tasks is to arrange for this kind of motivation.

The fourth element, *interpretation,* directs attention to parts of the first element, *situation,* and to past experiences of the learner, and it calls for predictions as to what is likely to happen if various courses of action are taken. This element, because it ties future actions to past experiences, is actually closely related to the element *goal.* The interpretations may be made without conscious awareness, or they may be conscious and deliberate. Whichever they are, interpretations permit the pupil to make trials on the basis of his predictions.

The fifth element is *action.* This includes the movements and the statements of the pupil. It pertains only minimally, if at all, to involuntary actions. The learner may be uncertain about his *interpretations* in a novel *situation,* so he acts tentatively, that is, he makes provisional tries. When these tentative actions are typical of the individual, he is characterized by creative activity. (Or there may be vacillation and an inability to make firm decisions as a consequence of personality disturbances. Or because of intellectual deficiency, he regularly gets the wrong answers.) He may be dissatisfied with what seems to be the obvious, wanting to see "what would happen if . . ." and either follows the rules routinely and solves his problems, or he discovers new solutions characterized as original or creative.

Element number six is called *consequence.* Whatever happens as a result of *action* by the learner, and is perceived by him as resulting from his action, will influence his future behavior. If consequences go unnoticed, or if he mistakenly assigns causal acts to effects that are not related to them, then systematic influences on learning will be lessened. Consequences, or the knowledge of consequences, either confirm or refute his predictions and tend to determine what interpretations he is likely to make on other occasions. If he is inaccurate in his observations of consequences, or if his interpretations are not consistent, then his actions may be reinforced or extinguished unpredictably. The teacher can be of great service in helping a pupil to observe the consequences of his actions accurately.

The final element is *reaction to thwarting.* If a learner meets conditions that prevent his reaching a goal, he is thwarted. His behavior at that point may take one of two general courses. He may engage in adaptive behavior,

---

as that of the teacher. How much help is given in selecting a goal may also depend upon whether it is a main goal or a subgoal, and whether achieving it is more important as an end in itself, or whether a consideration of the means to the goal is also a valuable objective.

such as making a new interpretation and launching another attempt, with some modification of his actions or with renewed vigor, resulting in his coming closer to attaining the goal. But making a new interpretation may also involve seeing the goal differently and changing his idea of what he can attain or how he wishes to attain it. The learner may also engage in nonadaptive frustration behavior when he reacts to thwarting. If he rigidly persists in repetitive acts that do not bring him closer to the goal, if he gives up, or if he produces random, erratic responses without much consideration of their appropriateness, then he is reacting nonadaptively. Such acts could happen to result in moving toward the goal, in which case they may be adaptive responses for that situation, and he is just lucky!*

When these seven elements of learning are related to some generally recognized problems of teaching, some directives may be developed for teaching. Cronbach mentioned the organizing of curriculum materials, the motivating of pupils, the evaluating of their work (and the teacher's), and the provision for individual differences as essential problems in teaching. Bringing together the seven elements of learning and the problems of the teacher, Cronbach listed the following acts of the teacher as they are associated with each aspect of learning:

Situation	Selects and arranges material to which the pupil is to respond.
Personal Characteristics	Uses aptitude tests and other data to judge what method and material the pupil is ready for.
Goal	Helps the pupil to understand what constitutes a desirable performance. Provides an encouraging atmosphere, sets attainable standards. Shows connections between the pupil's classwork and his personal aims.
Interpretation	Makes clear the characteristics of a desirable response. Arranges material meaningfully, and elaborates meanings by suitable explanation. Suggests suitable trial responses or methods of attack.
Action	Provides for the pupil to make active responses through practice, recitations, projects, etc.
Consequence	Monitors the pupil's performance to detect misunderstanding or faulty technique. Uses tests to show the pupil what progress he is making and what faults need to be overcome.
Reaction to Thwarting	Reduces emotional tension. Assists the pupil to reinterpret. Studies the pupil individually to identify causes of difficulty.

(1963, p. 83)

---

* *Serendipity* is applicable here. It means the attainment of a satisfying condition that was not even being sought.

The elements and the tasks that they present to teachers are sufficiently general to lie outside a definition of techniques or specific methods. If they are accepted as general enough to act as directives for teaching, they may be called principles of teaching, though most would not wish to accept them as *the* principles.

CONDITIONS OF LEARNING ARE BASIC TO TEACHING—GAGNE'S APPROACH

Theories have an intellectual appeal that is disarming, but can they explain learning? Gagne' (1965) took the position that learning cannot be accounted for by simple theories, by a small number of principles. Instead, he argued that generalizations that can be made about learning come only from observations of the *conditions in which learning occurs,* and that:

> If the outlines of a theory are identifiable, surely the latter must consist of the idea that complex forms of learning require simpler forms of behavior as prerequisites. As a generalization, this is certainly not novel. Perhaps, though, an articulate theory of learning might someday be based upon it. (p. vi)

The simpler forms of behavior that Gagne' stated may be prerequisites in identifying a theory are numerous, but he first described the elements of the learning event:

1. The learner, his senses, his central nervous system, and his muscles.
2. The stimulus situation, the events that stimulate the learner's senses.
3. A *response,* the action that results from stimulation and subsequent nervous activity. Responses are often described in terms of their effects, or *performances.*

Gagne' classified everyday observations about learning, so as to identify and distinguish varieties of situations in which learning occurs. He then went on to describe the conditions that control these occurrences. (The motivations and the attitudes of the learner are not included in this approach.) For Gagne', teaching or instructing means arranging the conditions of learning that are external to the learner. These conditions need to be constructed in a stage-by-stage fashion, taking due account at each stage of the just previously acquired capabilities of the learner, the requirements for retention of these capabilities, and the specific stimulus situation needed for the next stage of learning. (p. 26)

Stage-by-stage construction of conditions for learning, based on previously acquired capabilities and looking ahead for what is to be needed by a following stage of learning places a great deal of emphasis upon *prerequisites*. Gagne' suggested a hierarchy, in which one kind of learning is built upon another:

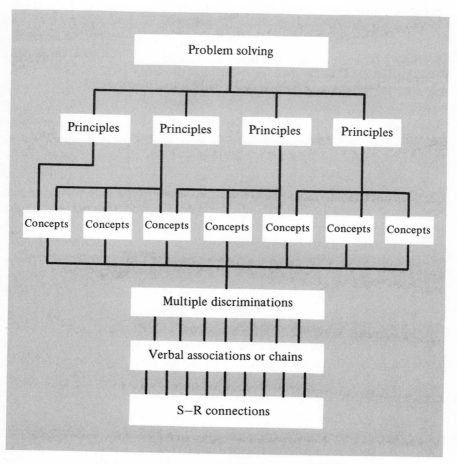

Fig. 3.1 Model showing Gagne's statement of prerequisites in learning.

The eight conditions for learning are based on eight types or basic forms of learning. Some of these basic forms are derived from what are usually called *theories of learning,* whereas others are based on ideas about learning, such as B. F. Skinner's, which their adherents refuse to call *theories.* Type one is called *signal learning.* This is simply Pavlovian conditioning. Conditions for type one learning are of two general categories; those within the learner and those in the learning situation. Within the learner must be a natural reflex that can be evoked by either an unconditioned stimulus or a conditioned one. The essential conditions in the learning situation are contiguity and repetition. The signaling stimulus must be presented very closely in time to the presentation of the unconditioned stimulus (from 0 to about 1.5 seconds apart). This contiguous pairing must also be repeated. Seldom if ever is the connection between signal and original stimulus sufficiently strengthened by a single pairing. For a more complete discussion of the importance of contiguity and other considerations in signal learning or association, see E. R. Guthrie's "Conditioning: A Theory of Learning in Terms of Stimulus, Response, and Association" (1942).

The second kind of learning, or type two, is called *stimulus-response learning.* Synonyms for this type of learning are *operant learning* and *instrumental learning.* (Thorndike's trial-and-error learning is not quite the same as operant learning, though it is considered the original S-R psychology of learning by Hilgard [1956]). The conditions necessary in the learner include the occurrence of a terminating act that is reinforcing. A response that terminates in reinforcement must be performed. As for conditions in the learning situation, the environment must provide an object or event that will result in satisfaction to the learner when he has performed the act. Also, contiguity and repetition are considered important. An excellent, brief summary of operant learning is presented in Fred S. Keller's *Learning: Reinforcement Theory* (1965).

Type three learning, or *chaining,* refers to the connection of a series of individual stimuli and their responses in a sequence. Gagne' spoke of non-verbal chains as simply *chains,* whereas the kinds that involve verbal behavior are said to be *verbal chains* or *verbal associates* (see type four). The prime condition within the learner is that each S-R connection must have been learned previously. However, because it is so difficult to know for certain that the necessary previously acquired discriminations have been accomplished, it is necessary to add external cues. Quite rapid learning may occur when very little additional cueing is necessary. As was the case with type one and type two learnings, contiguity and repetition are necessary conditions in the learning situation. It is also necessary that once the links of a chain are known, they be established in the *proper order*, and that reinforcement be present following the terminal link in a chain. Keller and Schoenfeld's *Principles of Psychology* (1950) contains an excellent chapter on chaining.

Type four learning is known as *verbal association*. This is concerned with establishing verbal chains, from very simple ones, such as in linking two S-R connections as in naming, to much more complex verbal chains, as in problem solving, where verbal response sequences act as cues or reasoning sequences. The previous learning of each link must have occurred, and mediating connections between each verbal unit and the next must have been learned. The mediating connections amount to verbal codes, that is, associations that tie the verbal units together. It is not difficult to learn a verbal chain, once the conditions within the learner are met, but there are also some conditions within the learning situation that are important. First, proper sequencing of verbal units is necessary. Second, the responses in the chain must be required of the learner, so that he is active, not passive. Third, external stimuli that furnish cues tending to establish orderly chain arrangements are helpful. Fourth, lengths of verbal chains should be provided that are correlated with the learner's span of immediate memory. Fifth, the confirmation of correct responses must be provided. C. N. Cofer's *Verbal Learning and Verbal Behavior* (1961) is an excellent source for further study.

Type five learning is *multiple discrimination*. In multiple discrimination, the learner does not merely learn connections one after another, as in a chain, but must respond simultaneously to many stimuli. The learner must establish various chains, and the discrimination involved may become quite difficult. Also, the learning of later associations tends to interfere with those learned earlier. The conditions within the learner are (1) the previous acquisition of each chain in the group that is to be learned; and (2) for each chain, the prerequisites for verbal-associate learning (type four) must have been established. The conditions in the learning situation are

1. All stimuli within chains that are to be associated must be presented one by one, on the initial presentation, so that the learner can set up each chain. Prompting is helpful, probably necessary, as an aid in making the associations.
2. Repetition will help reduce interference and subsequent forgetting.

3. The arrangement of repetitions should be optimal. How much repetition at a time and how much material per repetition has not been experimentally established yet.

4. There must be confirmation of responses (resulting in reinforcement).

Type six is *concept learning,* wherein the learner responds to objects or events as a class, e.g., tree, group, justice. The condition within the learner is that he must have previously acquired chains related to representative stimulus situations and that exhibit class characteristics peculiar to the concept. The conditions within the situation are

1. The related objects are presented simultaneously, or nearly so, with the requirement that the learner place them all in the same class.

2. New objects or events are presented, to which the learner must respond as he does to those in the concept.

3. Identification of additional instances of the concept must be required.

4. Reinforcement of correct responding should be promptly provided.

Type seven (along with type eight), or *the learning of principles,* is what is typically involved in formal instruction. "Principles are chains of concepts that make up what is generally called *knowledge*" (Gagne', p. 141). The condition within the learner that is necessary for the learning of principles is that the learner must already know the concepts necessary for the chain(s). The conditions in the learning situation are

1. The learner must be told what kind of performance, in general, will show that learning has been completed.

2. The concepts that will make up the principle must be invoked via instructions.

3. Verbal cues must be provided that will hint at the principle, although not really stating it.

4. A question must be provided that requires the learner to demonstrate the principle.

5. The learner may be required to state the principle (it has not been demonstrated that this is absolutely necessary for learning, though it may be useful for later instruction).

Type eight learning consists of *problem solving.* Problem solving is not merely using principles to achieve a goal. Instead, higher order principles emerge, which will facilitate handling later situations that might otherwise require problem solving. Once the higher order principles are learned, many situations cease to present problems. Conditions within the learner depend upon the previously learned principles that are relevant to the problem. Conditions within the learning situation are

1. The principles that must be put together to reach a solution and the stimulus situation that poses the problem must be contiguous—the learner must hold them in mind all at the same time.
2. There must be a recall of relevant principles.
3. Verbal instructions should be provided to channel the learner's thinking, such as statements of the goal and the general form of the solution.

Gagne's hierarchy of learning makes it possible to relate learning to the content of instruction in an orderly manner. "The importance of mapping the sequence of learnings is mainly just this: that it enables one to avoid the mistakes that arise from 'skipping' essential steps in the acquisition of knowledge of a content area" (p. 173). His suggested sequencing lends itself well to the three essentials in instruction, according to Gagne'.

1. Creating preconditions of learning that will ensure student motivation.
2. Managing instruction, including assessment of outcomes.
3. Ensuring that transfer of learning will occur.

Thus, by close examination of the conditions, both within the learner and within the learning situation, the adept teacher will be enabled to develop his own unique methods in teaching. He will become a more efficient decision maker.

Gagne' arranged the decisions to be made by teachers in priorities according to areas of concern:

1. Motivation.
2. Transferability of knowledge.
3. Assessment.
4. Conditions for learning.
5. The structure of knowledge to be learned.
6. Learning objectives.

Motivation comes first because it depends on personal interactions with the student, so that in a sense each teacher is a guidance specialist. In transferability decisions, the teacher must employ a great variety of techniques to ensure that acquired knowledge will be generalized. In assessment decisions, the teacher should be the person in the best position to know what questions ought to be asked. Decisions concerning the conditions for learning, many times, may be the province of a psychologist, who aids in predesigning the conditions. This specialist may also be required to help with decisions concerning the structure of knowledge. Many of the decisions regarding learning objectives are also made by agencies outside the teacher's domain. However, the teacher will be expected to define the relation of the objectives to human performance.

THEORIES OF TEACHING CANNOT BE BASED ON A THEORY OF LEARNING—GAGE'S MULTIFACETED APPROACH

If teaching is viewed as a part of a teaching-learning interaction, then it is not surprising to find researchers who, when they seek out generalizations about teaching, turn to what has already been accepted about learning. However, N. L. Gage (1964) pointed to W. K. Estes (1960) and Ernest R. Hilgard (1956) as examples of foremost learning theorists who have insisted that laboratory psychology and the study of school learning have not converged. Even in the textbooks of educational psychology, where it might be expected that the implications of learning theories might be greatly exploited, the specific connections are lacking. The generalizations that are drawn "bear only slight resemblance to the elaborations of the theories as portrayed in Hilgard's book" (1964, p. 268). Gage did not say that theories of learning have nothing to offer, but rather that the necessary connections have not been made between learning theory and teaching practice that would enable the educator to make full use of them. He also distinguishes between the two processes, teaching and learning, in such a way as to make it clear that theories of learning cannot alone suffice in education. Theories of learning aid in furthering the aims of behavioral science—i.e., in the understanding, prediction, and control of learning behavior—but not in the development of a science and technology of teaching. Teaching, dealing as it does with how an individual behaves in influencing another individual to learn, is not concerned with the same kinds of variables as is learning itself. It is therefore necessary to analyze teaching and to develop theories specifically for teaching. Gage went on to suggest the kinds of research that might establish better foundations for such theories.

The neglect of the development of theories of teaching becomes evident, as has been shown, when the paucity of written materials concerning this area has been noted. This neglect, according to Gage, is produced by two primary barriers. The first is that the development of a science of teaching is often rejected. Such rejection, however, does not necessarily preclude a theory of teaching, which may even incorporate such unscientific components as those subsumed under teaching as an art. Art may even contribute to a theory. "Although teaching requires artistry, it can be subjected to scientific scrutiny" (1964, p. 270). A case is also made for scientific inquiry into teaching for the sake of better understanding, even if no practical value should follow. Thus, the development of theories of teaching ought not to be contingent upon their having practical value, though such a desirable outcome would be welcomed.

The second barrier to the development of theories of teaching has been the view that theories of learning furnish most, if not all, of what is necessary to understand teaching. But the behavior of teachers is not necessarily comprehended by theories that are devised to explain the behavior of pupils. Gage views teacher behavior as independent variables, and the learning of pupils as dependent variables. The dependent variables ought to be well understood, if one is to be able to explain, predict, and control the effect of independent variables upon them. So although learning theories are necessary in the development of teaching theories, the latter ought to be separately constructed. The independent variables that determine learning are composed of the behaviors of the teachers, so that it is important for teachers to know not only how learning proceeds, and how it is facilitated, but also how to control their own behaviors in providing learning assistance.

Teacher education has thus far provided little for the neophyte teacher that is basic to teaching as a facilitator of learning. Instead, it is expected that an acquaintance with theories of learning will lead to the ability to draw inferences that will be useful in teaching. If the analysis and specification of teaching are carefully conducted, then it may be possible to sketch what this kind of examination might lead to.

Teaching is so broad a term that it is misleading and refers to no unitary phenomenon. A great many processes, behaviors, and activities are involved, so that the search for a single, unified theory of teaching as a basic concept may be fruitless. Gage suggested that *learning* has often suffered from the same kind of misapplication. Not learning but learnings are involved, under the several theories, and hence no single theory of learning has emerged. Even if the search is narrowed to theorizing about school learning, too many different phenomena and processes are included to be accounted for by a single theory.

After abandoning any attempt to develop *a* theory of teaching, Gage went on to analyze teaching in four different ways. He hoped to uncover processes or elements that might be brought together in some kind of theoretical framework. The analysis was conducted according to (1) types of teacher activities; (2) educational objectives; (3) families-of-learning theory; and (4) components corresponding to those of learning.

The *acitvities of the teacher* are so numerous, so diverse, that it is not expected that a single theory can encompass them all. Teachers engage in many kinds of activities—explaining, health, physical and mental, record keeping, assignment making, curriculum planning, testing and evaluation, and many others. Clayton (1965) listed the following:

The teacher

1. Identifies the expected outcomes of the process.
2. Analyzes the student and makes decisions about the student's present stage of learning.
3. Specifies the objectives of teaching in the light of the first activities.
4. Selects information and materials and makes decisions about methods.
5. Involves the student in activities presumed to lead to learning.
6. Directs and guides the learning activities.
7. Provides situations for using the learnings involved.
8. Evaluates the outcomes of the process.

(p. 13)

The categories of activities listed will be determined by the basic theoretical orientation of the educationist. A highly permissive approach leads to different teaching activities than does a more directive one.

Educational objectives are the desired goals that are established. Some objectives will be those set up by the teacher, whereas others will arise from pupil needs, interests, drives, and so on. A permissive educator is likely to prefer working toward as many pupil-determined objectives as possible, whereas a more directive one will wish to emphasize objectives considered important by the teacher.

Bloom and others (1956) have analyzed three classes of educational objectives. The *affective* domain is occupied primarily with feeling tones, emotions, and attitudes—degrees of acceptance or rejection. Here, interests, appreciations, values, and emotional sets or biases are stressed as important to the education of the individual. In the *psychomotor* domain muscular or motor skills are taught, involving the manipulation of objects, and acts requiring sensorimotor coordination, such as writing or printing. The *cognitive* domain embraces the intellectual processes—remembering and understanding, performing tasks or solving problems, and combining and ordering ideas, methods, or procedures. A complication that makes theorizing difficult is that the three domains not only overlap, so that some achievement is possible in all when one is the area of concentration, but achievement in one domain may diminish or increase in importance to the learner if a disturbance occurs in another domain. A pupil, for example, may have cognitive difficulties, accompanied by affective upsets, and his coordination, involved in achieving a psychomotor objectve, may be disturbed.

Families-of-learning theory as a category refers to groups of theories that are usually accepted as being similar. One such group of theories holds that *conditioning* is essential. Ivan Pavlov's classical conditioning, the substitution process; J. B. Watson's early behavioristic psychology; E. L. Thorndike's Law of Effect (consequences); E. R. Guthrie's learning by contiguity; Clark Hull's emphasis on acquired drives and rewards; Dollard and Miller's drive-cue-response-reward; O. H. Mowrer's two-factor theory, including both classical and reinforcement conditioning; and B. F. Skinner's operant or instrumental conditioning—all belong to this family of learning theories.

Classical conditioning is sometimes called *respondent conditioning* because respondent behavior refers to reflex behavior, responses that are elicited or evoked by stimuli. These responses are involuntary, not initiated by the learner. Certain stimuli just naturally evoke certain responses.

Food evokes salivation. It is called, in this case, an *unconditioned response.* Sounds, on the other hand, do not ordinarily evoke salivation. Yet, if a sound, such as that of a bell, is paired enough times with food, this sound, which had been neutral, will acquire the power to evoke salivation. It is then said to be a *conditioned stimulus* for salivation. The individual has learned to substitute one stimulus for another, and the sound alone will now evoke salivation—the conditioned response. The power to evoke will be lost, however, if the bell is presented alone too many times without the food. Such loss of the power to draw out the response, a kind of unlearning, is called *extinction.* J. B. Watson elaborated on this kind of conditioning, showing, for example, that responses to fear can be *generalized,* i.e., a child not only learns to respond with fear to a white rat that has been repeatedly presented to the child while a loud clanging sound is being made, but he also learns to fear other furry objects, not necessarily white, nor even alive.

E. R. Guthrie's theory is sometimes considerd an offshoot of J. B. Watson's. However, Guthrie did not follow Watson in building his theory on the conditioned reflex as a basic element of habit formation. Instead, he used a principle of associative learning. Stated as a law of learning, Guthrie's theory rests primarily upon his idea that "A combination of stimuli which has accompanied a movement will on its recurrence tend to be followed by that movement" (1935). Thus, the best prediction of what an individual will do under specified circumstances is that he will do precisely what he did the last time he responded under the same circumstances. Learning occurs completely on the first occasion—however, no two sets of circumstances are ever exactly alike, hence, gradual learning *seems* to occur. Guthrie added that the learner is conditioned (learns) by making movements in the presence of cues, and that his responses are extinguished when such movements cannot occur when the cues are present.

> If you wish to encourage a particular kind of behavior or discourage another, discover the cues leading to the behavior in question. In the one case, arrange the situation so that the desired behavior occurs when those cues are present; in the other case, arrange it so that the undesired behavior does not occur in the presence of the cues. This is all that is involved in the skillful use of reward and punishment. A student does not learn what was in a lecture or a book. He learns only what the lecture or book caused him to do. (1942, p. 55)

Because most behaviors are complexes of movements occurring in the presence of complex stimulus patterns, then the more stimuli associated with desired behavior, the less likely is it that the desired behavior will be interfered with by competing behaviors and/or other distracting stimuli. If one is to learn best, one ought to learn in the kind of setting in which he will be expected to exhibit the desired behavior and should go through all the movements involved as realistically as possible.

B. F. Skinner's ideas concerned another kind of conditioning, which he called *operant conditioning,* based on responses originated from or *emitted* by the learner, not on responses drawn out of him. Programmed instruction received a great deal of impetus from principles observed by Skinner in his laboratory research. Operant conditioning, sometimes called *instrumental conditioning,* arose from E. L. Thorndike's Law of Effect. The strength of an act can be altered by the consequences of that act. Thorndike spoke of a satisfying state of affairs as strengthening, and unsatisfying consequences as weakening, whereas Skinner spoke of reinforcement according to probabilities.

Positive reinforcers are those stimuli whose presentation to the learner results in strengthening the behavior they follow. A negatively reinforcing stimulus is one that strengthens the behavior that results in its removal. Punishment presents aversive or noxious stimuli, or removes positive reinforcers. Punishment weakens behavior, but does not extinguish it. Extinction is brought about by nonreinforcement. It is also accomplished by reinforcing responses incompatible with the responses that are to be extinguished, i.e., by the reinforcement of responses that cannot occur simultaneously with those to be extinguished.

The timing of reinforcements is important. If a response is reinforced every time it occurs, this is continuous or regular reinforcement. Such a schedule is best for novel learning and is often used in connection with the technique of successive approximations. The learner may produce a very remote approximation of the desired behavior and is then reinforced for it. After he has been reinforced enough times, he also adds to the behavior and is then reinforced for the progress made. Step by step, he moves toward the final behavior desired, and is reinforced for progress. This differential reinforcement, then, is applied on a continuous schedule for the most effective novel learning. However, an intermittent schedule is most resistant to extinction, so for retention, it is not desirable to reinforce every response. Thus, according to Skinner, one learns best when one is reinforced for learning. One unlearns (extinguishes) when repeatedly failing to receive reinforcement. New material is learned best via reenforcement for each step, even if only a small one, which represents improvement. Once learning is accomplished, retention is achieved best by occasional, not regular, reinforcement.

Identification theories are based on the learner's ability to imitate. Miller and Dollard (1941) showed that in order for learning to occur efficiently via imitation, the learner must have developed imitation techniques previously. Recently, Bandura (1962) presented a rationale for imitation as a learning mode.

Theory of Learning by Imitation

The teacher's role in promoting learning by imitation is preponderantly one of aiding in *social* learning. Bandura (1962) stressed the importance of an imitation or identification paradigm. Bandura opined that although learning is accomplished in some situations by other methods (e.g., via successive approximations, or step by step, with each bit of progress being reinforced), there are many situations in which this kind of learning does not predominate. Even in some step-by-step learnings, the process of imitation may occur and thereby shorten the learning time, especially when social models are provided. According to Bandura, the learning process receiving the most intensive laboratory investigation (instrumental conditioning) is not at all representative of the natural process of social learning. As a consequence, present-day social-learning theories fail to fit the facts of response acquisition in at least two important aspects:

1. Available theories are culture-free, that is, social agents are typically considered little more than inefficiently programmed reinforcer-dispensing devices. But social transmission of behavior is governed not only by the particular patterns of response-reinforcing contingencies, but by the behavioral *examples* they provide. Social agents are important as a *source of patterns of behavior*.

2. The unit of response acquisition is typically a large segment rather than small segments that are acquired through a slow, gradual process. "Following actual demonstrations by a model or verbal descriptions of the desired behavior, the learner generally reproduces more or less the entire pattern of behavior which must then be further refined, and maintained by the application of reinforcement procedures" (1962, p. 258).

Cognitive Restructuring

Organizing facts, concepts, and principles—called *cognitive restructuring*—is determined both by mental processes and by the nature of the subject to be learned. One family of learning theory specifies shifting the mental organizations of learners so that solutions to problems are facilitated.

> The cognitive restructuring paradigm of learning holds that the learner arrives at knowledge and understanding by perceiving the situation (the problem) before him and then rearranging it, through central cognitive processes, in ways that yield meaning of a rational, logically consistent kind. The teacher can engender this restructuring by pointing to, either physically or verbally, and by manipulating the parts of the cognitive configuration so as to make the structure he wants learned stand out as a kind of figure against the ground of irrelevancies and distractions. (Gage, 1964, p. 278)

The concept of cognitive restructuring is often preferred by (Gestalt) psychologists, who emphasize the importance of perception. Luchins (1961) viewed learning as a cognitive restructuring of problems. The learner acquires knowledge and understanding by perceiving the problem and rearranging its parts so as to find a meaning that is rational and logically consistent. Gage suggested that teachers can aid in this restructuring by pointing out parts of the problem patterns, either physically or verbally, and by working with the cognitive configuration so that the structure he wishes the learner to develop will stand out as does a figure against a background. Using the known principles of grouping, for example, such as similarity and proximity, the learner is virtually compelled to see the structure according to his natural tendencies. The teacher can take advantage of compelling qualities in the learner's cognitive structuring to identify the various aspects of problems. Suppose one is required to construct a curve whose shape is determined by known data—for example, a human growth curve. From the principle of good continuation it can be predicted that the probable tendency will be to give that line the same curvature, if one must extend it further in the absence of additional data. This family of learning theories therefore concentrates on matching intellectual structures with what is to be taught. Logical functioning is of great interest to those who find the cognitive restructuring approach useful. B. Othanel Smith (1962) studied logical processes of teachers and students, hoping to locate ways in which teachers might cue students in their thinking. Runkel (1956) studied the "collinearity" between the thinking of teachers and students. The cognitive structures of a teacher and a student are collinear with respect to a given set of objects when the criteria they apply in evaluating the objects are at least approximately the same. Runkel found that the higher the collinearity between students and teachers, the higher the achievements of the students as judged by the teachers. Suchman (1960) tried to improve the question-asking ability of children as they sought out explanations for simple scientific phenomena. Ausubel (1961) used "advance organizers" to aid in cognitive restructuring. (More will be said on this in Chapter 5.)

Components Corresponding to Those of Learning

It is sometimes assumed that because learning can be analyzed into basic elements, teaching can also be broken down into corresponding components. Some of the components suggested by learning theories are motivation producing, perception directing, response eliciting, and reinforcement providing; and theories including each of these might be developed.

Activities of the teacher, families-of-learning theory, and *objectives of education* should each provide sets of theories about teaching. The corresponding components of teaching, as listed above, may also furnish theories. So that all the components might not produce merely a hodgepodge of separate considerations, and in line with his insistence that teaching is quite generic, Gage offered a suggestion as to what a specific theory of teaching might be related to.

WHAT A SPECIFIC THEORY OF TEACHING MIGHT BE CONCERNED WITH, USING GAGE'S CATEGORIES

There is no attempt to develop a single theory to encompass all of the broad categories of learning theory—all are deemed necessary for accounting for "different kinds of persons learning different things in different situations" Gage, (1964, p. 276). Similarly, if one is to be specific, one must not attempt to accomplish specificity by lumping together teacher activities, objectives, and so on. Instead one must make selections from each of the suggested categories. Gage provides examples of such selections.

For his first example, Gage selected from the limited list of *activities of the teacher* that he has provided. He then selected from the *educational objectives*, and from the *teaching components corresponding to those of learning*. Finally, for illustration, one of the families-of-learning theories was chosen. Each of these selections represents specific activities, objectives, components, and learnings that could be present in a teacher-learning situation; hence, a great many such selections could be made, based on an even larger number of categories. However, Gage provided three sets of selections to make his point.

In his first selection, he chose the teacher activity "explaining." He also chose the "cognitive" domain for his selection from educational objectives, and specifically the aim of promoting student ability to extrapolate trends. As a teaching component, he chose one that amounts to the teacher's "directing student perceptions to the relevant part of his environment" (1964, p. 277). And from the families of learning theory, he selected the cognitive restructuring approach. Why these four selections? Given a teaching activity that involves explaining, so that learners may achieve an educational goal within the cognitive domain, Gage maintained that a family of cognitive theories of learning is the most suitable for drawing implications leading to a teaching component that parallels the learning component. More specifically, within the family of cognitive theories the cognitive restructuring one was specified. According to this paradigm, the learner acquires knowledge and understanding by rearranging his perceptions of the situation or problem before him. He does so via central cognitive processes, using methods for maintaining meaning of a rational, logically consistent kind. Now, the component of teaching that corresponds to cognitive restructuring is the manipulation of stimuli or the cognitive field so that the structure that the pupil is to learn stands out and is compelling, as is a figure against a background. The pupil is then largely bound by the structure that has been presented, and he apprehends because he must. The teacher does this by pointing at something, physically, or even verbally, using the principles of the grouping of stimuli (similarity, proximity, continuity, and so on), or by pertinent questioning, so that the significant qualities of the situation stand out.

Given an activity of the teacher, and the kind of educational goal that is involved, Gage's approach may be used to determine the message of the theory of learning most appropriate to the activity and objective. Then components in the teaching process will be found that correspond to what is known about learning. What governs the selection of a learning paradigm for this purpose? Gage examined the nature of the teaching activity and of the educational aim to determine which theoretical position is most likely to provide efficient, reasonable teaching assistance. In the first selection, conditioning and identification would not be indicated. Conditioning's successive-approximations approach is too slow; identification's emphasis on the imitation of a prestigious model doesn't fit; whereas stressing logically ordered content lends itself well to a cognitive approach, more specifically, to cognitive restructuring.

Gage also provided other sets of selections, in order to illustrate how the four analyses may be used. For one of these, he selected the mental hygiene *activity* of the teacher, the *affective* domain of educational objectives, the *conditioning* family-of-learning theories, and for the *component of teaching*, the arousing in the pupil of a desire to learn what the teacher wants him to learn. Within the affective domain of objectives, the more specific objective is that of the pupil's achieving emotional security. Within conditioning theories, positive reinforcement furnishes a logical choice. The corresponding component of teaching therefore becomes the dispensing of warmth and praise with a lavish hand. The final example that illustrates a version of a theory of teaching deals with an activity of the teacher that is called *demonstration*. The objectives chosen lie in the psychomotor domain—and the specific objective is the achievement of handwriting. The identification theory is chosen from the families-of-learning theory, and the corresponding component of teaching is the inducing of the imitation of what is demonstrated by a prestigious model with whom the pupil identifies. The pupil watches the teacher and imitates his actions.

These selections serve to show that the problem of the theorist is to synthesize many facets into a set of theories whose combinations might then be tested. What remained would be a number of theories of teaching that correspond to the families-of-learning theory that had been chosen, and that also correspond to the learning objectives and activities of the teacher.

Gage's approach is in agreement with that of others in that a large number of complex variables or teaching functions are considered important in effective teaching. He also recognized the importance of careful subject-matter preparation for teachers, each expert in his own domain. But teachers should also have at their disposal a great amount of information outside their own subject-matter areas. The teaching of learning theories to teachers has sometimes been questioned, especially by those who have failed to find widespread applications of learning-theory implications. But theories that will promote a better understanding of processes in learning, of *principles* that may be applied, may yet find use, as Gage has so clearly shown.

One source of difficulty seems to lie in the focus of instruction in learning theory. A course or two in learning theory is frequently taught in psychology departments, where the emphasis is not upon application, and when application is touched upon it is likely to be in areas of special education or clinical psychology, rather than in classroom practices. Time and effort are expended on experimental studies, dealing mostly with primates and the lower animals, with very little attempt at understanding human learning directly.

Along with an adequate knowledge of learning processes (including motivations), a teacher needs a logical, efficient information retrieval system, a personal one that quickly selects the appropriate teaching mode and activity that is indicated for specific combinations. The master teacher must develop power in his ability to analyze demands, to select tools for various applications, and to integrate their uses. However, no master teacher has yet arrived at a level of proficiency that even approaches the utilization of an exhaustive or systematic focus on relevant variables such as are suggested in Gage's approach.

RELATING THEORIES OF LEARNING AND THEORIES OF INSTRUCTION

Among those who have distinguished between a theory of learning and a theory of training is Arnett (1963) of the University of Aberdeen. A theory of learning should be concerned with "the systematic change in the relationships between inputs and outputs in an individual organism as a function of previous inputs" (p. 14), and a theory of training should not even be concerned with the learner, but with the instructor—what he should do in order to teach; what should be the rules by which he controls the behavior of the student so that he attains the stated training objective with maximum efficiency. From this viewpoint, Skinner's ideas, which have led to programmed instruction, do not belong in a theory of learning, but in a theory of instruction.

Essential factors that must be considered are

> 1. The student's reception of data from a "display."
>
> 2. An information store for the subject matter to be learned.

3. A teaching function, which amounts to selecting and ordering the information store, filtering, or biasing the probabilities (seeing to it that the student attends, faces certain problems, and produces certain responses).

4. A response evaluator, checking the appropriateness of input and output.

This is a general model of adaptive teaching.

An adaptive instructor, of course, is one who alters his decisions on the basis of changed conditions in the learner. It is extremely difficult to incorporate this feature into any kind of automated teaching device. The directive function of the teacher is an important one, and the ability to base directions on changing the inputs of the teacher becomes a critical factor in teaching effectiveness. But no teaching machine has ever performed this function well. The various contingencies are so numerous that only a computer can contain the necessary number of alternatives. Because at the time of writing (1963) no machine had yet done much more than alter its decisions in a very simple way, Arnett was rather pessimistic about the suitability of the then current efforts at developing the necessary flexibility in teaching devices: "In brief, then it is my own, perhaps pessimistic view that currently popular types of work are not suited to generating data which will improve our notions of how to teach, still less contribute to learning theory" (p. 18).

However, Arnett has some suggestions. First, a part of the difficulty in developing a theory of teaching is that the learner may be viewed as a teacher of himself. This makes it difficult to rely on any distinction between the operations performed outside the learner and the operations performed inside him, because they will be frequently of the same type. (Also, of course, the learner has his own filter, which admits only a part of the perceivable external world.) Arnett agrees with Skinner that as far as possible, those operations outside the learner should be manipulated. But he also feels that exteriorizing the control has not really been satisfactorily effected. A major weakness, as pointed out before as the reception of a display is that although exterior elements may have some effect upon selective attention, the learner may not be "completely coupled up" with the system. As research furnishes more data on the stimulus-analyzing mechanisms involved, the necessary control may be increased. (Later in this book, cybernetics is discussed. The discussion includes some concern with factors such as internal and external feedback and controls.)

Arnett suggests that the improvement of external control (a teaching function) may be effected by Pask's idea of working with paced tasks. With this increased control there is increased precision of the various manipulations that the controller may impose. The use of small steps also couples the learner more closely to the rest of the system—this is an aid to the focusing of attention, and to the production of more frequently observable responses. However, small steps are often coupled with techniques that are less flexible in other ways (for example, pacing). It may not yet be good teaching strategy to use a system of variable pacing, but it might help investigators of teaching theory to study more and more filtering activity as it occurs outside the learner rather than inside.

Many teaching efforts are exerted in domains that are not only interrelated with other domains; the objectives and the activities change so rapidly and are so transitory that only a computer could cope with the almost instantaneous decision-making tasks that might be imposed. Even when the necessary number and depth of learning theories have been developed, the problem of applying them, the problem of specification remains an important one. Teachers must continue to place activities, objectives, and teaching components in a hierarchy, dealing with those that can be most practically handled, rather than with those that may be most important to each learner. Even after better tools emerge—the appropriate ones—their effective use may hinge on the teacher's art, as well as upon his science.

References

1. Arnett, John, "The Relationship Between Theories of Learning and Theories of Instruction," paper presented at the Conference on Programmed Instruction and Teaching Machines, Berlin, July 1963.
2. Ausubel, David P., and Donald Fitzgerald, "Meaningful Learning and Retention: Interpersonal Cognitive Variables," *Rev. of Educ. Res.* (December 1961), XXXI, 500–510.
3. Bandura, Albert, "Social Learning Through Imitation," *Nebraska Symposium on Motivation*, M. R. Jones (ed.). Lincoln, University of Nebraska Press, 1962.
4. Bloom, Benjamin, Max D. Engelhart, Edward J. Furst, and Walker H. Hill, *Taxonomy of Educational Objectives, Handbook I: Cognitive Domain.* New York, David McKay Company, Inc., 1956.

5. Clayton, Thomas E., *Teaching and Learning: A Psychological Perspective*. Englewood Cliffs, N.J., Prentice-Hall, 1965.

6. Cofer, C. N. (ed.), *Verbal Learning and Verbal Behavior*. New York, McGraw-Hill, Inc., 1961.

7. Cronbach, Lee J., *Educational Psychology*. New York, Harcourt, Brace & World, Inc., 1963.

8. Dewey, John, *The School Journal*, Vol. LIV, No. 3 (January 16, 1897).

9. English, Horace, and Ava C. English, *A Comprehensive Dictionary of Psychological and Psychoanalytical Terms*. New York, David McKay Company, Inc., 1958.

10. Estes, William K., "Learning," *Encyclopedia of Educational Research*, Chester W. Harris (ed.). New York, The Macmillan Company, 1960.

11. Furst, Edward J., "Effects of the Organization of Learning Experiences upon the Organization of Learning Outcomes," *Jl. Exper. Educ.* (March 1954), XVIII, 215–228.

12. Gage, N. L., "Theories of Teaching," *Theories of Learning and Instruction*. The Sixty-third Yearbook of the National Society for the Study of Education, E. R. Hilgard and Herman G. Richey (eds.). Chicago, The University of Chicago Press, 1964.

13. ———, "Paradigms for Research on Teaching," *Handbook of Research on Teaching*, N. L. Gage (ed.). Chicago, Rand McNally & Company, 1963.

14. Gagne', Robert M., *The Conditions of Learning*. New York, Holt, Rinehart and Winston, Inc., 1965.

15. Guthrie, E. R., "Conditioning: A Theory of Learning in Terms of Stimulus, Response, and Association," *The Psychology of Learning*. Forty-first Yearbook of the National Society for the Study of Education, Chicago, The University of Chicago Press, 1942.

16. ———, *The Psychology of Learning*. New York, Harper & Row, Publishers, 1935.

17. Hilgard, Ernest R., *Theories of Learning*. New York, Appleton-Century-Crofts, 1956.

18. Keller, Fred S., *Learning: Reinforcement Theory*. New York, Random House, Inc., 1965.

19. ———, and William N. Schoenfeld, *Principles of Psychology: A Systematic Text in the Science of Behavior*. New York, Appleton-Century-Crofts, 1950.

20. Krathwohl, David R., Benjamin S. Bloom, and Bertram S. Masia, *Taxonomy of Educational Objectives: The Classification of Educational Goals, Handbook II: Affective Domain*. New York, David McKay Company, Inc., 1964.

21. Luchins, Abraham S., "Implications of Gestalt Psychology for AV Learning," *AV Communications Review*, Vol. IX, No. 5 (1961), 7–31.

22. Miller, N. E., and J. Dollard, *Social Learning and Imitation*. New Haven, Conn., Yale University Press, 1941.

23. Mowrer, O Hobart, *Learning Theory and Behavior*. New York, John Wiley & Sons, Inc., 1960.

24. Osgood, Charles E., "The Similarity Paradox in Human Learning: A Resolution," *Transfer of Learning*, Robert F. Grose and Robert C. Birney (eds.). New York, D. Van Nostrand Company, Inc., 1963.

25. Pask, Gordon, and B. N. Lewis, "An Adaptive Automaton for Teaching Small Groups," *Perceptual and Motor Skills*, Vol. 14 (1962).

26. ———, and B. N. Lewis et al., "Adaptive Teaching Machines," *Ann. Summ. Rep. No. 1*, USAF, Contract AF61 (052)-402, 1961.

27. Runkel, Philip J., "Cognitive Similarity in Facilitating Communication," *Sociometry*, Vol. XIX (1956), 178–191.

28. Silverman, Robert E., "Theories and Models and Their Utility," *Educational Technology* (October 15, 1967), Vol. 7, 1–6.

29. Skinner, B. F., *Science and Human Behavior*. New York, The Macmillan Company, 1953.

30. Smith, B. Othanel, and Milton O. Meux, Jerrold Coombs, Daniel Eierdam, and Ronald Szoke, *A Study of the Logic of Teaching*. Urbana, Ill., University of Illinois, 1962 (mimeo).

31. Suchman, J. Richard, "Inquiry Training in the Elementary School," *Science Teacher* (November 1960), Vol. 27, 42–47.

4

Ordering Educational Goals

Why should a particular psychological theory come to dominate educational thinking? McDonald (1964) has traced a number of factors. Preferences for a learning theory are not merely matters of choice governed by reason, and the determinants change from period to period. At one time, a prevailing philosophy that fits a psychological effort may be quite influential. Pragmatism and functionalism were so wedded, during the twenties and thirties. A movement toward progressive social thought then helped shape educational psychology. During the same period, J. B. Watson launched his behaviorism, which was followed by Hull and Skinner. But Gestaltists and field theorists presented compelling alternatives, and the twenties and thirties offered an expanding view of psychology's domain. The forties and early fifties then moved toward eclecticism, and learning theory began to lose ground as a determiner of educational practices.

At present, many educators view the arrangement of objectives in education in a hierarchy of importance. Some feel that this is a necessary

step, at least if evaluation is to make sense. The statement of objectives
in precise, behavioral terms, rather than in vague, ambiguous, albeit ideal
statements, is hailed by many. Researchers in curriculum, who favor
precise measurements of the degree to which objectives are met, and
also individual differences of all sorts, want to know the exact nature of
educational aims, so that outcomes may be compared with them. "These
are the workers who have argued for fairly precise statements of objectives, who have insisted on measurement of effects, and who have asked
only that the ideas underlying the proposal make some kind of general
theoretical sense" (McDonald, 1964, p. 23).

Does the task of arranging according a hierarchy of educational aims
imply that these aims must be specific? Most think so. Does such an
ordering also imply a narrowing of subject matter to prescribed goals?
Do enrichment and transfer become more restricted as objectives are
made more specific? Proponents simply answer that related and even
peripheral issues need not necessarily be rejected when objectives are
clearly established. However, specificity, not ambiguity, and order, not
confusion, are to be preferred in any determination of what children
ought to learn. Does greater precision eliminate pupil sharing in setting
up classroom goals and subgoals? Will greater specificity and order in
creating a structure of objectives result in restrictions of evaluations to
those aims listed? The reader is left to draw his own conclusions from
the following discussion. The determination of *what* will be taught,
however, is not necessarily bound up with a logical arrangement derived
from the structure of thinking processes, nor with definite statements as
to what the learner will be asked to do or say when he is showing
whether or not he has attained the objectives.

Gage's suggestions on theory building include an analysis of educational objectives. One of the best known, most carefully prepared hierarchies of educational objectives is that constructed by Benjamin Bloom
and others. Two taxonomies have been completed, one in the cognitive
domain and the other in the affective domain (Bloom et al. [1956] and
Krathwohl et al. [1964]). For the purposes of their discussion, Bloom
and his associates referred to the cognitive area as that which includes
remembering and recalling, thinking, problem solving, and creating. They
expected that this classification scheme could help in gaining "a perspective on the emphasis given to certain behaviors by a particular set
of education plans" (1956, p. 2). Insofar as the purposes of the present
book are concerned, the taxonomy contributes viewpoints that may be
used in analyzing teacher effectiveness and hence suggests an area from
which principles may be derived. According to the authors, "it was the

view of the group that educational objectives stated in behavioral form have their counterparts in the behavior of individuals" (1956, p. 5). It was felt that a taxonomy should not be merely a listing of test materials and techniques, but that a relatively small number of classes of intended student behaviors could be set up systematically. The word *intended* is used, because there might be considerable disparity between the behavior intended or specified by the objectives and the actual behaviors shown by students after completing corresponding units of instruction.

After reviewing major theories of learning, the authors of the taxonomy were forced to accept Hilgard's (1964) and Gage's (1964) view, that no single, unified theory of learning is sufficient to account for all learning phenomena. They therefore saw their method as providing at least the range of phenomena that such a theory must account for. They arranged the educational behaviors chosen in order from simple to complex. Actually, a hierarchy of classes of behavior from any of the acceptable theories of learning or teaching would need to take some cognizance of this view.

A close examination of the domains treated by the taxonomy revealed what seemed to be a significant thread connecting them. There appeared to be a scale of degrees of consciousness or awareness. The implications for theory are exciting!

> If the level of consciousness can be demonstrated to be an important dimension in the classification of behavior, it would pose a great range of problems and point to a whole new set of relationships which would be of interest to researchers in the field of educational psychology. One might hope that it would provide a basis for explaining why behaviors which are initially displayed with a high level of consciousness become, after some time and repetition, automatic or are accompanied by a low level of consciousness. Perhaps this would provide a partial basis for explaining why some learning, especially of the affective behaviors, is so difficult. Perhaps it will also help to explain the extraordinary retention of some learning—especially of the psychomotor skills.
>
> (1956, p. 20)

Although the builders of this taxonomy have made no claim that it establishes a base for theory construction, it is easy to agree with Gage, who saw the analysis of educational objectives as a fertile field for possible theories. Methods for developing curricula and instructional and testing techniques have been suggested as appropriate provinces of utilization. The interest stimulated in a hierarchy of awareness has resulted in some careful inspections of the literature with the aim of bringing some order out of the chaotic nature of the field. Research on retention, growth, transfer, and relationships between measures of scholastic aptitude (intelligence) and what has been learned about the development of classes of behavior can now be more readily assembled in orderly fashion, so that generalizations can be drawn, in addition to the usual correlations. In applied developments, programmed instruction especially is expected to become more effective, as it makes use of the taxonomy, utilizing the hierarchy of awareness. More difficult to apply, but even more important, could be the teaching function that requires an organization of learning experiences directed toward learning outcomes.

The taxonomy takes into account the classroom settings in which the teacher exercises a directive function, and where the required order and sequence minimizes the objectives or goals set by pupils. "The formulation of educational objectives is a matter of conscious choice on the part of the teaching staff, based on previous experience and aided by consideration of several kinds of data" (1956, p. 26). But choosing and ordering the objectives makes use also of learning theory and of the prevailing philosophy of education. The psychology of learning contributes in that it offers information particularly about the learning-forgetting processes, whereas the philosophy of education provides criteria for determining what knowledge is most important and how it shall be used.

THE COGNITIVE DOMAIN

Knowledge

The simplest, most specific level of the taxonomy is the knowledge level. At this level, behavior and test situations emphasizing memory for ideas, material, or phenomena are evident. Three areas of knowledge are described. *Knowledge of specifics* involves the *task* of recalling specific and isolable bits of information. Knowledge of specific facts and terminology constitute the *content*. Many teachers go very little beyond this level in teaching and in testing. *Knowledge of ways and means of dealing with specifics* involves the *task* of organizing, studying, judging, and criticizing ideas and phenomena. Knowledge of conventions, trends, and sequences, classification and categories, criteria and methodology makes up this *body* of information. To reach this objective requires more of the learner than simple recall or the acquiring of a store of specific facts and names. To teach for this objective requires more than imposing drill and rote memory tasks. *Knowledge of the universals and abstractions in a field* implies the *task* of arriving at knowledge about the major ideas, schemes, and patterns by which phenomena and ideas are organized. Knowledge of principles and generalizations and knowledge of theories and structures make up the *content*.

Comprehension

The level of comprehension does not refer to the complete understanding or the fullest grasp of what is being communicated, but rather to the understanding of communications, so that objectives, behaviors, or responses are included that are more broad than those associated merely with, for example, reading comprehension. One aspect of comprehension is that of *translation*. The *task* here amounts to acquiring the ability to move a communication into another language, using other terms or other forms of communication. Translation may be similar to simple recall (e.g., "Say it in your own words"), or it may become quite complex, when analysis, synthesis, or application are required. *Interpretation* includes a *task* involving the ability to translate and to perceive relationships between parts, along with restructuring a communication so that it has meanings related to the student's own background of experience and ideas. In behavioral terms, the task is identified ". . . when, given a communication, the student can identify and comprehend the major ideas which are included in it as well as understand their interrelationships" (1956, p. 93). In *extrapolation* the *task* is acquiring the ability to translate and interpret, and being able to extend the trends beyond the given data in such a way that implications, consequences, corollaries, and effects may be suggested.

Application

Application usually requires more of the learner than does comprehension. If given a novel problem, he will apply the appropriate abstraction without the aid of cues as to the selection or use of that abstraction, when he is properly carrying out the task involved. At the level of comprehension, it is only known that the learner *can* make the application; at the level of application, he actually *does* make it. Correct application is required in transfer (though of course, negative transfer, interfering with application, is possible). Thus, factors important to affecting transfer are important at the application level. Efficient learning techniques in problem solving, learning concepts and generalizations—as opposed to learning specifics—and the development of facilitative work attitudes and self-confidence and control all make for increased efficiency in application.

Much has been written about transfer, and some of the thinking in this area has led to paradoxes. In studies of retroactive inhibition in memory, the most interference occurs when later learnings contain similar content to the original learnings. But in applications to novel problems, the more nearly similar the new problem is to elements of those already met, the more likely the learner is to solve it. The application level of the taxonomy implies that teaching needs to utilize or experiment with those factors contributing to transfer that have already been found to be useful, and further, to integrate this level with the rest of the taxonomy.

Analysis

Analysis is

1. Separating material into its constituent elements.
2. Finding the relationships among these elements.
3. Recognizing the pattern(s) of organization of the parts.

Cues, or devices that have been used for conveying meaning or for establishing conclusions are a part of analysis. Analysis is used as an aid to more complete comprehension, as a prelude to evaluating the material, and perhaps, as an exercise in itself. Analysis approaches comprehension at a lower level of the taxonomic hierarchy and evaluation at a higher level.

Analysis as an objective may itself be analyzed into three tasks:

1. Separating and *classifying the parts or elements.*
2. *Making explicit the relationships among the elements.*
3. *Recognizing the organization principles* that bind the communication together.

The synthesis level requires the student to put together a number of elements into a structure or pattern. These elements come from different sources and, when synthesized, form a structure that did not previously exist. Thus, synthesis allows for creative behavior by the student, though it is not entirely free creative expression that is involved, because limits are set by the problems, materials, or framework established in the educational setting.

Because synthesis objectives may be found at most levels of education, it is to be expected that relatively small tasks that develop synthesizing ability would be presented early in a student's educational program, whereas larger tasks would be imposed and attacked later. The synthesizer is a producer, rather than a consumer, and it is for this reason that a great deal of value ought to be attached to this objective. The claim is also made that the able synthesizer becomes efficient in reaching a variety of objectives, and is highly motivated because of the satisfactions obtained when something of one's own creation emerges. A synthesis, however, may be lacking in both utility and art—a patchwork or even a botched job—whereas at the other extreme are the immortal creations of the world's greatest minds.

A synthesis may be

1. A unique communication.
2. A plan or proposed set of operations.
3. The derivation of a set of abstract relations.

Implications for teaching involve the usual considerations for a creative teaching-learning situation. (These will be discussed in detail when the topic of creative teaching is developed.)

Evaluation

"Evaluation is defined as the making of judgments about the value, for some purpose, of ideas, works, solutions, methods, materials, etc." (1956, p. 185). Though all of the preceding behaviors or levels of the taxonomy are found at this stage, evaluation requires in addition a consideration of *values*. It acts as a connecting link between the cognitive behaviors and the affective behaviors, though it is still primarily cognitive.

In fact, it is present in virtually all cognitive behaviors; and if it is characterized by quick decisions based upon shaky or little evidence and dubious considerations, then the pronouncements made are called *opinions*. Sometimes opinions are made within a framework of awareness, but much of the time they are formed at a preconscious level and based on prejudice or self-interest. *Judgments* are formed according to distinct criteria and hence are consciously directed, making use of relatively adequate comprehension and analysis.

Two types of standards of criticism are involved in evaluation. The first is based on *internal* tests, such as consistency, logical accuracy, and the absence of internal flaws. But internal perfection may be insufficient, when measured by considerations outside the product. A second type of evaluation is based on the application of *external* criteria that have to do with ends, and with the means for achieving those ends. Efficiency, economy, and utility are such criteria. Thus, a perfect product, as seen by a producer, may not be suitable for a consumer, if it fails to meet the external evaluative criteria.

THE AFFECTIVE DOMAIN

Although it is not at all difficult to see that the cognitive and affective domains of educational objectives overlap, confusion may mount when it comes to determining how much overlapping occurs and how overlap may therefore be used advantageously for instruction. Merely to insist that the development of cognitive objectives will result in *appropriate* affective behaviors is to underestimate the need for a taxonomy of both domains, developed with an eye to their interdependence. The taxonomy does not claim to have found *the* facilitating intersections, but the care and research lavished upon the effort have at least resulted in an orderly arrangement. The authors suggest that ". . . the order and principles of arrangement should be of value in the development of a theory of learning which would be relevant to the complex as well as simple types of human learning." (Krathwohl et al., 1964, p. 6)

Receiving (Attending)

The *task* is first to sensitize the learner to the existence of certain phenomena and stimuli. The objective at this level is achieved when the learner shows a willingness to receive or attend to the specified stimuli. Thus, *awareness* is the lowest level of attending, with no implications as to recall, but the mere consciousness of something. To notice, at this level, does not imply interest in what is noticed. The next higher level of *receiving* is *willingness to receive*. This means that the learner does not actively seek to avoid attending, but that he is neutral, insofar as making judgments about what he is attending to. Above this level is that of *controlled* or *selected attention*. The *task* may amount to training the sensory faculties to a closer awareness of that already being received. It may also involve control of attention, so that given certain stimuli, the learner will be aware of them.

Responding

At this stage, the student is actively attending. He is ready to comply, so that a minimum behavior for this level is *acquiescence in responding*. He may be even further committed, in which case he shows *willingness to respond*. If he goes yet a step further, then he may show *satisfaction in response*.

Valuing

"Behavior categorized at the valuing level is sufficiently consistent and stable to have taken on the characteristics of a belief or an attitude" (1964, p. 180). Many of the objectives listed by teachers that use the term *attitude* are included at this point. The minimal level is *acceptance of a value*, and the appropriate term is *belief*. To prefer is to value somewhere between mere acceptance and commitment to that value, so the next level is *preference for a value*. Finally, one may have convictions about values and act on them, and hence reach the level of *commitment*.

Organization

Because situations arise in which the learner has more than one relevant value, it is then necessary for him to organize his values, determine their interrelationships and establish which ones are dominant and pervasive. At the level of *conceptualization*, the student is able to note the relationships of a value to those already held or being internalized. When he begins to bring his values into an ordered relationship with one another, he has reached the level of *organization of a value system*. If the organization is such that harmony and internal consistency prevail, this may provide a philosophy of life—quite often such an ideal state of organization does not exist.

Characterization by a
Value or Value Complex

Once the values have been arranged hierarchically and have become a part of the learner's behavioral controls, he may be described by his pervasive tendencies. He may also be said to have built his beliefs, ideas, and attitudes into a world view (*Weltanschauung*). When the behavior control consists of a predisposition to respond in a certain way, this is a *generalized set*, "a persistent and consistent response to a family of related situations and objects" (1964, p. 184). When a greater inclusiveness is involved and there is an emphasis on internal consistency, then the values tend to characterize the learner, so that the objectives are then called *characterization objectives*.

The affective domain of educational objectives has not been systematically explored. Although the generally accepted viewpoint is that affective orientations are disruptive, few attempts have been made at discovering whether the variables involved may be subjected to systematic control. It is generally agreed that some affective states are facilitative to learning, whereas some are disruptive, and that some kind of optimal level exists that will be motivating. Cognitive measures are relatively easy to construct, because they are presumed to be revealed by products of learning. However, affective measures may either impede or accelerate productions, and the degree to which they do so is difficult to determine, because the effects are difficult to isolate. The taxonomy does seem to provide a step toward analysis of the factors involved, because it suggests how the presence of affective components may be detected and implies some probable effects.

Klausmier and Goodwin (1966) have made comparisons of parallel processes from J. P. Guilford (1958) and from Bloom's taxonomy, in the cognitive domain. The comparison begins at the *comprehension* level, which Guilford calls *cognition*—discovery, rediscovery of recognition. Then, for Guilford, memory is simply the retention of what has been cognized, whereas Bloom does not state it as an intellectual process. Guilford relegates both application and analysis to *convergent thinking*. In convergent thinking, one arrives at a right answer or at least at a recognized best answer or a conventional one, on the basis of known, remembered information. Guilford's *divergent thinking* corresponds to

Bloom's synthesis stage. Divergent thinking requires the learner to arrive at a number of unique responses that are not completely determined by known and remembered information. Both Guilford and Bloom describe an *evaluation* level.

PSYCHOMOTOR ABILITIES

The committee of examiners who built the two taxonomies has not yet constructed the third, the psychomotor domain taxonomy of objectives. However, Guilford (1958) has identified six factors believed to be common in many kinds of motor performances. *Strength, speed, impulsion, precision, coordination,* and *flexibility* are suggested as important in producing learning outcomes. *Impulsion* involves the rate at which movements are originated from nonmoving positions. A sprinter is impelled at a certain rate from the starting blocks, but he develops a certain *speed* after he leaves them, whereas a tennis player is concerned with accurate body movements or *precision. Flexibility* is required in bending or moving the joints and in stretching the muscles. *Strength* and *coordination* have the usual referents, concerned with power and with integration of efforts. What makes it especially difficult to establish a psychomotor domain of objectives is that so many perceptual motor tasks involve both psychomotor and cognitive elements. Various *sets,* or predispositions to respond, are obviously of key importance to the learning of psychomotor skills. Sets may be viewed either as outcomes, or results of previous learnings, or they may be acquired via anticipations that are cognitive. Woodworth (1906) referred to sets as *situation-sets,* or adjustments to environmental objects, and *goal-sets,* or inner directivity that unifies series of goal-directed activities.

WRITING BEHAVIORAL OBJECTIVES

Robert Mager believed that educational units of any size ought to be prepared with the following questions in mind:

(1) What is it that we must teach?
(2) How will we know when we have taught it?
(3) What materials and procedures will work best to teach what we wish to teach?

(1962, p. vii)

The questions are not so new, but the ways in which he proposed to answer them are not even yet commonly practiced. The three questions must be answered in the order presented, if instruction is to proceed effectively. Many teachers insist that they do decide upon what is to be taught, obtain tests for achievement, and plan for the effective use of materials. However, Mager and others insisted on written, *behavioral* objectives, so that tests may be more specific and teaching procedures more systematic. Objectives written by most teachers are ambiguous, vague in intent, and not to be interpreted with any acceptable degree of reliability. Furthermore, their objectives are often of low validity, so that what they teach and test for bear only a faint relationship to their stated objectives. Although it is true that programmed instructional materials, with their highly specified requirements, have focused upon behavioral objectives, it is also probable that teachers who cannot specify their objectives well do not carry out other important aspects of good planning. Many feel that they are too busy with the details of everyday teaching, and that because they at least have in mind the general nature of their objectives, they do not need to be more specific.

If objectives are to be behaviorally specified, how can this be accomplished? Being specific in *behavioral* terms suggests stating exactly what the learner will be *doing*, or *saying*, when he demonstrates that he has achieved the aims of an instructional sequence. Walbesser (1967) listed four requirements for the construction of objectives:

1. Words denoting the stimulus situation which initiates the performance should appear in the description of the objective.

2. An action verb which denotes observable behavior must be contained in the description.

3. A word denoting the object acted upon must be contained in the description.

4. A phrase which indicates the characteristics of the performance that determine its correctness or acceptability must be included in the description of the objectives.   p. 18

An example of a well-stated behavioral objective is

> *Given drawings of acute, obtuse, straight, and right angles, the pupil will correctly identify each angle by writing its name below it.*

Well-stated objectives not only serve to clarify procedures and evaluations for the teacher, they also are useful to the pupil, when shared. A student who knows the specific objectives will spend less time acquiring a bag of tricks derived from understanding the instructor, than in engaging in activities relevant to student success in achieving the objectives.

Sometimes, what passes for a set of objectives is merely a course description, such as may be found in a school catalogue. A description is intended only to tell something about what is contained in the course and how it will proceed. Whereas a course objective ought to be a clear description of its desired *outcome,* a course description tells what the *course* is about. An objective describes *learner* behavior. If a teacher can use an objective in teaching his students to perform according to the intentions of another teacher who wrote the objective, the objective has been communicated meaningfully. Words such as *know, understand,* or even *really understand, appreciate,* and so on are open to misinterpretations. Mager suggested that verbs be chosen that are open to fewer interpretations. *Write, recite, identify, differentiate, solve, construct, list, compare* and *contrast* require more specific responses than do ambiguous directives.

An objective has not necessarily been well written if it is specific as to outcomes, however. It must also specify the conditions under which the learner is to meet the criterion. This is the *given* of the specification. For example—"Given a quadratic equation, the learner will solve it, unaided, within two minutes." An objection sometimes raised is that such objectives may be easily written for highly structured subject matter areas, but not so easily for such areas as human relations. Mager, however, provided an example of a behavioral objective for a human relations course:

> The student is to be able to prepare an analysis of any five of the ten case studies given him at the time of the examination. This analysis should attempt to discuss the cases according to the principles developed during the course, and the student must show evidence of having considered each problem from at least two of the participant's points of view by restating this in his own words. References and notes may be used and up to 24 hours may be taken for the writing of the five analyses.
>
> (1962, p. 50)

Mager's final summary for writing objectives follows:

> 1. A statement of instructional objectives is a collection of words or symbols describing one of your educational *intents.*

2. An objective will communicate your intent to the degree you have described what the learner will be *Doing* when demonstrating his achievement and how you will know when he is doing it.

3. To describe terminal behavior (what the learner will be *Doing*): (a) identify and name the overall behavior act; (b) define the important conditions under which the behavior is to occur (givens and/or restrictions and limitations); and (c) define the criterion of acceptable performance.

4. Write a separate statement for each objective; the more statements you have, the better chance you have of making clear your intent.

5. If you give each learner a copy of your objectives, you may not have to do much else. (p. 53)

Walbesser (1967) added to Mager's suggested list of verbs of low ambiguity, in writing objectives. His list includes: *distinguish, name, describe, state a rule, apply a rule, demonstrate,* and *interpret.* All of these verbs give clear directions for action. He also developed a Game of Hierarchy, in which he suggested a method of formulating instructional sequences. In cases where behavioral objectives are related so that they can be ordered from less complex behaviors to more complex related behaviors, a hierarchy can be constructed as an aid to teaching.

Suppose you were interested in providing instruction that would help a learner acquire the most complex behavior. . . . How might you proceed instructionally? That's one of the fascinating applications of behavioral hierarchies. The behavioral hierarchy suggests one possible instructional path. For those learners who did not already possess the most complex behaviors, you would begin instruction with the least/most (correct answer is *least*) complex task which the learner does not already exhibit. Naturally instruction would begin by helping those learners acquire the simplest behaviors, the least complex, which they had not already acquired. Then instructions would proceed to the next level of complexity and so on through each of the behaviors considered prerequisite to the final complex task. (Walbesser, 1967, p. 5)

Thus, not only may educational objectives be categorized by levels of complexity, but instructional procedures may be made more effective by the employment of hierarchies of task complexity, within each of the categories suggested by Bloom.

It is not surprising that those interested in developing a technology of education would be the most vocal in extolling the virtues of a careful statement of objectives. Burns listed five "basic principles" that guide the conceptualization and development processes:

1. Learning is change in behavior.
2. Behavioral changes resulting from learning are observable and measurable.
3. Learning is an individual process.
4. Learning is varied. Research into how learners learn has failed to produce a best or universal method.
5. Everyone can learn.

(October 30, 1967, pp. 1 & 2)

Burns felt that:

There is no more important contribution being made by modern learning theorists and educational technologists than the development of a sound body of knowledge relating to the conceptualization, development, and implementation of learning objectives. (September, 1967, p. 1)

He suggested some practical steps:

1. All teachers in training should develop skill in expressing objectives in specific behavioral terms.
2. All practicing teachers should be exposed through in-service training experiences to the theory of behavioral objectives and the practical aspects of expressing them in writing.
3. All teachers, individually or in a group, should be required to establish a list of specific objectives for each area (course, subject, grade level, ability level) taught.
4. Teachers should experiment, at first with small projects, with allowing students to set their own learning goals.
5. Teachers, supervisors and administrators should demand that published materials be developed from carefully defined and published learning goals.
6. Research should be initiated to establish procedures aimed at discovering the real needs of students. A profitable approach should actively involve the students in the location and defining process.

7. Published materials should be designed for less variable learner populations. The "all purpose" text designed for all students pursuing a subject at a given grade level has always been a "dead-end street" since the first one was published.

8. Teachers who so desire and who have the aptitude for it should be allowed time to develop some of their own teaching materials. These projects can be aimed at meeting a few specific objectives. If repeated often enough the small projects grow into sizable subject matter areas.

9. Teachers should experiment with lists of objectives, letting the learner choose the sequence in which he wishes to achieve. Observing and recording the sequence behaviors should produce insight into how learners learn.

10. Teachers should experiment with alternative yet similar objectives, letting students choose what they desire to learn. Observing and recording the choosing behavior of the learners should again produce insight into the learning process.

(Sept. 15, 1967, pp. 2, 3)

Some of these practical suggestions were reviewed by Slack (1967), who noted that the establishment of educational objectives, laudable as it is, is primarily a political and economic process. Publishers, writers, and purchasing agents (decision makers in the buying of books), he averred, are the major parties to a transaction in the market, whereas the minor parties are the student and the teacher, except when the learner prescribes his own objectives or the instructor writes his own materials. The political decision-making process forces the teacher to accept materials he has not selected. A sequence of decision filters influence the kinds of materials that eventually reach students, and what they see is often outdated, inefficient, and unattractive. Slack interpreted John Dewey's *transactionalism* as a concept of learning that takes place when there is a simple buyer-seller relationship between two parties, the teacher and the student—without the interposition of these filtering agents.

RATIONALE FOR OBJECTIVES

Even carefully constructed objectives, sequenced according to a logical hierarchy, are not necessarily valid ones. If the achievement of behavioral objectives does not eventuate in support and furtherance of the broader objectives of the curriculum, the school, the system, or the community, it may be difficult to show cause for their use. In fact, whenever a rationale for objectives is sought, the nagging question always arises, "Just why should the student learn this, anyway?" Should teachers be the sole determiners or should students share the information about objectives, and even have a part in determining them?

But the question is not simply one of providing opportunities for students to determine what they should learn. Most college students, for example, have for so long been accustomed to the provision of prescribed dosages of the "essential" knowledge provided by textbooks, they do not readily depart from the standard practice. The standard practice is to assume that if it's in the book, it should be learned because it might be on the examination. It has been this writer's experience that even when graduate students are permitted to write objectives, with express permission to delete or add to what is in the book, they are unable to break away from traditional practice. They still follow the text, almost without exception. And when they are asked to provide a rationale for their objectives, many will simply state that a given objective should be achieved because it helps one to understand the chapter!

When knowledge for knowledge's sake is the only rationale, however, it may well be that the whole idea of objectives should be discarded. But the movement toward closer articulation between the work of teachers in the field and what they learn in college is a healthy one. Feedback from the students may well lead to more "realistic" objectives in such courses as human growth and development, educational psychology, and personality theory. Teachers ought to be able to insist that their foundations courses have transfer value. Vigorous insistence on objectives as worthy of attainment may be a means for bringing theory and practice closer together.

How can the Why of objectives be determined? Thus far, no set of criteria exists for a rationale. However, it would seem that the rationale for teacher education should be stated on the basis of what the teacher actually needs to be able to know and do. Because education's tasks are burgeoning along with the knowledge explosion, then one answer is to compress what teachers must know. A simple (perhaps too simple) solution is the judicious paring of offerings in college. Teachers are seldom quite satisfied with the preparation for teaching that they obtained in college. If they can be weaned away from the textbook long enough, they may be able to cooperate with university personnel in setting up useful educational objectives, for they are supposed to profit from practicing what they have been taught.

THE SYSTEMATIC USE OF QUESTIONS
IN TEACHING-LEARNING

The judicious employment of questions as a technique has enjoyed a position of importance in education since the days of the ancient Greek philosophers and before. The term *Socratic method* often brings to mind a picture of the eminent scholar, probing, correcting, directing, maneuvering, teaching almost exclusively by asking a continuous stream of questions. It is less appropriate at this point to ask whether Socrates' often loaded questions did, in fact, teach, than it is to note that systematic questioning is hardly a novel technique. Socrates' sequences were usually in the form of a logical progression calculated to bring about the solution, or possibilities for several solutions, to problems. However, questions may be sequenced in many other ways, planned in advance, to induce adequate responses on various levels of a wide range of complexities. Most teachers probably feel that they question pupils sufficiently and helpfully, and many are somewhat justified in that contention. Still, it is too often the case that a teacher may not perceive his efforts accurately—the hard-nosed disciplinarian, for example, insists that he frequently "uses reinforcement," when even the casual observer notes that his reinforcers are conspicuous by their absence. Just so, the teacher who thinks he questions sufficiently and well may be one who questions primarily for evaluation, for labeling pupils, or in a rhetorical sense, requiring no answer but the one that he himself immediately provides. Probes, directives, and cues in the form of questions can be arranged in a progression, in a hierarchy, and planned in advance so that the teacher may more adequately cope with individual differences in pupils. This is to say that questions may be based on objectives, at various levels, and may be of differing degrees of complexity. A taxonomy of objectives ought to provide an excellent platform from which to launch barrages of questions. Question-asking skill can therefore be taught to student teachers, so that it is not necessary for them to acquire this ability through years of experience. Norris M. Sanders looked at Bloom's taxonomy of objectives and found the basis for interrogative sequencing. Bloom and his associates had already suggested means of *testing* whether each level of the taxonomy was being achieved. Sanders, in the book *Classroom Questions: What Kinds?* (1966), showed some interesting and constructive ways of using questions at each level, in order to *instruct* more effectively.

> The objective of this book is to describe a practical plan to insure a varied intellectual atmosphere in a classroom. The approach is through a systematic consideration of questions that require students to *use* ideas, rather than simply to *remember* them. (p. 2)

Bloom's categories in the cognitive domain were first carefully examined, and statements were set forth in terms of what the student does at each level of the taxonomy. Then question types suitable for leading students to think in these categories were constructed. Teachers like to think that they teach on a variety of levels of discourse, and that their questions are aimed at promoting thinking in a variety of ways. Sanders asserted, however, that the taxonomy of question types, so arranged that classes of questions are sequential rather than arbitrary, will be helpful to many teachers. For example, a question that requires only that the student exercise his *memory* has a definite place in the instructional effort—but when too many such questions are in evidence, the teacher is not only testing at a superficial level, he is probably teaching at that level too. If subject matters have been well handled, students ought to be able to *translate,* to *interpret,* to *apply,* and sometimes to *analyze, synthesize,* and *evaluate.* Sanders suggested that the teacher who is using his ideas best will be prompted to ask himself: "What opportunities are there for application questions? What opportunities are there for synthesis questions? and so on." These opportunities are not merely presented at the end of instructional units, as in tests, but at the time of discussion; hence, skill in asking questions is developed to enhance skill in instructing. A second benefit to be derived from a knowledge of the sequence of questions is an increased ability to evaluate instructional materials. Finally, the taxonomy of questions, employed by a teacher, makes it more likely that he will induce learning by doing, actively involving even the child who is sitting quietly at his desk. That child may be quite involved in the learning activities, if he is asked to do more in his thinking than merely to remember facts.

A question determines the kind of thinking students engage in by

1. The nature of the question itself, in relation to the category in the taxonomy.
2. The knowledge that the student has at the time of the questioning.

3. The instruction that precedes the asking of the question.

Some teachers pride themselves on asking many *why* and *how* types of questions, feeling that this practice requires students to use more than memory in their responding. However, *how* and *why* types may also require only memory, if students are merely expected to reply with pat answers that have previously been provided by the teacher, or elsewhere in the instructional materials. The instructional sequence as well as the questioning ought to encourage students to work out answers, not merely to remember them.

The taxonomy of objectives is not only sequential, it is cumulative in nature. This sequential-cumulative structure has also been used in some programming of instructional units. In the construction of a program, it has been called the *lattice technique*. In the taxonomy's lattice, for example, only *memory* may be required. However, if the requirement is that of *translation*, then memory is also involved. And memory and translation are both involved, when the learner is engaged in *interpretation*, and so on up the hierarchy. The chart Sanders used to illustrate the idea appears below, except that the categories have been abbreviated:

						Eval
					Synth	Synth
				Analy	Analy	Analy
			Appln	Appln	Appln	Appln
		Interp	Interp	Interp	Interp	Interp
	Transl	Transl	Transl	Transl	Transl	Transl
Mem	Mem	Mem	Mem	Mem	Mem	Mem

(From *Classroom Questions: What Kinds?* p. 10.)

Sanders devotes most of his effort to expanding upon the most effective use of questions at each level of the taxonomy, beginning with *memory*.

Memory

Memory utilizes either the recognition of something that has been learned or the recalling of it. Probably the easiest questions to ask and to answer are those that simply require the pupil to repeat some specific information. Memory type questions may ask the pupil to recall or recognize *facts; definitions, generalizations,* and *values;* and *skills.* At first thought, it may seem that values belong to a higher category, and although it is true that they may, they also have a place at lower levels, including memory. For example, at the memory level, the student merely needs to repeat what has been said, even though it includes a statement of values, which he can often do with little understanding of meaning. Once the learner can recall or recognize statements of values, he may then be required to interpret, apply, analyze, and so on. Sanders stated that definitions, generalizations, and values should be given attention for four reasons:

1. This form of knowledge is generally the most important—the most worthy of learning.
2. Teachers will find it much easier to compose questions that require a variety of intellectual activities if they concentrate on generalizations and values.
3. Educational research indicates that widely applied generalizations and values are less likely to be forgotten than most other forms of knowledge.
4. Educational psychologists who have studied the "transfer of training" conclude that the best way to prepare students for an unknown future is to instruct them in the use of generalizations and values that are likely to have fruitful application.

(pp. 24, 25)

The word *skill* is often used as a catchall for many sorts of meanings. Unless the teacher is reasonably certain as to what he means when asking a pupil to use a skill, he may require its use before he has adequately prepared the pupil in the skill itself. Teachers should first develop skills at the memory level, so that the pupils are questioned on definitions and characteristics of the skill before being asked to exercise it.

Sanders points out three weaknesses of the memory category of questions:

1. Facts that are only memorized are soon forgotten.
2. Memorized knowledge does not necessarily represent a high level of understanding.
3. Other intellectual processes are likely to be neglected when there is a concentration on memory.

Translation

There are many ways by which to communicate the same idea. When a student changes from one way of communicating an idea to another, he is translating. One of the most common forms is the statement in one's own words of the gist of a statement. Questions at this level are aimed at requiring the student to do more than quote back from memory. He may show by a diagram or draw a picture the ideas intended by a given communication. The teacher may wish to require students to merely recognize a translation, at first, and then to be able to translate. The use of sociodrama to illustrate ideas is a good example of translation—and if the mechanics and art of the production are not overdone the niceties of the play do not submerge the ideas being dramatized.

Interpretation

Although memory is used in all cognitive processes and translation is also basic to most, Sanders asserted that all the higher levels are resident in embryonic form in interpretation. Thus, a complete definition of interpretation cannot be made without reference to those higher levels. However, he did describe interpretation by discussing its functions. Interpretation requires the student to show relationships between two ideas; or given an idea and a relationship, the student must furnish an idea that follows from the evidence. Interpretation questions may also require a student to discern relationships of different kinds:

1. Comparative relationship (Determining if ideas are identical, similar, different, unrelated, or contradictory).
2. Relationship of implication.
3. Relationship of an inductive generalization to supporting evidence.
4. Relationship of a value, skill, or definition to an example of its use.
5. Numerical relationship.
6. Cause and effect relationship.

Sanders, 1966 (p. 43)

Two other characteristics of questions at the interpretation level are

1. Explicitness about what the student is to do—there is usually only one and never more than a few ways of thinking through to the answer.

2. Objectivity—the pattern of thinking required by the question can be predicted, so the question is objective.

Application

Application questions require the student to leave the setting in which the knowledge or skill has been acquired in order to transfer it to other, often real life, situations. Application questions deal with knowledge useful in explaining or problem solving. They also deal with wholes rather than with parts of skills and ideas. Finally, application questions are based on previous learning, so the student is placed on his own, being given few directions or instructions after the question has been asked. Bloom et al. discussed differences between the interpretation and application categories:

> A problem in the . . . [interpretation] category requires the student to know an abstraction well enough that he can correctly demonstrate its use when specifically asked to do so. "Application," however, requires a step beyond this. Given a problem new to the student, he will apply the appropriate abstraction without having to be prompted as to which abstraction is correct or without having to be shown how to use it in that situation. (1956, p. 120)

Regardless of whether a teacher is real-life-experience oriented toward problems of application or subject centered, he can and should discover ways of influencing students toward applying what has been learned to situations outside those in which they have been learned. The former orientation may tend to result in too much emphasis on establishing props of reality in a familiar pattern—that is its weakness. The latter may tend to result in too much emphasis on intellectual mastery, stopping short of action. But either approach ought to allow for application questions that are appropriate for the classroom.

Analysis

At this level, it is not sufficient for the teacher to ask the student to "Analyze the following . . ." unless the student fully understands what is meant by *analyze*. However, a student may be taught to analyze via a sequence of questions that draw him along a path of logic that leads to analysis. Sanders treated analysis as a formal procedure in logic based on the rules for reaching valid and true conclusions. He therefore differed from Bloom, who said of analysis:

> The breakdown of a communication into its constituent elements or parts such that the relative hierarchy of ideas is made clear and/or the relations

between the ideas expressed are made explicit. Such analyses are intended to clarify the communication, to indicate how the communication is organized, and the way in which it manages to convey its effects, as well as its basis and arrangement. (1956, p. 205)

Sanders said that Bloom's definition needs to relate thinking in analysis more explicitly to systems of reasoning—otherwise, it overlaps the definition of interpretation. On the other hand, Sanders limited the analysis level of questioning, perhaps unnecessarily, to those who can understand formal logic. "Students should not be asked analysis questions until they have had special instruction in some phase of the parts and processes of reasoning" (pp. 110–111). However, it should be pointed out that he also felt that teachers in elementary schools should offer instruction and practice in the process of reasoning.

Synthesis

Synthesis is putting components together, and the synthesizer is creative when this results in knowledge or skills that are new to him. It is Sanders's position that the synthesis level involves creative efforts, and leading questions are not so closely tied to synthesis thinking as with the other categories of the taxonomy. Instead, at this level, the emphasis is upon a classroom atmosphere that fosters originality and rewards it. However, there are possibilities for synthesis questions, and Sanders reported their characteristics. These questions should not limit students to subject matter and thought processes that are either stated or are implicit in the questions. They are to understand that an answer or solution does not need to take any particular form that the teacher might have in mind. Hence, divergent thinking is employed, starting with a specific problem, but moving toward a variety of possible answers. Another characteristic of synthesis questions is that a product is required, as the solution.

The weaknesses of synthesis questions are

1. Questions may require synthesis that leads to trivial answers.

2. Questions may require competency that is too high for students.

3. The answers to synthesis questions are often difficult to evaluate—why is one answer considered creative, a desirable product, whereas another is insignificant?

Evaluation

Sanders speaks of two steps in evaluation—setting up the values that are appropriate, and determining the extent to which the idea or object being evaluated measures up to those standards. If the student is not required to take the first step (because the standards or values are already specified), then the question is actually one of interpretation rather than evaluation. Thus interpretation and evaluation questions pose similar tasks. But interpretation requires the discovery of the relationship between a correct, objective answer and the answer given by the learner. Evaluation, on the other hand, is more subjective, because the student must utilize his own value judgments in the case where the standard or value cannot be proven to be correct, and also in the case where the thing to be evaluated cannot be proven to either violate or illustrate the standard.

Because evaluation questions are easy to construct, and answers may depend on so many subjective factors, these questions may lead to fruitless arguments. To prevent this, a teacher should instruct students in the ground rules. "Like analysis, the process of evaluation requires preparatory instruction, which falls mainly in the memory and interpretation categories" (p. 143). Facts and values are not the same, and students need to be made aware of the difference. Preparatory instruction would then include exercises using questions that require students to differentiate between statements of fact and statements of values. They must also learn that although all values are opinions, all opinions are not values. Opinions that are not values are those that result from lack of information or are simply predictions. Finally, before students can handle evaluation questions successfully, they need to know that knowledge of purpose is necessary for them to determine the quality of anything. Instruction would therefore utilize tasks stated something like: "Establish a purpose and appropriate standards for evaluation of each of the following: . . ." (p. 146).

How far should the teacher go in commiting himself to the systematic use of questions? The decision is his, of course, but the very least he can do is to use all of the seven types of lattice-technique questions that are appropriate. However, if he wishes to be conscientious about the questioning phase of instruction, then he will deliberately plan for the use of questions at various levels. Planning may include developing questions designed to improve students' transfer ability. In this case, he will develop sets of application questions. Or, he may wish to bring out some special skill or concept, and will construct questions in advance in such a way that the skill is developed and exercised. Perhaps he will feel that some of the seven categories have been neglected. In that case, planning would include concentration on questions of the type that bolster the neglected areas, possibly weaving the entire course around the hierarchy of thought processes. This would require that the teacher know the lessons well, and that he be able to communicate them successfully. He must then carefully compose the questions, in advance, not as he goes along. Even then, some will not result in the desired responses. But if they are prepared in advance, the teacher can always return to the ineffective questions and revise them —were they too difficult, were they poorly stated, or did they simply require additional instruction before they were used? Thus, like good test items, good questions survive the test of continued successful use.

To compose good questions, one ought to have first of all mastered his subject matter. If he merely composes questions with the textbook in hand, he is likely to be making up memory questions. To teach according to the unique needs of different pupils, the teacher should be so well versed in his subject matter that he can compose questions on all levels suited to the various student abilities. Also, unless the teacher is confident of his own subject matter mastery, he will be less likely to deal frequently or adequately with the synthesis and evaluation categories of questions, because he will be unable to produce convincing judgments of quality work.

Sanders suggested a technique that is useful for the teacher as he prepares a topic for instruction. While he is studying the topic, he should dig out the generalizations, values, definitions, and skills that ought to be emphasized. These are the leads that will help him move to higher-level questions. There are textbooks that, to some extent, defeat this end. The authors have written them so carefully that too many issues are closed, or the alternatives are clearly set forth, leaving the student with little to do but nod in agreement. The principle exercise the student gets is that of remembering. "The result is that the creative process and the controversy of competing ideas are hidden from the students" (p. 158). This, too, points up the importance for the teacher of being able to present subject matter from other sources. Sanders noted six ways of bringing out ideas that are useful in instruction and evaluation, and that suggest frequent departures from the textbook domain:

1. A contradiction to information offered in the text.
2. A different interpretation or evaluation than offered in the text.
3. Additional evidence to support a point made in the text.
4. A different line of reasoning to arrive at a conclusion made in the text.

5. A new example of the use of a generalization, value, definition, or skill in the text.

6. More recent or accurate information on a topic presented in the text.

(p. 159)

The additional information provided may take the form of oral statements, audio-visual presentations, or copied articles to be handed to students. Inexpensive paperback books may also be used as supplementary sources. The teacher who teaches important concepts in various ways rather than by a single approach is most likely to compose questions that will be based on different levels of thinking. It is suggested that teachers try to anticipate some of the points at which students are likely to make errors. In fact, because many errors are caused by faulty memory for facts that need not be memorized anyway, teachers may occasionally pose questions that permit of open-book responding. If the objective is primarily that the student be able to follow directions, to analyze a passage, and so on, the emphasis is not on memory, but on higher levels.

Questions that are designed for grading students ought to reflect the kind of thinking required in instruction. For tests, a teacher should not use a variety of questions for instructional purposes and then resort to questions requiring memorization on tests. On the other hand, it is poor practice to instruct via memory questions and test via other categories. Sanders suggested that teachers compose both test questions and instructional questions at the same time, in order to reduce the probability of nonparallel items. Summarizing:

1. The greater depth a teacher has in a topic, the more potential he has for writing a variety of good questions. When preparing a lesson or unit, a teacher should look for the kinds of ideas that are important and susceptible to use in thinking.

2. Textbooks help a teacher present an orderly sequence of subject matter but are written in a manner that encourages only the use of memory. Higher-level questions often require the withholding of conclusions drawn in the text until the students have had an opportunity to do some thinking. Questions in the higher categories frequently require sources of information in addition to the text.

3. Almost any idea or skill can be taught in several ways, featuring different kinds of thinking. The teacher should be aware of all possibilities and choose the most appropriate according to his objectives.

4. Questions classified in the higher categories can be missed by students on lower intellectual levels. For example, an application question may be missed because of an inability to remember, translate, or interpret information. The teacher should bear this in mind when ascertaining the causes of errors in students' solutions.

5. Questions used to evaluate student progress should call for the same kinds of thinking as those used in instruction. It is not right to instruct on the level of higher categories of thinking and then evaluate only the ability to remember.

After a teacher has acquired some skill in constructing and using questions on each of the levels of the taxonomy, there may be the danger that he will enjoy seeing students work their way through higher-level intellectual exercises so much that he may neglect what Sanders called the "bread-and-butter" memory questions. The teacher who will constantly refer to the lattice presented in this chapter, however, will be reminded that a certain amount of memory requirement is resident in each of the higher levels. Objective questions should be provided along with those requiring subjective answers. Teachers also need to take care that they are making clear the logical organization of their instructions. This is especially important in line with the insistence in this chapter upon going outside the textbook's continuity to use supplementary sources. Another reason for not spending a disproportionate amount of time on higher-category questions is that it takes longer for a student to respond or to think out the solutions than it does, on the lower levels, in responding to more objective types of questions. Hence, a variety of questions is desirable, but not at the expense of everything else. Some subject matters call for simple, straightforward answers, not high-level analyses. As teachers gain skill in using the taxonomy, it is also hoped that they will acquire an ability to use each level appropriately.

References

1. Bloom, Benjamin S. (ed.), Max D. Engelhart, Edward J. Furst, Walker H. Hill, and David R. Krathwohl, *Taxonomy of Educational Objectives: The Classification of Educational Goals, Handbook I: Cognitive Domain.* New York, David McKay Company, Inc., 1956.
2. Burns, Richard W., "Objectives and Classroom Instruction," *Educational Technology* (September 15, 1967), Vol. VII. No. 17, 1–3.
3. ———, "The Theory of Expressing Objectives," *Educational Technology* (October 30), 1967), Vol. VII. No. 20, 1–3.
4. Gage, N. L., "Theories of Teaching," *Theories of Learning and Instruction.* The Sixty-third Yearbook of the National Society for the Study of Education. Chicago, The University of Chicago Press, 1964.
5. Guilford, J. P., "A System of the Psychomotor Abilities," *Amer. Jl. Psychol.,* (1958), 71, 164–174.
6. ———, "Three Faces of Intellect," *Amer. Psychologist,* (1959), 14, 469–479.
7. Hilgard, Ernest R., "A Perspective on the Relationship Between Learning Theory and Educational Practices," *Theories of Learning and Instruction.* The Sixty-third Yearbook of the National Society for the Study of Education. Chicago, The University of Chicago Press, 1964.
8. Klausmeier, Herbert J., and William Goodwin, *Learning and Human Abilities.* New York, Harper & Row, Publishers, 1966.
9. Krathwohl, David R., Benjamin S. Bloom, and Bertram B. Masia, *Taxonomy of Educational Objectives: The Classification of Educational Goals, Handbook II: Affective Domain.* New York, David McKay Company, Inc., 1964.
10. Lindvall, C. M. (ed.), *Defining Educational Objectives.* Pittsburgh, Pa., University of Pittsburgh Press, 1964.
11. Mager, Robert F., *Preparing Objectives for Programmed Instruction.* San Francisco, Fearon Publishers, 1962.
12. McDonald, Frederick J., "The Influence of Learning Theories on Education (1900–1950)," *Theories of Learning and Instruction.* The Sixty-third Yearbook of the National Society for the Study of Education. Chicago, The University of Chicago Press, 1964.
13. Melton, A. W., "The Taxonomy of Human Learning: Overview," *Categories of Human Learning.* New York, Academic Press, Inc., 1964.
14. Sanders, Norris M., *Classroom Questions: What Kinds?* New York, Harper & Row, Publishers, 1966.
15. Slack, Charles W., "The Politics of Educational Objectives," *Educational Technology* (July 30, 1967), Vol. VII, No. 14, 1–6.
16. Walbesser, Henry H., *Constructing Behavioral Objectives,* series of unpublished papers, Bureau of Educational Research, University of Maryland, 1967.

17. ——, "An Evaluation Model and Its Application," Washington, D.C., American Association for the Advancement of Science, 1965.

18. Woodworth, R. S., "Imageless Thought," *Jl. Phil. Psychol. Sci. Meth.*, 1906, 3, 701–708.

5

Ordering Knowledge

The problem of determining which knowledge will be most useful to learners is not new. Since the days when philosophers gave advice on what knowledge ought to be acquired by a "gentleman," men of letters have glibly assured us that certain learning contents were makers of the educated man, the polished individual, or the gentleman. Selective ignorance even indicated great stature. The man of letters did not concern himself with the knowledge held by tradesmen. The businessman and the merchant learned about techniques, skills, facts, and figures that were sometimes "beneath the man of noble birth and higher learning."

This volume will not treat on what knowledge is most worthy for the value placed on various contents shifts with the times, and the patterns of change are themselves often unpredictable. The concern here is with recent efforts to improve the effectiveness of teaching by examining the logic and psychology of knowledge that are presently accepted as desirable, the acquisition of which may be subjected to teaching-learning processes having common elements.

PATTERNING AND SEQUENCING

Searles (1967) viewed order as having two facets—one concerned with patterns and another with sequences. Thus, a nonrandom arrangement that forms a pattern of related aspects is an ordered one. Or an arrangement in which one part precedes another may also be an ordered one. How is the structure of knowledge to be ordered? If it is so ordered that some parts of a topic are prerequisites to other parts, then a hierarchy can be established, according to the logic of the topic. Some knowledge structures are best apprehended when perceived in patterns or wholes. *The Fifth Annual Phi Delta Kappa Symposium on Educational Research* (1964) presented efforts to examine the structure of knowledge according to *logic*, but it also discussed the *psychological* ordering of knowledge.

Ordering here refers to sequencing: the placing of concepts, principles, ideas, and so on, one after the other in such a fashion that the sense of the statement, paragraph, or chapter is readily apprehended. Teachers frequently feel that the arrangement of topics in a textbook does not fit into the scheme of instruction that they are following. They therefore teach the chapters in a different order. Writers of programmed textbooks place a great deal of emphasis upon the logical ordering of content, so that learners may more easily grasp related ideas.

What seems to make the best sense in sequencing (ordering), when viewed objectively and in accordance with the structure of the subject matter, is not always best matched to a particular style of learning. Students preparing to become teachers learn that the logic of deduction moves from the general to the specific, and that of induction is synthetic, moving from components to their embodiment into a larger whole. Both methods are logically ordered. Content may be compressed, as when fewer words are used to make the same point, or when symbols represent some of the words. When speech is too expanded, the end of a statement or group of statements may be so far removed from the beginning that the learner has difficulty in putting it all together. In case of either compression or expansion, the psychologic as well as the logic becomes important. Sometimes a piece of subject matter is presented in dense form —it is filled with new ideas and terms. The author must thin it out by presenting fewer new ideas in each statement and explaining each more carefully. A comparison of programmed textbooks with conventional ones makes it apparent that the programmed text attempts to avoid both extremes—too dense and too compressed.

LOGICAL AND PSYCHOLOGICAL STRUCTURING

McClellan (1961) said that the distinction between logical and psychological ways of ordering in education is taken for granted, but that the continued use of distinctions that have served in the past has "a certain logical oddness" (p. 145). He quoted from Charles S. Pierce (1924) in providing an example of a distinction between the logical and the psychc logical:

> The psychological question is what process the mind goes through. But the logical question is whether the conclusion that will be reached, by applying this or that maxim, will or will not accord with the fact. It may be that the mind is so constituted that that which our intellectual instinct approves will be true to the extent to which that instinct approves of it. If so, that is an interesting fact about the human mind; but it has no relevancy for logic whatsoever. (McClellan, p. 146)

Psychological ordering has to do with the making of judgments; and logical ordering has to do with the basis upon which the judgments are made. McClellan pointed out that Bode (1927) approached the distinction between logic and psychologic in much the same manner as is implied by present-day hierarchies. *Psychological* referred to ways of organizing knowledge. *Logical* referred to a formal structure of content. However, it is sometimes difficult to distinguish between a psychological ordering and a logical one.

> We showed that if the words "logical" and "psychological" were to have any meaning in making a distinction that is important in educational discourse, they would have to qualify, in coordinate fashion, different varieties of the same kind of thing (certain relations or connections). (McClellan, 1961, p. 156)

Thus, the question becomes not only "What shall be taught?" but it also asks about what is of the least and of the highest complexity and difficulty, and what is the order of worth within a curriculum, a subject matter, or a unit. Furthermore, it may be necessary to ask what order of processes will most effectively cope with the content.

LOGICAL AND PSYCHOLOGICAL PARALLELS

Bellack (1964) credited Ausubel (1964) with a major contribution to a theory of instruction with his

> distinction between the "organized bodies of knowledge that represent the collective recorded wisdom of recognized scholars in particular fields of inquiry" and the "corresponding psychological structures of knowledge repre-

sented by the organization of internalized ideas and information in the minds of individual students of varying degrees of both cognitive maturity and subject-matter sophistication in these same disciplines." He then goes on to present a model (reminiscent of the Herbartian view) of the psychological structure of knowledge and of the factors that influence its accretion and organization, based on the principles of *subsumption*. (Bellack, p. 277)

If it be acceptable that logical arrangement deals with ordering what may be found in textbooks or other knowledge sources, and that psychological arrangement deals with ordering the corresponding mental processes that utilize the textbook content, then it is easier to understand some of the attempts to structure knowledge, but difficulties may arise in separating their domains.

Ausubel's *principle of subsumption* shows one educator's manner of accounting for the ordering of knowledge *psychologically*. He stated that the subsumption process explains why one's organization of the content of a subject matter in his mind consists of a hierarchy. In that structure, the most inclusive concepts are found at the apex, and progressively less inclusive, more highly differentiated subconcepts and factual data are subsumed. Ausubel agreed that logical and psychological ordering differ in the kinds of processes that may be classified under each kind of arrangement. For psychological organization of knowledge, there are the laws of meaningful learning and retention. For logical organization, the laws are found in the logic of clasification. Still, both kinds of organization utilize the logic of classification and are subject to the same principle of ordering knowledge. Both integrate elements according to the greatest generality, inclusiveness, and explanatory power, while also relating and integrating the most inclusive array of subject matters. Both logical and psychological processes of organization may be described as processes of subsumption, the placing of the less inclusive categories under the more inclusive.

However, though logical and psychological arrangements may obey similar laws, the arrangement of the component elements differs. Subsumption may govern both, but in the psychological hierarchy, new learnings are subsumed under those relevant, broader concepts that already exist in the cognitive structure of the learner, whereas the logical structuring of knowledge is aimed at establishing topical relatedness and homogeneity. But a minimal degree of subject-matter sophistication is first required if logical and psychological structures are to parallel each other. When the individual has become an expert and a specialist in his knowledge, then his psychological structure corresponds somewhat to the logical structure of the knowledge in that discipline. His expertness permits him to easily reorganize his psychological structure according to the most homogeneous and systematic ordering of the relationships between the facts, the concepts, and the propositions of the topic.

Teachers apply the principle of subsumption when they develop outlines of topics. For example, the most inclusive, most general heading is numbered I, then a less inclusive one is A, and so on, as in the following familiar outline.

The more specific, less general the topic or concept, the more the number of more inclusive topics under which it will be subsumed. Teachers find it useful to instruct pupils in arranging a body of knowledge in this way because it is an orderly way of relating the components meaningfully. Many essays begin as outlines, which are then filled in with the details. But the logic of the subject-matter structure must also fit the psychologic. Those things to be learned must be relatable to what is already known. They are not merely catalogued in memory as isolated facts, but they are placed within the appropriate area of subsumption. The learner may more meaningfully and easily learn what is in the subject matter outline if it can be fitted into the more inclusive outline that already exists in his own thinking. The learner sorts the data, so to speak, fitting it into his own cognitive structures.

Ausubel advocated a strategy for deliberately manipulating cognitive structure, by using "advance organizers." Advance organizers differ from summaries and overviews in that these organizers are presented at a higher level of abstraction, generality, and inclusiveness than is to be found in the material that follows them. The summary or overview is presented at the same level as the learning material. The principle of subsumption is applied when advance organizers are used—the organizer provides a structure that permits (1) incorporating and retaining the lesson material and (2) increased discriminability between lesson material and any interfering concepts that may already exist in the learner's cognitive structure. (Ausubel referred to these two functions of the organizer as the "enhancement of proactive facilitation" and the "minimizing of proactive inhibition.")

There have been many other notable attempts to utilize hierarchical arrangements. Teaching according to readiness stages and the teachable moment have been mentioned in Chapter 2, as means for fitting the logic of subject matters to the psychologic of the developing stages of intellectual maturity. Classifying according to the maturity of psychological structures and the complexity of logical contents has received a great deal of attention from Piaget (1958). Elkind and Flavell (1963) have interpreted Piaget's psychology.

THE DEVELOPMENTAL STAGES OF PIAGET

From birth to age two the child undergoes a period of development that Piaget characterized as *sensorimotor*. Reflex behaviors become modified with experience. There is a beginning of activities initiated toward external objects and events. Intentional behavior emerges, and some using of means toward ends becomes evident. Novelty in objects arouses interest, and the child begins to try new ways of using objects. New means of moving toward goals are attempted.

From ages two to seven, the child evolves gradually through a period of *preoperational thought*. Here, the child is egocentric; he centers his attention upon the most striking feature of an event, ignoring some other important factors; he lacks the ability to strike a balance between assimilating new material into the existing cognitive structure and accommodating or adjusting to the environment, and his cognitive organization is unstable. The child thinks in specific images rather than abstractly, and he tends to attribute human powers to inanimate objects. Concepts of time, causality, space, measurement, number, quantity, movement, and velocity are understood when applied to concrete situations, but not as abstractions.

At seven to eleven years, the period of *concrete operations* obtains. The child can perform only concrete problem-solving operations at first, but moves toward the ability to attack abstract problems. The nine possible groupings of the operations that were named suggest levels of teaching:

1. Primary Addition Classes
2. Secondary Addition Classes
3. Bi-univocal Multiplication of Classes
4. Co-univocal Multiplication of Classes
5. Addition of Asymmetrical Relations
6. Addition of Symmetrical Relations

7. Bi-univocal Multiplication of Relations
8. Co-univocal Multiplication of Relations
9. Preliminary Groupings of Equalities
(Klausmeier and Goodwin, 1966, p. 225)

Some teachers have difficulty in instructing the very young because they fail to recognize that certain basic operations are not utilized by the child. If a child has difficulty in grouping or classifying on more than one level, or on the basis of more than one commonality, then some kinds of problems will be beyond his solution. In the stage of primary addition, a child will be able to establish simple hierarchies of classes of things, but will be unable to reclassify or regroup a thing into a new class at the same time that one of his groupings still exists. For example, he may correctly classify types of cups according to materials, e.g., *plastic* cups. When shown three blue plastic cups and five red ones, however, he may not be able to state that there are more red, when asked "Are there more red cups or plastic cups?" because he cannot disturb the category he has already made (plastic) in order to utilize a new one (red). He thinks in terms of only one classification scheme at a time.

In secondary addition, the child is able to deal with classes that are equivalent. He recognizes that all of any group is composed of the members of a subgroup and all other members that are not in that subgroup. For example, in the group or class of horses, there are white horses and all other horses, which are not white. And the class, horses, also has an equivalent, black horses and all others not black.

Biunivocal multiplication of classes occurs when the child can divide up a group or class into subgroups of the same rank. He knows that *horses* refers to Percherons, Arabians, and so on. But he can also put two classes together to make a third class, such as white horses and pacers, to make white pacing horses.

The fourth kind of operation is said to be necessarily present, but Piaget has not yet demonstrated that it is.

When ordering is accomplished according to size, rank, height, weight, and so on, this is called addition of assymetrical relations. The teacher is realistic in requiring of most children that they arrange things in serial order at this stage.

In the addition of symmetrical relations, the child can recognize reverse relationships. For example, he sees that if Alice is a sister of Bertha, then Bertha must be a sister of Alice. He can also go beyond this to understand that if Roy is a brother of Bertha, then he is also a brother of Alice.

In biunivocal multiplication of relations, the child is able to deduce that two objects may be equal in one respect, but unequal in another, or in several others. A wooden rod may be the same size as a plastic one, but the wooden one weighs more. Also, the same sized metal rod weighs more than the wooden one. The child can exercise his deductive power to say that the metal rod also weighs more than the plastic one. At this time the child can also state correctly that when a given amount of liquid is poured from a wide, low jar into a narrow, tall one, the amount remains constant. Similarly, he can also solve other conservation problems dealing with weight, volume, and mass.

Piaget did not demonstrate the existence of the eighth type of operations.

In preliminary groupings of equalities, the child can recognize the truth of the statement heard in geometry classes, "When quantities are equal to the same quantity they are equal to each other." Number concept emerges. The child begins to realize that if a third statement can be made, the equivalency of the first two must be established. (If Smith is as tall as Jones, and Brown is as tall as Jones, then Smith and Brown are as tall as each other.)

The period of developing *formal operations* extends from eleven to fourteen years. The learner is able to manipulate ideas abstractly. He does not have to solve problems by using concrete manipulations, and can engage in problem solving according to logical operations. He can also divorce himself, upon occasion, from the present, to generate various orders of possibilities for the future.

Although Piaget's disregard for age and intelligence data and his rather sharply defined categories have been deplored, those who have performed similar experiments seem to support his general contentions (D. Elkind, 1961, 1962, 1964; K. Lovell, 1961; and J. Smedslund, 1963). And others are likely to agree with his central theme, that there are levels of maturity that must be considered in the ordering of learning experiences. The psychological processing of inputs changes according to a hierarchy that develops with age. And there is also a hierarchy of learning to which one may be systematically exposed, when he reaches a given maturity level.

INSTRUCTIONAL UNIT DESIGN
BASED ON CONCEPT FORMATION

Piaget is usually associated with the sequence of concept levels that develop in the child, but Asahel Woodruff focused not only on concept formation, but also on a cognitive cycle as a complete energy system, very much like that of a computer. The model of the cognitive cycle is reproduced in Figure 5. 1.

Not shown on the diagram is Woodruff's list of concept types, arranged according to topical organization:

Concepts of Processes and Consequences ("sequences")
 Natural forces and processes
 Social actions and effects
 Personal actions and effects
 Persons seen as sets of behaviors
Concepts of Structure
 Anything seen spatially or dimensionally ("organizational structure")
Concepts of Qualities ("analysis")
 Any characteristics of a referent which we wish to handle in the abstract
 (color, size, style, traits, etc.)

(Woodruff, 1967, p. 104)

To plan a unit of instruction, a conceptual statement ought to assume the form of "A description of the properties of a process, structure, or quality stated in a form which indicates what has to be demonstrated or portrayed so a learner can perceive the process, structure or quality for himself" (1967, p. 102). Instruction is aimed at changing behavior, so it is useful to think of a unit of instruction as being built around the desired behavior that is the learning outcome. Woodruff does not feel that concepts are significant variables in behavioral acts that are simple, specific, largely reflexive—those that are responsive to classical conditioning. Nor does he accept very simple operants, acquired via instrumental learning, as complex enough for concepts to be significant. When behavior is simply conditioned, logic is not involved in the learning. "Thus the suggested form of an instructional unit is that of a terminal behavior and all of the subordinate concepts, operants, symbolic data, and vocabulary required to produce it" (Verduin, p. 108).

An instructional unit may be designed according to (1) a terminal behavior or (2) the acquisition of a concept or concepts, whichever outcome is desired. If the outcome is the acquisition of a desired terminal behavior, then Woodruff suggested, as did Mager and Walbesser, that the unit of instruction ought to be specific about the capabilities to be acquired and the abilities that are prerequisite to that instruction. Following these determinations, there should be a sequence for the learning (conditioning) experiences that will be used for helping the learner to reach the terminal behavior. (Programmed instruction and other very systematic instructional procedures illustrate this sequence.) If the desired outcome is the acquisi-

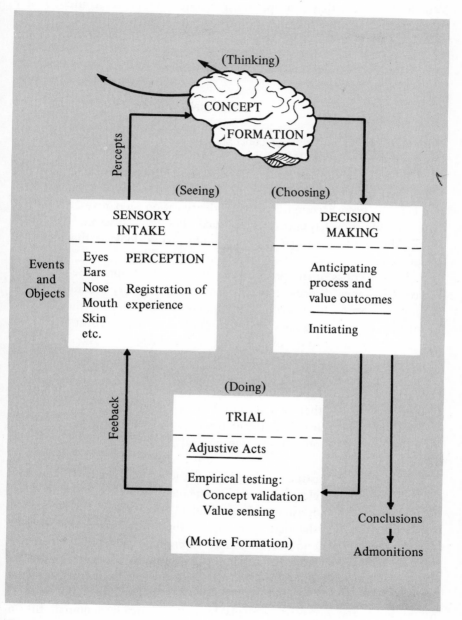

Fig. 5.1. (From "Concept Formation and Learning Unit Design," p. 104, in
Verduin's *Conceptual Models in Teacher Education,* American
Association of Colleges for Teacher Education, 1967.)

tion of concepts, the instructional unit should contain a concept statement identifying all components that are contained in the concept. Woodruff believes that concepts must dictate content, for content is not merely selected, rather it comes from the concepts that are to be acquired. He would build a hierarchy of conceptual objectives, not of content objectives. His sequential taxonomy appears in Figure 5. 2.

DESIGNING AN INSTRUCTIONAL UNIT

Based on the acquisition of concepts, the starting point is with sensory inputs, the percepts of Woodruffs' cognitive cycle, which make possible what he calls (a) *identification.* If this step is necessary, reference materials may be provided, but if prior identification of the relevant phenomena has been accomplished, this identification step may be omitted. Once identification has been accomplished, then the learner may be helped to (b) differentiate, to take a closer, more precise look at the identified phenomena.

If the concept is of the *process* type, it is one that affects behavior and behavioral change. Process concepts may be formed (i) according to the natural processes and procedures in the cognitive cycle. Or they may be formed by (ii) drawing conclusions through analysis or synthesis or from the other technical processes shown in the hierarchy. As the learner builds concepts of processes and consequences, he also reaches the (d) recognition-of-value level. Affective and cognitive elements of a concept are formed at the same time. Finally, the (e) formation of a principle occurs.

If the concept is that of a *structure,* then (c) forming a class concept follows upon the learner's differentiating the relevant phenomena. Then (d) the learner simply forms more general groups from less general, or more specific ones.

In designing an instructional unit, the teacher will need to know how he will present the elements for initial perception to the students. Two factors govern his decision: (1) a student may already have enough background so that he does not require the initial perceptual process; (2) the student may not have had any appropriate perceptual experience. In case he has not, the teacher must first supply adequate perceptual materials. The unit should indicate the sequence to be used, the media, the materials, and the directions that will be used to direct the learner's attention. If the necessary percepts have been already acquired, the instructional unit should require recall and review. Appropriate stimuli should be provided and the learner should be aided to focus upon relevant

(e) FORMATION OF A PRINCIPLE
Assumes a repertoire of specific instances of a process and its consequence, and requires discovery of invariable relationships among them.

(d) RECOGNITION OF VALUE
Assumes concepts of processes and consequences, and requires perception of how people feel about the consequences.

(d) FORMING MORE GENERAL GROUPS
Assumes awareness of pervasive common characteristics and their differentiation from irrelevant differential characteristics.

(c) FORMING OF PROCESS CONCEPTS
   (i) NATURAL PROCESSES AND PROCEDURES

   (ii) TECHNICAL PROCESSES TO ASSIST OR TO GUIDE THE FORMING OF A CONCLUSION OR DECISION
     Analysis
     Synthesis
     Evaluation
     Problem solving
     Self-directed learning

(c) FORMING A CLASS CONCEPT (GENERAL)
Assumes differentiation of characteristics to be used for classifying objects or events.

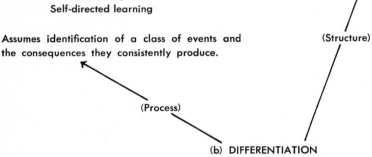

Assumes identification of a class of events and the consequences they consistently produce.

(Structure)

(Process)

(b) DIFFERENTIATION
Assumes identification, and requires more precise perceptions to find differentiating characteristics.

(a) IDENTIFICATION
Assumes no prior learning, but requires sensory ability to perceive, and referential materials to be perceived.

Fig. 5.2. Woodruff's Hierarchy of Conceptual Objectives (1966). (From Verduin's *Conceptual Models in Teacher Education,* American Association of Colleges for Teacher Education, 1967.)

components and to put them together. This response-requiring situation should be one in which the learner's decision, using the concept acting upon it, should result in consequences that with help may be interpreted as to meaning and value.

The next step in unit design takes into consideration the balance between the inputs of the learner and the discussions concerning interpretation, due consideration being given to the learner's readiness. Learning may move onto the perceptual level, at which the learner merely identifies or differentiates. Or the unit may be geared to move up to an organizing level, through discussion aids. Learning may also begin on the organizing level, if the learner already has the percepts and subconcepts necessary. A fourth possibility is that the learner may move back and forth between levels, as new percepts are brought in to support or suggest organizing ideas. Thus the teacher, even with a carefully designed unit of instruction, needs to know the level for which the learner is ready.

The unit of instruction should also include various teaching strategies and verbal patterns that the teacher may use to advantage, set up according to their levels of meaningfulness. Some of the possibilities for strategies and verbal patterns are found in Smith's "The Logical Aspects of Teaching," Bellack's "The Language of the Classroom," Taba's "Teaching Strategies for Cognitive Growth," Flanders's "Interaction Analysis," and Gallagher's "Structure of the Intellect," all described in *Conceptual Models in Teacher Education*, by Verduin (1967).

Another step in designing an instructional unit is to designate the limited number of inputs of symbolic materials that the learner will be expected to store in his memory, for example, *vocabulary* related to the concept, *nonverbal signs* and symbolic strategies, and *data essential to communicating* about the concept and for using it in making decisions.

The final consideration in instructional design is that provisions must be made in the unit for the motor learnings that may be required for using the concept, or the terminal behavior in situations that require adjustment. If overt behavior is required by the unit, then the motor learning that must accompany this behavior must also be considered.

IMPLICATIONS OF WOODRUFF'S IDEAS

Many schools do not utilize sensory inputs adequately. The older emphasis on sense training and object teaching has been ignored. Instead, much content is handled via verbal, symbolic knowledge. If this is done before sensory input has occurred, concept formation is not adequately fostered. Few educators state objectives in terms of behaviors and their concepts, which therefore are drawn from the content instead of being used to outline the content necessary to form them. Because sensory inputs came to be recognized as important in the *adequate* formation of concepts, media and materials were developed from which learners could supplement their perceptual experiences from the "real world." Finally, because teachers need to be quite well acquainted with the idea to be taught before they begin to teach it, they ought to be able to *show* students, not merely *tell* them, so that students may then build the concepts themselves.

PROGRAMMING INSTRUCTIONAL UNITS

Most teachers have at least seen a programmed instruction textbook. A few have worked through a program, and some have even used programs effectively, in either the book form or with teaching machines. Some courses are being offered, either for the users of programs, or for those who would like to be able to construct their own. The term *construct* is an apt one, for the writer of a program does not simply write one, as one does a book. He builds it carefully, bit by bit, and painstakingly tests it on a student or two at a time, revising it several times before it is deemed fit for public use. This chapter is not intended to present a history of the development of programmed instruction, nor to analyze programming or teach how to program. The intent is rather to familiarize the reader with the place of programmed instruction in the systematic ordering of topics to be learned. It will be noted that both logical and psychological ordering are utilized in programming.

Sidney Pressey, in the nineteen-twenties, aroused some interest in an experimental machine that was essentially a device for testing, using multiple-choice items. But in using this machine students learned, and the right answers that it furnished served as a convenient means of self-evaluation as well as of evaluation by the teacher. However, programmed instruction has become virtually synonymous with linear programming, a development of B. F. Skinner, who employed Ebbinghaus-type completion items. Carpenter (1964) has discussed the psychological basis for programs, in *Systematic Application of Psychology to Education,* and the following discussion is based on pages 200–219 of that book. Additional references are listed at the end of the chapter.

REINFORCEMENT

Some kind of reward or reinforcement (the terms are not technically equivalent) has been shown to facilitate the learning of rewarded responses or response patterns. Among those who have emphasized the powerful influence of consequences upon learning (conditioning) is E. L. Thorndike, who promulgated the law of effect:

> When a modifiable connection between a situation and a response is made, and is accompanied by a satisfying state of affairs, that connection's strength is increased: When made and accompanied by an annoying state of affairs, its strength is decreased. (Thorndike, 1914, 1921, II, pp. 2–4)

Skinner revised Thorndike's formulation, and spoke in terms of response probabilities (instead of the strength of a connection), and these are increased via reinforcement, reduced via punishment, and extinguished via nonreinforcement. To apply the idea of reinforcement to a unit of instruction suggests that the reward or reinforcement be made contingent upon the successful acquisition of certain behaviors. However, learners have too often been expected to acquire novel learnings in pieces that are too large, and complex and for which the learner does not have adequate concepts. One way to increase the certainty that the learner will be able to complete each learning task and hence be rewarded and therefore learn is to cut up the task into smaller ones. Thus, the principle may be stated:

> *Units of material to be learned will be small enough to permit the student to respond successfully almost every time a response is required.* Carpenter (p. 201)

Successful responding (being a "satisfying state of affairs") not only tends to ensure learning, it also reduces the likelihood of fear of failure on subsequent responses. Because the student is required to respond to every small piece of information, that is, respond to every frame, his *responses are frequent*, compared with the usual frequency of responding required when conventional textbooks are used.

Most written materials, prior to the advent of programmed instruction, made no provisions for informing the student of his progress at frequent intervals. Teachers supplemented the textbook offerings by verbal feedbacks, when feasible, but their efforts had to be distributed among many pupils. Each individual could not expect frequent feedback or knowledge of results with respect to his responses. Thus, instructional programs that are carefully composed must provide another necessary adjunct to efficient learning:

> *The learner will be provided with knowledge of the appropriateness of his responses. Programmed units provide correct answers or some evaluative aid, for each learning task.*
> Carpenter (p. 202)

To allow for the uniqueness of individuals, that is, to adjust for individual differences, is a laudable aim. However, it is an ideal objective, to be striven for but only approximated. One way of allowing for individual differences is to permit each learner to proceed at the rate that is best for him. Self-pacing may be disadvantageous in a few situations, as when a pupil will not go beyond what he is definitely asked to do, but generally, it is considered to be better than forced pacing, which holds some back and leaves others behind. Self-pacing means that

> *The flow of material is under the control of the learner.* Carpenter (p. 207)

Woodruff (1951) emphasized the desirability of *overt* responses. Most programs require the learner to make overt responses before moving from one item to the next; usually, the learner is to write something. But the necessity for overt responding has not been definitely established. For one thing, efficiency is involved. The student who merely thinks an answer moves more rapidly through a program than does one who must write it. But efficiency may be purchased at the expense of thoroughness or permanence. The argument as to whether overt responding is always, sometimes, or seldom necessary has not been settled.

Good teachers do not give up on slowly responding pupils. They restructure questions and provide hints of various sorts so that the pupil who is groping, but has some knowledge, may arrive at the correct answer. Sometimes a question may be highly redundant, so that the answer is almost given away by the wording of the question. Programmed instruction utilizes all kinds of cues or prompts designed to ensure correct responding. Cues may range all the way from maximal helpfulness, so that for most learners the frame seems a little silly, to aids that are rather subtle. The frame may be structured as a rhyme, so that the response to be furnished rhymes with the preceding line. The initial letter of the response word may be furnished by the frame, or, occasionally, the final letter of the answer or the number of letters may be provided. A definition of a new term may be given, followed by an example that requires the learner to fill in the term that is defined. An effective program is neither overcued nor undercued, but it is skillfully, often subtly cued.

> *The cueing system is used to keep errors at a minimum.* Carpenter (p. 209)

Too often, readers of conventional textbooks read, assume they understand, and move on, only to have to return again and again to assimilate material they thought they understood. A program induces the learner to pause frequently to note any differences between what he thinks was the intent of the subject matter before him and what the writer actually intended. The availability of aids to self-evaluation on the spot, and a program structure that requires occasional pauses, is a better learning facilitator than looking up answers in the back of the book, or turning back in the book. Frequent exercise of self-evaluation tends to strengthen habits of self-evaluating.

> *Self-evaluation is stimulated.* Carpenter (p. 210)

Programs not only reinforce the learner's continued responding, they tend to induce him to reach toward higher levels of learning. Students who had not thought of themselves as capable of going beyond elementary concepts in subject matters such as mathematics, physics, and so on have been agreeably surprised at what they can do through the use of programmed instruction. These students' behavior is reinforced for improvement, not merely for factual acquisition.

> *The teaching agent reinforces improvement.* Carpenter (p. 211)

At first, the reinforcers, or rewards, may be extrinsic ones. Praise from other people, or written into the program, or even some reward or prize may be given. However, with increased ability, the learner is increasingly moved by intrinsic motivation. He often finds himself learning well beyond his expectations, and his learning is not necessarily compared competitively with the learning of others. He no longer need worry about marks.

It is easy for a student to engage in woolgathering, especially when a textbook of uninspiring content lies before his reluctant eyes. Many are the distractions that may easily capture and hold his attention. The printed page itself may simply become a busy array of unrelated stimuli, so that any thread of meaning is lost. The student may skip a line and hardly realize it. He may wander away from the material and back again, only to resume at the paragraph before or the one after the place where he left off. Some textbook writers have tried to make topics more attractive by the liberal use of color, by increasing print size at certain points, and by underlining key statements or stating them in isolation. (Markle calls these "emphasis prompts.") Programmed instruction also makes use of these devices, but its principal contribution is the presentation of a small bit of material that is sufficiently isolated from other frames to keep attention from wandering, and if it does, it wanders easily back to the correct place. Often, masks are provided, so that only the item or frame before the immediate attention of the learner is seen until the mask is moved.

> *Distracting stimuli are minimized.* Carpenter
> (p. 211)

For an individual to develop strength, he must learn to stand on his own feet. So the cues that have been inserted to ensure his correct responding must gradually be removed. The task imposed must become more difficult as it becomes easier for him to accomplish it in part. This *gradual cue reduction* in programmed instruction is called *fading.* The rate at which cues are reduced, or even the amount of cueing that is desirable in the first place, is a matter that has not been experimentally determined. Presumably these factors are a function of learner abilities, the structure of the topic, and the availability of supplementary sources.

If a student is not informed of the results from a test until long after he has passed on to another topic or unit, it is likely that his errors will be difficult to rectify. Busy schedules, overloading, and so on may prevent a teacher's grading examinations and returning them for days after the examinations have been given. In a classroom discussion, some students have to wait for others to speak, and it may be such a long time before their turn comes that they forget or the time for their contribution has passed.

Immediate knowledge of results seems a desirable attribute of programmed instruction. How immediate this ought to be is a moot point. The good student develops an ability to depend more and more on a kind of internal feedback (more on this, in the treatment of cybernetics) and less and less on external checks. However, for all learners it is not too much to expect that they should at least have feedback sources available, if needed, immediately.

MATHETICS

Mathetics is a systematic method of arranging a unit of instruction proposed by T. F. Gilbert (1962) that reverses a major dimension of programmed instruction; sequences, or chains, are taught backwards. As an applied science, mathetics is not confined to subject matter but is applicable to behavioral skills also. It requires a systematic analysis of cognitive and motor skills and then their reconstruction. Major Robert Gerry has said, "In essence, a matheticist describes in behavior terms the sequence of performance leading to desired mastery and constructs from this behavior model exercises which permit attainment of this mastery" (1963, p. 1).

There is a great deal of similarity between mathetics and the usual (Skinnerian) form of programmed instruction, in that both forms rely strongly upon reinforcement (praise, confirmation of progress, and so on), both stress step-by-step progress, and both allow for self-pacing of learning. However, there is also a basic difference between them. The assumption in programmed instruction is that frequent, easily gained success is intrinsically rewarding. A learner who has had difficulty in even getting started in a given subject matter now finds that he can make small, successful steps toward acquiring the terminal performance, or desired goal—but the actual goal behavior is not engaged in until the learning task parts have been completed. Mathetics agrees that success is rewarding, but insists that the most important factor in the motivation of the student is that he desire mastery sufficiently strongly in the first place to work for it. In addition, the system itself is arranged so that the learner does not have to depend upon the confirmations written into the program (another's word) to find out that he is performing correctly. Awareness of one's mastery is evident with each step, because he performs the terminal behavior, but with varying degrees of help, early in the learning phases.

As was the case with programmed instruction of the linear or branching types, there will be no effort here to describe the details of how to make lessons or learning prescriptions via mathetics. The general ideas of the system will be presented, suggesting the possibilities of mathetics as a very systematic approach to teaching—and to self-teaching, once the lessons are developed.

Programmers insist that objectives be stated specifically and in behavioral terms. Once it has been determined that the learner possesses a personal objective in learning the material, the first step in *task analysis* is taken. Gerry points out that it is very important for cooperation to be established between a subject-matter expert and a matheticist. Although the latter need not be well acquainted with the task area, he must at least be able to describe the essentially functional elements of the task. Task analysis or function analysis requires that the instructional aims be defined quite specifically, so it may require either the help of the master (the subject-matter expert) or at least the availability of source materials that clearly contain the required content. (The master may even be indispensable for some highly specialized subject areas.)

After task analysis has been completed, the next step is *prescribing or representing the behavior* that is to be taught. A *chain* is composed of links that are called *operants*. An operant, in this case, refers to a stimulus-response link. A very detailed description is made, and it usually contains three kinds of operant arrangements, *chains, multiples,* and *generalizations.*

Chains

Chains consist of sequences of S-R units. For example, when a stimulus (S) and its associated response (R) are described in a laboratory experiment of the Skinner type, the Skinner Box is the (S), and the cord pulling (or bar pressing) is the associated (R). This is one link, which is then followed by the S-R association or the link of a light (S) coming on, and its association with (R), cord pulling or lever pressing.

A third link in the same example consists of the (S) appearance of food and the associated (R) of eating the food. Thus, there is a three-link chain of behavior.

Another type of operant arrangement that could be described or represented in the *synthetic prescription* would be a *multiple,* or *multiple discrimination structure.* There is no particular or necessary order of the operants or units; each link contains stimuli that are similar in some respect, but may occasion responses that are incompatible with other links in that structure. For example, turning right is incompatible with turning left. In this multiple discrimination structure, the stimulus condition might be "red light," with the associated response "turn right," and another condition might be "blue light," associated with the response "turn left." Yet a third response, incompatible with both of the first two, could be "remain" in response to the stimulus "white light." (For detailed accounts of chains and multiple discriminations, see Gagne's *The Conditions of Learning.*) Such learning situations are common, in which the learner must discriminate or select different responses on the basis of perceived differences in various stimulus situations. The matheticist attempts to note such possibilities in advance of actual learning, so that he will know where to expect that there might be discrimination difficulties.

A *generalization* operant is the third possible arrangement. Stimuli occasioning the same single general response but not occurring except as individual stimuli make up a generalization operant. Learners may also have difficulties with generalization.

The *synthetic prescription* is composed of chains, multiple discrimination structures, and generalization operants. After this prescription has been made and all the task-related operant arrangements have been described, the process of *condensation* of the prescription is carried out. The first writing only approximates the way it will finally look. The final appearance of the prescription is called the *nth Px.* The emphasis in mathetics is on economy, so the Law of Parsimony is applied to the condensing of operants for greater efficiency. The simplest adequate prescription is sought. The matheticist not only tries to sequence behavior toward mastery in a logical way, but he also tries to consolidate various steps as completely as possible within a range that the learner can be expected to negotiate. This greatest possible consolidation of sequenced behavior is called the *operant span.* Operant spans or units are represented in a structure called an *exercise,* which is a lesson segment, just as in popular terminology. Because he is thus far "arm-chairing," the matheticist first makes his prescription very comprehensive, so that the first operant spans that he describes are likely to be too great for a learner to handle at one time. These can then be pared down in successive revisions or approximations. Trial runs are made, using a single learner at a time and carefully noting the student reactions. Notes are made and improvements suggested, and the lesson is revised until learners no longer have difficulties with it.

The Analytic Prescription

The synthetic step amounted to a description of the practical learning performance—what is to be expected of the learner. Next, an analysis must be made of the learning behavior of the master, the subject-matter expert, using analytic theory derived from a condensation of the preceding synthetic prescription. A search for a model is begun by combining and generalizing adjacent operants or links in chains, until a much more generalized, more simplified description of the behavior emerges. Common properties are located, and they are used to facilitate the use of symbols, such as S_1, S_2, R_1, R_2, and so on. Once the schematic representation has been decided upon, a model that will involve all the operations that have been distinguished is built. Again, there follows a condensation, as the model itself is revised.

Characterization

Now that the behavior units that will be necessary in learning have been described, their characteristics may be analyzed. If they seem to present generalization and discrimination difficulties, these are noted. Two kinds of recognition are necessary: (1) a (significant) stimulus must be found that will generalize to all situations to which the response is appropriate; (2) the response must be related to the appropriate stimulus for a given situation, so that competition between stimuli for a given response will be diminished.

Just how does the matheticist actually go about accomplishing the characterization of a mastery prescription? First, he identifies as many instances of generalized stimuli as he can in the prescription. (These are the stimuli that occasion the same response.) The learner will have generalization problems if different stimuli that ought to occasion the same or similar responses do not. The matheticist reduces such difficulties by teaching generalized operants in one exercise, i.e., conditions are arranged so that only the desired responses are forthcoming in the presence of the stimulus conditions. This can be done by *mediation*, the use of an act that intervenes between the desired response and the stimulus that must occasion it. This intervening act serves as a competing response that is of greater weight or strength than the desired response, but that also sets the stage for the desired one to occur. Another way of saying this is that the mediator is something already in the knowledge (response repertoire) of the learner—if this already well-known thing is used to relate the new stimulus to the response to the well-known thing, then it has mediated. Suppose the learner already responds with "0.1 meter" to the stimulus "decimal = 0.1". He may then readily make the response "0.1 meter" to the stimuli "decimeter" and "dm." Thus, what he already recognizes and responds to has acted as a bridge between what he is learning and his responses.

Another way to facilitate generalization is via *graphic focus*. This amounts to providing layouts that will call the learner's attention to the generalization problem. Diagrams may be used that employ contrasting colors, or capital and lower case letters to make something stand out; the use of symbols at strategic points on diagrams are also useful. Photographers achieve graphic focus by only dimly developing one part of a picture, while sharply bringing out the area that is to be the center of attention.

Generalization may also be taught by *sequence facilitation*. A technique that tends to reduce competition between desired and undesired responses to two or more stimuli will facilitate generalization. If two stimuli evoke two competing or incompatible responses or operants, then generalization is not operating. However, if two different stimuli evoke the same response, then generalization is in effect. Sequence facilitation aids in learning to generalize by first teaching (helping both stimuli to evoke the response) the weaker (least likely to occur) of the competing responses, and then using sequences that will bring the response up to strength.

Next, the characterization of the prescription requires *analysis for discrimination or competition*. All behavior that lies within the domain or even outside it, that may appear to compete with learning the new material is studied. Does the stimulus of any operant tend to bring out any incompatible responses just as readily or more so than it does the desired response? If so, graphic focus, sequence facilitation, and mediation should be used to reduce the competition.

Operant interaction analysis is the concluding stage of the characterization of the prescription. Suppose that both elements (stimulus and response) have some common features with both elements of another operant, but the responses of one are incompatible with the responses of the other. The desired operant must be learned by being reinforced, and elements may be used as mediational behavior that will reduce the competition between the incompatible responses. Also, the incompatible response will be less essential to the desired chain of behavior, and it will tend to weaken, thus lessening its competitive power.

If it is possible to use mediators or a special strategy to facilitate its structure, an entire multiple discrimination set may be presented in one exercise. However, if such help is not available, the exercise that requires discrimination may be divided into subsets, each of which contains operants that are competitive, but that also facilitate operants in other subsets. The first exercise would demonstrate the first subset of competitors, the second exercise would demonstrate the first and second subsets, and so on in collective, cumulative fashion.

The Final Prescription

The aim is to reduce competition and to improve operant interaction. More efficient learning sequences may be afforded by following these rules:

1. The earliest operants presented should be those that (a) produce facilitation between domains, or (b) seem most likely to be in competition with other domain operants.

2. Later operants should be those that (a) are most likely to be facilitated by other domain operants, or (b) afford the greatest competition.

The Lesson Plan

Now that preparations and analyses have been made a lesson plan may be developed. The idea is to begin with task accomplishment and gradually include larger and larger behavior segments until all the behavior engaged in includes a chain of stimuli and responses. The responses are usually expressed as a form of overt behavior. The stimuli are usually expressed as elements that occasion responses, or as reinforcing consequences of responses.

Each unit of behavior, or operant span, within an exercise is fully *demonstrated* or presented in one exercise, is partially instructed as a *prompted* effort in the next exercise, and is expressed so as to require the learner to accomplish it totally in the third exercise. This stage of total accomplishment of the desired behavior unit is said to have been *released. An exercise therefore consists of demonstration, prompting, and releasing.* The release consists of successively longer operant spans until the last release combines all behavior from the beginning efforts to the full task accomplishment. The making of lesson plans would be accomplished in this same way, using both synthetic and analytic prescriptions, though an analytic prescription usually describes covert behavior. The lesson plan may be illustrated as shown in the table (each S——R represents an operant).

Exercise #	Demonstrate	Prompt	Release
1	S_3——R_4		
2	S_2——R_3	S_3——R_4	
3	S_1——R_2	S_2——R_3	S_3——R_4
4		S_1——R_2	S_2——R_4
5			S_1——R_4
			(Gerry, p. 14)

Composing the Exercise

First, how is the operant *demonstrated?* There are three basic conditions: (1) attention to the stimulus; (2) a correct response as the result of attention; (3) an immediate result that is reinforcing must be produced by the response. First, an attention director is provided, so that the learner may observe the relevant or discriminative stimulus, and identify it for what it is. Also, the learner's response should be appropriate, so explicit instructions must be provided. Thus, the demonstration phase of an exercise has two functions, to direct attention and the identification of the proper stimuli for learning, and to compel the learner to respond correctly while under stimulation.

Now, how is the operant prompted? The prompt is a restatement of critical elements from the *demonstration* that precedes this phase. Thus, it may be considered partial instruction and is used immediately after the demonstration. The prompt not only mediates the student behavior until the discriminated stimulus acquires full strength to evoke his responding, but also chains the learner's present behavior to the terminal operant—it hooks up the full accomplishment with the partial accomplishment.

How is the operant *released?* Essentially, the student simply completes the behavior sequence unaided. The release is from the necessary influences of the instructional sequence. Thus, the prompting phase may be unnecessary when mastery has been attained within fewer exercises than have been planned.

Final Refinement

The final refinement is a stage of proofreading and copy editing the lesson. The tasks involved may be carried out by others, but the matheticist is consulted for approval of any changes made. Then the lesson is ready for trial testing on subjects who are similar to those who will be eventually taught by it. The trial is on a person-to-person basis, with the instructor noting student reactions. This close individual scrutiny may uncover ambiguity, overcomplexity, or inefficient format, so it may lead to one or more revisions.

The foregoing description makes evident the extremely systematic nature of mathetics. The approach is said to have high reliability, so that more than one group of matheticists working separately will produce lessons that are similar, if provided with the same set of objectives. Analysis of tasks will result in similar prescriptions. Validity is also high, because the behavior is directly related to the prescription. However, the approach is sometimes difficult to understand, and precision of implementation demands careful study of the designs to be produced. D. F. Pennington and C. W. Slack (1962) have elaborated upon these ideas, as presented by Gerry's article. Learning by doing is emphasized, and because task simulators are used instead of teaching machines, other kinds of behavior can be taught besides verbal and written skills. This learning by doing is called a *transactional approach*.

It is common to speak of the learner's moving toward a goal via small, progressive steps, and the goal is called the *terminal behavior*. However, it may be seen that mathetics starts with the last thing that the individual learns in that sequence—a reversal of the direction in programmed instruction. The learner is first taught where he is going and what he will be doing when he has become competent. Each step he takes is reinforcing because it is connected with the final performance. The learner gradually increases the amount that he does on his own, without support, until he can perform the entire task unaided. Because he clearly sees evidence at each step of his increasing ability, he is increasingly aware that he can do more each time and is highly motivated to continue. Matheticists claim that their method (1) saves time and lesson space; (2) sustains motivation; and (3) requires a greater degree of active functioning by the student than does the usual form of programmed instruction. The third consideration is derived from the fact that the unit of measure is not a frame, but an operant—the amount of behavior that is changed by the lesson—and the response is not merely constructed or chosen, but is a combined task simulation and some sort of constructed response.

THE TEACHER AS PROGRAMMER

The application of what O'Keefe (1967) called "eight basic aspects of programming" can characterize a teacher as a programmer, with or without the aid of a teaching machine or a programmed text:

1. *Specification of goals or objectives* in advance of class time. Admittedly, even if the teacher adheres rather strictly to the pursuance of these goals, pupils will learn a great deal more than what is specified, but specification of goals provides definite directions, rather than vague, random meanderings. The sequence calls for development of priorities or hierarchies of concepts, so that some concepts may serve as prerequisites for understanding others.

2. *Only one concept at a time is taught.*

3. *New concepts or skills should be mastered before other new ones are introduced.*

4. *Newly learned concepts should be related to those already learned.*

5. *Practice that will encourage pupils to use both old and new learnings should be provided.*

6. *Dissimilar concepts may be introduced,* often as opposites of those learned, or as paired associates, after the mastery of certain basic concepts. It is easier for the child to learn concepts that are contrasting than to learn those that are confusingly similar.

7. *Reinforcement should be provided that is appropriate for each child.*

8. *Stability and structure* for the learning should be provided for the learner. He acquires coping abil-

ity, secure in the knowledge that he will not be pushed too rapidly, nor bored with insufficient progress, and that the order of the things learned will make sense.

"PROGRAMMING" OTHER INSTRUCTIONAL MODES

The principles applied in programming may also be useful in improving other modes of instruction. Motion pictures, for instance, have not been really exploited. Films are frequently used for motivational purposes, but both their content and presentations can be structured for improved instruction. Many projectors are now equipped with controls for the immediate stopping of the film, so that rate of pacing can be more easily controlled by the teacher or the student. Breaking up the material to be learned into small bits is now facilitated by the development of single-concept films, short instructional units in cartridges that are quickly, easily inserted, without the usual preparation required in threading a projector. It is also quite practical to show printed programs via film. Slides and filmstrips may be used in programmed form, and recorded sound instructions may supplement the programs.

What has been said of films is also true of video tapes, with the added advantage that video tapes may be erased for modification. (Video tapes are especially advantageous in simulations and in microteaching, both of which are dealt with later in this book.)

Field trips need not be merely occasions for entertainment or change of pace. Phases (steps) may be planned in advance, so that the principles found so useful for programmed instruction may also be applied to a field trip. Students may be given opportunities to acquire many concepts that will be useful on the trip well in advance of the trip. Audio-visual aids may be quite motivational, not only during this preparation phase, but as a review, after the trip. A few possible checklist items for field trip preparation would question whether the field trip is a logical extension of subject matters currently being studied. If it is, then the teacher already has a possible basis for entering-behavior or the baseline of present knowledge. If pupils have been stimulated to consider trip possibilities in connection with a topic, the anticipation of a trip will provide motivation for classroom learning as well as for the trip itself. Discussions designed to promote awareness of what will be necessary for getting the most out of the trip will also be helpful. As they await the trip, students will accept suggestions for preparing checklists of things they wish to see and do during the trip. They may also defer certain questions, at the teacher's suggestion, until they can be answered by their own observations. Each pupil's contribution to the preparation should be reinforced. It may be decided that the trip is worthy of a report in the school newsletter, or the class bulletin, and if many pupils, not merely a chosen few, are permitted to list their observations, the increase in attentiveness during the trip will be gratifying. If the class is very large, it will probably be worthwhile to try to divide it into groups, so that guides or other leaders may provide more personal supervision.

During the trip, if possible, each student should be permitted to ask questions and should receive adequate answers. On some trips, it may be possible for pupils to manipulate some controls, produce objects, and so on. If the trip is to be maximally instructive, then shy children who would remain on the fringes, hearing little, with questions unasked and unanswered, ought to be given their share of instruction. Some areas abound with distractions, noises, and so on, so much that the trip will be improved if only very small numbers are guided through at a time. Many cues should be provided, and then gradually withdrawn. In factories, where there are production processes arranged to assemble complete products, pupils, if not properly cued, may get lost in following some minor process. When possible, frequent questioning by the teacher should occur on the spot where operations are carried out, so that more meaningful feedback can be utilized.

After the trip, review should be immediate. Short, frequent reviews are desirable during a field trip, but are not always feasible. During the review is also a time for establishing predispositions for other trips. Learning gained in the planning stage may be synthesized during and after the trip.

Analyses of other instructional modes can be made, using the principles found useful in programmed instruction. Group discussion, for example, can be systematically used for instruction, as well as for insights into group dynamics. Even that most inefficient mode, the lecture, may be so structured as to become increasingly effective. (When so structured, however, it may assume an aspect that differs considerably from what is ordinarily understood to be a lecture.)

LOGICAL STRUCTURE OF TEACHING

This chapter has presented some logical and psychological considerations with respect to the intellectual processes of the learner and of what is to be learned. There has been some treatment of systematic applications of psychology to various modes in teaching-learning, e.g., Albert E. Hickey and John M. Newton (see Verduin, 1967) on the logical structure of teaching. They used a conceptual model to illustrate the logical ordering of teaching, based on "logic space." The model points up (1) the relationship of the subconcepts of conceptual elements to the major concepts, and (2) the relationship between general rules, principles, or laws and specific instances or examples of the principles. The model is shown in Figure 5.3.

It may be seen that the "tree" has its basic, more general structure at the bottom, or trunk, whereas the less general, more specific sub-structures form branches and their interrelationships. Thus, any of the very elemental ideas or terms could be extended by adding more subchains or branches. So that the tree need not be extended indefinitely, however, some starting points are specified. The logic tree is a diagrammatic form of the subsumption process, as described by Ausubel (1963). It may also be seen as an inverted lattice, often used in structuring a segment of programmed instruction. However, the lattice places the more specific processes at the bottom of the structure, with increasingly more complex processes being erected on the steps provided by the simpler ones. Hickey and Newton's logic tree is built so that it can specify various means of dealing with the analysis and organization of concepts. It does not dictate what methods are to be used in teaching, but it does make the salient points that are to be taught explicit rather than implicit.

Starting points will be determined by the prerequisites of the content area and by their mastery by the student. Suppose, in the example, pupils already understand the effects of temperature changes in air, know the composition of air, and can handle the conception of weight. From these understandings, they may be led to a knowledge of how temperature changes in air may result in air movements. Their knowledge of air's composition and weight may be used in developing the concept of air pressure. If it is desirable at the time to go on to more advanced ideas, they may then use the concepts of air movement and air pressure to form a relationship or rule about air pressure and air movement interactions, and about high- and low-pressure areas. Finally, all may be combined to develop principles in the overall study of weather, or meteorology. Thus, the tree provides the advantage not only of specifying the relative inclusiveness of its parts, but of indicating their mutual relationships as they contribute to a larger structure.

Hickey and Newton have also constructed a Model of Logic Space, indicating planes that represent specific concrete, specific abstract, and general abstract events that knowledge may encompass. Induction and deduction

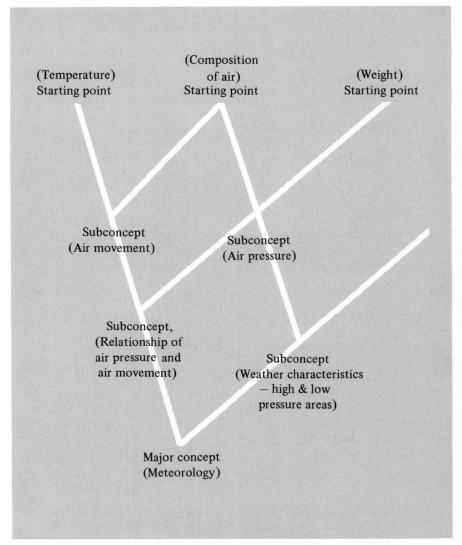

(Temperature)
Starting point

(Composition
of air)
Starting point

(Weight)
Starting point

Subconcept
(Air movement)

Subconcept
(Air pressure)

Subconcept,
(Relationship of
air pressure and
air movement)

Subconcept
(Weather characteristics
— high & low
pressure areas)

Major concept
(Meteorology)

Fig. 5.3. A Logic Tree (Hickey and Newton). (From Verduin, 1967, p. 83.)

may be used in moving either from specific to general (inductive direction) or from general to specific (deductive direction). At each level, learning may be facilitated via synthesis or analysis. Although knowledge can be specified in multidimensional terms, it is suggested that it can be taught only in a single dimension for a sequence, because a pupil is limited as to the amount of attention he can give. The teacher must therefore convert from a multidimensional consideration to a single-dimensional sequence. He must also decide upon the degrees of abstractness or concreteness he will use in his terms. Will the subconcepts be attended to by words, for instance, perhaps in lecture form, or will there be a concrete experience?

Hickey and Newton experimented with a program for teaching the concept, law of demand. They wished to know the effects of analysis versus synthesis, that is, of *direction;* they also were interested in the effects of frame *positions* in the various concepts, and in what influence would be related to the *order* of presenting the subconcepts. They were interested in determining the effects of each instructional sequence on the number of student errors, on the speed of completion of each sequence, and on the transfer of learning. It was found that performance is more rapid when principles are stated first, followed by more rudimentary definitions. Transfer was not superior when the program moved from elements to principles —however, it was not inferior in this direction, either. They found no advantage in learning subconcepts first and then retaining them till needed for further development—i.e., they could be learned at the time of need and integrated into the whole process just as well.

LOGICAL ORDERING OF TIME SEGMENTS

Searles (1967) suggested that the appropriate application, at the moment of readiness, makes for the most logical use of time. (This is in agreement, of course, with many others, such as Havighurst, Piaget, and Gesell.) However, at this point, he is not speaking of readiness in the usual sense, but of some effects on the learner and teacher of the time of day during which instruction is occurring. Students may be sleepy in the early morning, hungry before lunch time, and on edge just before dismissal, or in anticipation of a pep rally or following one. Mondays may be difficult and Fridays are well-known letdown times. But teachers learn to live with these nadirs, or to discover ways of shoring up the low spots.

Searles stressed the effects of more subtle dimensions of time. He assumed that there are episodes in the instructional process, so that it proceeds in bursts, not in a smooth, continuous flow. These episodes are partial determiners of instructor and learner verbal behavior, and range from five to fifteen minutes in length, or about four per hour. Whatever the length of an instructional episode, there are four distinct phases, and ideas concerning these are presented by Allen and Gross (1965) and by B. O. Smith (1962). Each episode may be seen as composed of the *entry,* the *development* phase, and the *exit*. In the entry phase, contact between the learner and the instructor and what Searles called the "search image" takes place. The search image has to do with the immediate learning task, which, as viewed by the search image, is generally small, well-ordered, and learnable. Learning tasks are found in the cognitive (thinking) domain, in the affective (emotional) domain, or in the psychomotor (skill) domain. Searles limited his discussion to the search image in the thinking or cognitive domain.

Entry

The entry phase has several functions as it establishes contact between the instructor, the learner, and his search image. One function is to provide rules of procedure for classroom dialogue. The line of logic that is to be followed is developed. Also, a decision is made as to whether the main aim of the instructional session will be to produce something or to get the child engaged in some kind of process. There is some overlap, of course, with tasks that have preceded this one and with larger overall tasks, of which this one may be a part. The entry phase amounts to the establishing of the ground rules and the objectives of the instruction. The child gets an idea of what he is expected to learn and how he will learn it.

Development

During this phase logical considerations are uppermost. The instructional unit is likely to be broken up into its parts via analysis. It will then be rebuilt via synthesis. How small the parts will be, or what they will consist of, will depend on the nature of the knowledge to be analyzed. A poem may be analyzed verse by verse, whereas a statement to be analyzed grammatically may be treated word by word.

Closure

Closure is effected after the components have been restored to their proper places. That is, the knowledge or subject matter has been analyzed and put back together again. It is important that pupil closure coincides with the closure of the teacher—otherwise the pupil may break away from the instructional process. If the pupil feels that he has finished before the teacher shows evidence of it, the pupil will not be likely to attend to further discussion. If the pupil has not yet reached closure, however, though the instructor is winding up the discussion, it may mean that the instructor has been too abrupt, trying to fit what he is teaching into too brief a period. The tapering off process ought to be well timed, so that pupils and teacher reach closure together. If a summary is used, it should simply remind the pupils briefly and then lead out of the discussion to terminate it. Pupils should have achieved the necessary insights, but they should not have to endure too many reiterations of what they have learned.

Exit

The closing phase aids the learner in moving on to the next search image and so serves a connecting function. One excellent way to exit is to provide reviews that overlap into previews of things to be learned the next day or the next week. Overviews or advance organizers are also useful in the exit phase. Also, this is an appropriate time for providing inviting glimpses of possibilities that may be uncovered by the student if he will but move along into the next phase of learning.

It is customary to say that readiness to learn emerges because of maturation, though many educators are ready to insist that environmental stimulation is the important determiner. However, there is general agreement that learning proceeds more meaningfully, more efficiently, and more pleasurably when the logic of knowledge reasonably parallels the psychological development of the learner. Greater retention and transfer to broader applications also accompany the matching of subject-matter logic and learner development.

References

1. Allen, Dwight, and R. E. Gross, "Microteaching: A New Beginning for Beginners," *NEA Jnl.*, Dec. 1965, 25–26.
2. American Educational Research Association, *Criteria for Assessing Programed Instructional Materials*, 1962 Interim Report of the Joint Committee on Programed Instruction and Teaching Machines. Re-Printed in *Audio-Visual Instruction* (1963), 8, 84–89.
3. Ausubel, David P., *The Psychology of Meaningful Verbal Learning*. New York, Grune and Stratton, 1963.
4. ———, "Some Psychological Aspects of the Structure of Knowledge," *Education and the Structure of Knowledge*, Stanley Elam (ed.), Fifth Annual Phi Delta Kappa Symposium on Educational Research. Chicago, Rand McNally & Company, 1964.

5. Bellack, Arno A., "Knowledge Structure and the Curriculum," *Education and the Structure of Knowledge,* Stanley Elam (ed.), Fifth Annual Phi Delta Kappa Symposium on Educational Research. Chicago, Rand McNally & Company, 1964.

6. Brethower. Dale M., *Programed Instruction and Programming Techniques —The Analysis of an Educational Technology.* Ann Arbor, Mich., The Institute for Behavioral Research and Programmed Instruction, 1962.

7. Bruner, Jerome S., *The Process of Education.* Cambridge, Mass., Harvard University Press, 1960.

8. Carpenter, Finley, and Eugene E. Haddan, *Systematic Application of Psychology to Education.* New York, The Macmillan Company, 1964.

9. Coulson, John E. (ed.), *Programmed Learning and Computer-Based Instruction.* Proceedings of the Conference on Application of Digital Computers to Automated Instruction, October 10–12, 1961. New York, John Wiley & Sons, Inc., 1962.

10. Cram, David, *Explaining Teaching Machines and Programming.* San Francisco, Fearon Publishers, 1961.

11. Crowder, Norman A., "Automatic Tutoring by Intrinsic Programming," *Teaching Machines and Programmed Learning,* A. A. Lumsdaine and Robert Glaser (eds.). Washington, D.C., National Education Association, 1960.

12. Deterline, William J., *An Introduction to Programmed Instruction.* Englewood Cliffs, N.J., Prentice-Hall, Inc., 1962.

13. Elam, Stanley (ed.), *Education and the Structure of Knowledge: Fifth Annual Phi Delta Kappa Symposium on Educational Research.* Chicago, Rand McNally & Company, 1964.

14. Elkind, D., "Children's Conceptions of Right and Left: Piaget Replication Study IV." *Jl. Genet. Psychol.,* Vol. 99, 269–276.

15. ——, "Children's Discovery of the Conservation of Mass, Weight and Volume: Piaget Replication Study II," *Jl. Genet. Psychol.,* Vol. 98, 219–227.

16. ——, "The Development of Quantitative Thinking: A Systematic Replication of Piaget's Studies," *Jl. Genet. Psychol.,* Vol. 98, 37–46.

17. ——, "Quantity Conceptions in Junior and Senior High School Students," *Child Development,* Vol. 32, 551–556.

18. ——, "Discrimination, Seriation, and Numeration of Size and Dimensional Differences in Young Children: Piaget Replication Study VI," *Jl. Genet. Psychol.,* Vol. 14, 275–296.

19. ——, "Quantity Conceptions in College Students," *Jl. Soc. Psychol.,* Vol. 57, 459–465.

20. ENTELEK, Inc., *Programmed Instruction Guide* (a computer-based catalog of information), Newburyport, Mass., 1967.

21. Evans, J. L., Robert Glaser, and L. E. Homme, "The Ruleg System for the Construction of Programed Verbal Learning Sequences," report prepared under Cooperative Research Project No. 691(9417). Wash-

ington, D.C., U.S. Office of Health, Education and Welfare, 1960 (mimeo).

22. Flavell, J. H., *The Developmental Psychology of Jean Piaget*. New York, D. Van Nostrand Company, Inc., 1963.

23. Fund for the Advancement of Education, *Four Cases of Programed Instruction*. Washington, D.C., U.S. Office of Health, Education and Welfare, Title 7, National Defense Education Act, 1964.

24. Gagne', Robert M., *The Conditions of Learning*. New York, Holt, Rinehart and Winston, Inc., 1965.

25. ——, and Kenneth B. Henderson, "Research on Teaching Secondary School Mathematics," *Handbook of Research on Teaching*, N. L. Gage (ed.). Chicago, Rand McNally & Company, 1963.

26. Gerry, Robert, "Mathetics: A Behavior-Oriented Approach to Learning," published at Lackland Military Training Center, Lackland Air Force Base, San Antonio, Texas, April 1963.

27. Gilbert, T. F., "Mathetics: A Technology of Education," *Jl. Mathetics*, Vol. I, No. 1 (January 1962), 7–73.

28. Green, Edward J., *The Learning Process and Programmed Instruction*. New York, Holt, Rinehart and Winston, Inc., 1962.

29. Hendershot, Carl H., *Programmed Learning: A Bibliography of Programs and Presentation Devices*, 4th ed. Bay City, Mich., Carl Hendershot, Publisher, 1967.

30. Hickey, Albert E., and John M. Newton, *The Logical Basis of Teaching, I: The Effect of Sub-concept Sequence on Learning*. Newburyport, Mass., ENTELEK, January 1964.

31. Hughes, J. L., *Programmed Instruction for Schools and Industry*. Chicago, Science Research Associates, 1962.

32. Inhelder, Barbel, and Jean Piaget, *The Growth of Logical Thinking from Childhood to Adolescence*. New York, Basic Books, 1958.

33. Jacobs, Paul I., Milton H. Maier, and Lawrence M. Stolurow, *A Guide to Evaluating Self-instructional Programs*. New York, Holt, Rinehart and Winston, Inc., 1966.

34. Klausmeier, Herbert J., and William Goodwin, *Learning and Human Abilities*. New York, Harper & Row, Publishers, 1966.

35. Lovell, K., "A Follow-up Study of Inhelder and Piaget's 'The Growth of Logical Thinking,'" *Brit. Jl. Psychol.*, Vol. 52, 143–154.

36. ——, *The Growth of Basic Mathematical and Scientific Concepts in Children*. London, University of London Press, Ltd., 1961.

37. Lysaught, Jerome P., *Programmed Learning*. Ann Arbor, Mich., Foundation for Research on Human Behavior, 1961.

38. Markle, Susan, *Good Frames and Bad: A Grammar of Frame Writing*. New York, John Wiley & Sons, Inc., 1964.

39. ——, L. D. Eigen, and P. K. Komoski, *A Programed Primer on Programing*, Vols. I and II. New York, The Center for Programmed Instruction, 1962.

40. McClellan, James E., "The Logical and the Psychological, an Untenable Dualism," *Language and Concepts in Education*, B. Othanel Smith

and Robert H. Ennis (eds.). Chicago, Rand McNally & Company, 1961.

41. National Education Association, *Selection and Use of Programed Materials*, Washington, D.C., 1964.

42. O'Keefe, Ruth Ann, "Effective Programming for the Classroom," *Montessori for the Disadvantaged*, R. C. Orem (ed.). New York, G. P. Putnam's Sons, 1967.

43. Peirce, Charles S., *Collected Papers*, Charles Hartshorne and Paul Weiss (eds.). Cambridge, Mass.. Harvard University Press, 1924.

44. Pennington, D. F., and C. W. Slack, "The Mathematical Design of Effective Lessons," *Applied Programmed Instruction*, Stuart Margulies and Lewis D. Eigen (eds.). New York, John Wiley & Sons, Inc., 1962.

45. Pipe, Peter, *Practical Programming*. New York, Holt, Rinehart and Winston, Inc., 1966.

46. Pressey, S. L., "A Simple Apparatus Which Gives Tests and Scores—and Teaches," *Teaching Machines and Programmed Learning: A Source Book*, A. A. Lumsdaine and R. Glaser (eds.). Washington, D.C., National Education Association, 1960.

47. Searles, John, *A System for Instruction*. Scranton, Pa., International Textbook Company, 1967.

48. Skinner, B. F., *Cumulative Record*. New York, Appleton-Century-Crofts, 1959.

49. ——, "The Science of Learning and the Art of Teaching," *Harvard Education Review*, Vol. 24 (Spring 1954), 86–97.

50. ——, *The Technology of Teaching*. New York, Appleton-Century-Crofts, 1968.

51. Smedslund, J., "The Acquisition of Transitivity of Weight in Five-to-Seven-Year-Old Children," *Jl. Genet. Psychol.*, Vol. 102, 245–255.

52. Smith, B. Othanel, and Milton O. Meux, Herrold Coombs, Daniel Eierdam, and Ronald Szoke, *A Study of the Logic of Teaching*. Urbana, Ill., Bureau of Educational Research, University of Illinois, 1962 (mimeo.).

53. Thorndike, E. L., *Educational Psychology*, 1914, 1921, II, 2–4.

54. Verduin, John R., Jr., *Conceptual Models in Teacher Education: An Approach to Teaching and Learning*. Washington, D.C., American Association of Colleges for Teacher Education, 1967.

55. ——, "Concept Formation and Learning Unit Design," *Conceptual Models in Teacher Education*, John R.Verduin (ed.). Washington, D.C., American Association of Colleges for Teacher Education, 1967.

56. Woodruff, Asahel, "Characteristics of an Effective Instructional Unit," paper, Academic Year Study, State University College, Geneseo, New York, 1966.

57. ——, *The Psychology of Teaching*. New York, Longmans, Green and Co., Ltd., 1951.

58. ——, "Putting Subject-Matter into Conceptual Form," paper prepared for TEAM project meeting, February 6, 1964.

6

Classification of Pupils and Teachers
for Effective Instruction

THE GROUPING OF CHILDREN

Children have always been grouped according to some sort of criterion. The most common procedure since the nineteenth century has been to place them in like age groups. Thus, all six-year-olds may enter the first grade, and when they are seven they are promoted to the second grade, and so on. Improved means for assessing intelligence, however, revealed that a pupil's chronological age and his thinking abilities were not very closely related. The more intelligent child was found to think as did older children, and the less intelligent thought more like younger ones. Furthermore, although one child might be more mature in his development, say, of reading ability, another might be more adept in mathematics, and such differences were often found in the same child. Age grouping generally placed children of about the same physical development together, but hereditary factors and differences in growth rates made even this basis a poor one for grouping. It remained, at best, a convenient but manifestly unsatisfactory administrative device for categorizing a school population that, it was assumed, had to be graded.

In the nineteen-twenties, educators began testing other bases for grouping, and the nineteen-fifties saw a fresh upsurge of interest in pupil grouping as a means of fostering learning. When age is used as the criterion for grouping children, not only are the group members found to be of different mental ages, but they differ greatly in motivation and in interest areas. Because of wide differences in ability, the competition among pupils is frustrating to those who are not qualified to compete with others of their group and hence are treated as failures.

Grouping "Normal" Children

One of the traditional means of coping with inequalities in the abilities of those of the same age is simply to accelerate those who are doing exceptionally well and to retard those who cannot keep up. The rest, the "average" of the group, then continue at the normal rate. Grade skipping (double promotion) and failure (withholding promotion) have been practiced for many years. The apparent disadvantage in this practice is that the child who is double-promoted may be smaller and not so well developed physically and socially as those in the older-age class into which he is moved. Thus his adjustment to his new social group is made difficult. Terman (1925) and others, however, showed that few gifted children are weak and neurotic, and because nonpromoted children did not have to compete with the new group on such uneven terms, they could, perhaps, keep up after a fashion. But to be held back is defeating to some children, who do not even attempt to compete with those younger than themselves. Their status is lowered, their self-esteem suffers, and learning does not proceed optimally. In some cases, another repetition of content that they had not liked very well in the first place brings on more boredom and even rebellion. Even yet, many do not realize that the low-intelligence child is not just a normal child only not so far advanced. He learns more slowly, and even learns in different ways.

Perhaps age-grade promotion's greatest evil is the too-long semester or term. Flexibility could be increased by a switch to quarterly promotion periods. Promotions (and nonpromotions and accelerations) come more frequently, but the jumps are not so extreme. The logic of breaking up the promotional units into smaller time segments has led to even greater flexibility—allowing each pupil to progress at his own rate through an entire course of study. (This is one of the principles of programmed instruction —self-pacing.) This plan is not so new as might be supposed. Pueblo, Colorado, used it from 1888 to 1894 by developing complete outlines of each subject in such a way that each student could progress at his own rate. Another "modern" technique was also applied—no marks were assigned. The Dalton, Massachusetts, plan divided subjects into the non-academic and the academic groups. This plan, put into effect in 1920, divided each subject to be covered in a year's work into monthly "jobs," with each job consisting of about twenty "units." When a child had completed all the jobs, he could move on to the next set.

Others have experimented with the length of instructional periods as independent variables upon which learning abilities may depend. The studies of massed versus distributed practice had indicated in general that there are optimal sizes or pieces of content that a learner may acquire most efficiently. If the chunks of information are too large, they are not learned quickly and easily, and if too small, there may be a time waste. Similarly, pupils become fatigued if required to remain still or in the same situation too long. Whereas pupils once remained several hours in their seats or on benches, they may now change activities as frequently as every half hour or even every fifteen minutes. It has been suggested, however, that the amount of time spent per instructional period may also be a function of the degree of interest held by the pupils.

Homogeneous Grouping

English and English (1964) defined homogeneous grouping as "sectioning according to ability" (p. 2). According to L. J. Bicak (1965), *homogeneous grouping* is a very general term, and it may refer to ability grouping, interest grouping, or grouping according to physical characteristics or to many other criteria. The intellectual, social, or cultural development of pupils may serve to determine how they ought to be grouped. Although it is often assumed that special grouping practices are quite widespread in this "progressive era of education," Ekstrom (1961), who reviewed the major experimental studies on homogeneous grouping, found that in recent years there has been relatively little investigation into grouping practices. What studies there were utilized various experimental designs and showed no consistent pattern of results. Bicak wanted to know

1. Whether pupils of comparable ability would differ in overall achievement when some were taught in homogeneous classes and others in heterogeneous classes in eighth-grade science.

2. Whether these pupils, so grouped, would differ in achievement as measured by an application test.

3. Whether they would react differently to attitude questionnaire items.

He found no significant differences in the achievements of pupils of comparable ability. There were also no significant differences in their reactions to questions concerned with their attitudes toward membership in their groups, the class procedures, the subject matter taught, the nature of the work in the class, and the teaching techniques used.

Acceleration and retardation of pupils by grade levels may be accompanied by *ability grouping*. When effective means are available for determining individual differences within a grade level, then pupils may be grouped according to differences in measured ability. *Ability grouping* usually refers to classification according to academic ability. The bases for determining degrees of difference may be intelligence test scores, previous marks and present ones, industry and application, and teacher ratings. Sociometry, as a means of determining some aspects of interpersonal relations obtaining in groups, has also contributed to ability grouping. Occasionally, membership in a group may be strongly contraindicated, even though the prospective member has demonstrated equivalent academic ability.

The effectiveness of ability grouping could conceivably vary, depending on the grade levels at which it is employed.

A double-track plan of ability grouping, in Portland, Oregon, divided nine grades into fifty-four units. During each semester, the usual procedure was to cover three units, but those who had shown the ability to do so were permitted to cover four units during this time. This acceleration plan made it possible for rapid learners to complete the nine-year course in seven years. By 1915, the plan had been discontinued, though some schools have used modifications of it since that time.

Recently, Walter R. Borg reported in *The Psychology of Education* (Clark, 1967) on a large-scale experiment conducted in two adjacent, closely comparable school districts in Utah. Differences in the effects of ability grouping on students were studied. In one school district, ability grouping was used by adjusting the rate of the presentation of materials. In the other school district, random grouping was used, with differences in the curriculum principally being in the amount of enrichment. Over a period of four years, data were collected for the purpose of appraising the long-term effects of the two types of grouping for pupils in elementary school, in junior high school, and in high school. During the first year, there were more differences that favored the ability-grouped pupils *in elementary school*. However, from that time on, differences declined, and no significant differences were found between those who had ability grouping with acceleration and those who were randomly grouped with enrichment. However, there was some slight advantage in achievement for the two grouping systems, wherein superior pupils were grouped by ability and slow pupils were randomly grouped.

The only average students who benefited from ability grouping were those at junior high school level, where science achievement was greater than with random grouping. Also in junior high, the ability grouping of superior students led to greater mathematics achievement. For slow students, the random grouping was again more favorable.

The sociometric data collected indicated that in the intermediate grades, ability grouping did not result in a permanent loss of leaders in groups of average and slow pupils. But superior students tended to lose sociometric status when placed in ability-grouped classrooms—though the status was regained after a period of adjustment to the new grouping. Both average and slow pupils had better chances of gaining social recognition in ability-grouped classrooms, as compared with random grouping situations. The effects of ability and random grouping were not different for boys and for girls.

Ability grouping appeared to be associated with more favorable attitudes toward teachers than was random grouping, for both the superior and the slow pupils, but not for average pupils. Girls had better attitudes toward school than did boys, with greatest differences at the superior level. As to pupil problems, the random grouping condition resulted in more problems for the superior and average groups than did ability grouping. For all ability levels, grouping pupils randomly resulted in more favorable self-concepts than did ability grouping. Inferiority feelings and other negative personality characteristics assumed to accompany ability groupings were not found, however, when ability groupings were *appropriate*. For slow pupils at the junior high level, heterogeneous classrooms seem to provide better environments.

Grouping the Handicapped

Alice Noel (1966) suggested that *both* academic and mental health aspects of a training program for crippled children are necessary. (It had been assumed that such children need to be separated from others, and that the emphasis should be on mental health.) She taught severely handicapped children (with multiple handicaps) the idea that learning can be fun by encouraging them to find this out for themselves. They participated in group sessions to develop self-discipline. (Some communications were necessarily by Morse code and finger spelling.) They read magazines and newspapers and wrote stories and letters. They learned conversational French and creative writing, and applied arithmetic skills to actual practices in banking, cooking, and fund drives. Reduced emphasis on mental health and increased use of group sessions and attention to academic learning resulted in achievement not usually expected of the severely handicapped. These children also developed the attitude that they ought to learn the subject matter that normal children were learning. They were still separated from the other pupils, but the move toward parallel academic involvements tended to make them suffer the effects of separation less.

Grouping the Emotionally Disturbed

Kounin, Friesen, and Norton (1966) questioned whether emotionally disturbed children should be removed from the others, to be placed in a group of their own, or should be handled individually. They video taped thirty classrooms, each of which contained at least one emotionally disturbed child, from the first through the fifth grade. As expected, disturbed children showed less school-appropriate work than did nondisturbed children. However, teachers who handled nondisturbed children's behavior well also were relatively successful with disturbed children. Teachers who had the know-how in handling group movement, who could readily arrange for change and variety in learning activities handled both types of children better. Kounin et al. concluded that these successful teachers not only had a lower deviancy rate in their classrooms, but also produced a classroom climate that prevented deviant behavior from disrupting the behavior of other children.

Containing the misbehavior of a deviant child has been discussed in some detail in an interesting book by William J. Gnagey, published by the National Education Association (1965). In *Controlling Classroom Misbehavior*, various means for coping with the "ripple effect," or the spread of behavior from one classroom area to others, are discussed.

It may be argued that the disrupting effect of a behavior disturbance in a correctional institution is likely to be greater than in other groupings, because so many may be expected to engage in that kind of behavior. R. E. Walther, former superintendent of the Dallas Juvenile Home, suggests some ways of using group participation as a reward for the successful establishment of a desirable person-to-person adjustment with an adult in the institution. Under this approach, removal from group activities is viewed by the child as punishing.

Clark (1967) suggests that normal children may even gain by being grouped with emotionally disturbed children. If the experiences can be arranged so that the undisturbed learn to become tolerant of people who are difficult and to help those less fortunate than themselves, then both groups may gain. "Watching and helping a classmate gain control over his impulses can help a child learn more about how, when, and why he must control his own impulses" (p. 127). It should be apparent that more research is needed that notes comparisons between classes with disturbed children and those without. Even where disturbed children have been separated maximally—i.e., placed in schools for disturbed children only—should the extremely agitated be separated from the less disturbed?

If homogeneous grouping is sectioning according to ability, what kinds of ability are involved? Ability in each of the subject matters offered in school? The ability to control the emotions? The ability to communicate? Or must the ability to socialize at a generally common level of functioning be the criterion?

> Whenever children are grouped together on one ability or factor, we find that they are ungrouped in a thousand other ways. When reading time comes we can divide a class into redbirds, bluebirds, yellowbirds, or even chartreusebirds, but the teacher can count on having a lot of *different* birds within any one nest. (Clark, p. 128)

THE GROUPING OF TEACHERS

Team Teaching

Teachers have been engaged in cooperative efforts for many years, but it was not until the nineteen-fifties that team teaching, systematically practiced and experimentally examined, received a great deal of public notice. A shortage of qualified teachers, during the period of the great population explosion in the postwar years gave impetus to redoubled efforts in handling the overflow pupils. Harvard began an internship plan that grouped four or five novices to work together with a master teacher. The Harvard plan led to the Teaching Teams Project, in Lexington, Massachusetts, under Robert H. Anderson. Francis S. Chase (1953) of the University of Chicago stated that teaching teams, under the leadership of exceptional teachers, would be one means for utilizing maximally the teaching talents that were available. He suggested teaching aides for clerical and nonprofessional duties, also. This kind of grouping would provide guidance for inexperienced teachers and make possible better salaries for the experienced ones, and also provide for them a more responsible role. J. Lloyd Trump (1966) has probably been more extensively involved in projects and writings on team teaching than anyone else because he served as Director of the Commission on the Experimental Study of the Utilization of the Staff in the Secondary School.

The history of experimentation with team teaching will not be recounted here. Instead, some of the possible groupings and their implications for teaching will be examined. It should be noted, however, that though the nineteen-fifties were the years of greatest *public* interest in team teaching, as early as 1941, the Troy State Teachers College in Alabama had organized the staff into teaching teams of an interdisciplinary nature. Those interested in the early, by now almost classical, beginnings of the team teaching movement will wish to read further about the work-study-play school plan of William A. Wirt developed in Indiana around 1900. Pupils were divided into two platoons, and classes were scheduled so that half the time was spent in studying academic subjects and the other half was used for learning via activities. (Teacher grouping does not occur in isolation, because pupil grouping is also necessary when team teaching is used.) Two classical examples were the Winnetka Plan and the Dalton Plan. Anderson (1966) described team teaching as

> a pattern of horizontal school organization that has emerged as an alternative to the self-contained elementary-school classroom and the departmentalized arrangements found in most secondary schools and some elementary schools. (p. 80)

And he defined it as

> a formal type of cooperative staff organization in which a group of teachers accepts the responsibility for planning, carrying out, and evaluating an educational program, or some major portion of a program, for an aggregate of pupils. (p. 83)

Trump (1966) suggested a gradual introduction to team teaching by a simple combination of the classes usually taught by two teachers so that each teacher may teach the elements of the subject matter that interest him most and that he is most competent to teach. Next, these two teachers could systematically work together in planning their units of study, and other teachers could be added to the team, which now would cut across subject-matter lines. Clerks and instructional assistants and technological aids would be provided. Occasionally, the subject-matter expert would be a community consultant, not ordinarily a member of the school staff. All team members would be involved in planning, teaching, and evaluating.

According to Anderson, an ideal conception of team teaching ought to provide for the participation of all team members in drawing up the over-all objectives for the program. This would include the pupils, wherever possible. At least once a week the team members should work on the more immediate objectives. Planning should also include more than mere interest in what each team member is doing, so that each team member will submit his own lesson plans for possible modification by the others. An extra advantage of this mutual assistance is that any team member may be able temporarily to fill another's shoes in an emergency. It is difficult for some teachers to teach in the presence of colleagues but the experience is valuable for both the observer and the observed, and hence should be occasionally practiced. If it can be arranged, team members should participate weekly in evaluation sessions aimed at improvement of the program. Finally, Anderson suggested that each team member ought to be privileged to hear a careful and objective analysis of his own teaching episodes. During these conferences, specific suggestions and ideas for professional improvements are to be made. Although all of these requirements for an ideal approach are not likely to be met in most schools, at least some move toward fulfilling each of them is desirable. In early elementary grades, it may be that most teachers will teach all their own subjects, much of the time. However, in moving up the academic scale, it will become increasingly necessary for specialists to be employed in each area.

Thus far, insufficient data of a conclusive nature have been accumulated to indicate specific outcomes from the standpoint of teacher responses to team teaching. However, generally speaking, though it may be difficult initially to pursuade teachers to enter into a hierarchical arrangement, those who have worked in teams have elected to remain on them and are favorably disposed toward the approach. Skills are usually increased, and team members spend more time working than under the traditional method. Teachers feel that they learn more about their pupils, though they must become less inclined to feel that a class belongs to them. Team teaching seems to be able to promote the mental health of those who continue successfully on teams, and it may be hoped that this may result in fostering better mental health in pupils. Although pupil achievement has not been measurably changed when team teaching arrangements are compared with the traditional, it has been suggested that standardized tests are not often applied to the areas greatly effected by team teaching. Pupil enthusiasm, for example, has not been measured, nor has pupil capacity for self-direction, pupil interpersonal relationships, efficiency in study habits, and other long-range implications.

The present stage of team teaching is one of experimentation. Even where staffing has followed these patterns, the ideal has not been ap-

proached. Anderson (1966) listed seven characteristics of team teaching
that represent contributions by various authors, and that may be expressed
as advantages:

1. Specialization in teaching functions.
2. Flexible subgrouping of pupils.
3. Flexible, efficient use of school resources.
4. Ease of using professionals and non-professionals
   as supplementary teachers.
5. Wider range of resources and technologies used.
6. Ease of training apprentices and beginning teachers.
7. Stimulation of team members' professional growth.

(p. 89)

GROUPING FOR DIVISION OF LABOR AND FOR MORE EFFICIENT DECISION MAKING

It has been said that learning in groups is an inefficient process, because
so much is said that is irrelevant and because many excellent ideas remain
unspoken, giving way to the utterances of the more aggressive or the more
emotional group members. But there are some advantages in group participation as a learning aid. The focus is upon *participation.* Mitnick (1958)
found that the influence of a film-showing alone was insignificant in
changing the attitudes of viewers. But when the film was followed by a
group discussion, expressed attitudes changed significantly. There is less
likelihood that a single point of view will prevail when there is free and
open group discussion. When a group is assigned a comprehensive problem, the division of the problem's facets into areas that can be separately
researched and reported upon has obvious time-saving advantages. This
division of labor also has another advantage, in that group members may
criticize the findings of other group members and require greater validity
and reliability in what is accepted.

To be an active decision maker in a group is educationally valuable and
tends to reinforce the conclusions of the group. Individuals who share in
making policies or in formulating a set of findings are more likely to follow
up the group decisions with congruent actions. Kurt Lewin (1958) has
written an interesting report on group decision making. Problem solving
in groups has also been studied. Two considerations are uppermost in most
such studies—initial learning and transfer. Unfortunately, the research
findings are not in agreement. Most researchers (Fox and Lorge [1962];

Hall, Mouton, and Blake [1963]; Hoppe [1962]; Lorge and Solomon [1960]; and Tuckman and Lorge [1962]) reported the average performance of small groups superior to the performance of individuals. However, Duncan (1959) pointed out that in problem solving, the best individuals outperform the *averages* of groups. When group members have experience in working together and have received some instruction in groups, the group tends to improve. An individual learner may not do so well in small groups in the *initial* learning, but there seems to be increased *transfer* when he works in a group (Hudgins [1960]; Klausmeier, Harris, and Wiersma [1964]). During initial learning, small groups develop an understanding of the problem more quickly than do individuals, remember important information better, and tend to test out a greater variety of methods. They also bring out more possible solutions and verify them more reliably. But when these same group members are later required to solve new problems involving transfer ability, they do not perform as well, on the average, as they did in the group. The assumption is that they had not been required to participate as actively in the group as they would as individuals.

Many teachers who do not prefer to use group work as a general instructional device, use it as a means for breaking the ice in a classroom. Students in small groups quickly engage in some conversation, even those who would remain silent when in a very large group. Contagion from behavior disruptions is less likely to spread to an entire class, when it begins in a small group, than when the offender is in a larger one.

THE ADAPTIVE CONTROL OF GROUPS

The adaptivity of a teacher or a teaching system requires that the instructional component furnish its influencers contingent upon the responses of the learners. To some extent, any attempt at grouping students according to some perceived similarity is adaptive. However, the following description indicates one of the more extreme forms that can be assumed in adaptation to learners. An adaptive control system, according to Lewis (1963), can interact with a three-person group to achieve several objectives, among them:

1. *To teach:* assisting in group coordination and optimizing decision making in the group.
2. *To aid performance:* a less positive teaching func-

tion, preventing the reduction of group efficiency to below a point of acceptability.

3. *To test:* the discovery of pressuring techniques that will induce the group to yield required information.

The teaching function is of primary interest at this point. A group consists of transmitters of information and receivers. When one transmits, the other two should be receiving, or decoding the transmitted information. Successful receiving requires the convergence of transmitter and receiver to a common set of concepts (conventions). What makes communications an easy subject for experimentation is that it occurs externally, but what makes it difficult is that it usually occurs simultaneously with a continuously changing background of assumptions that each person is making about the other.

Lewis chose to study communication in a small group by assigning a communicating role to a person who was initially unacquainted with the best ways of carrying it out, and was merely told what concept he was to convey. Thus, participants saw the communicating task as an educational game. There was a fixed universe of discourse, consisting of eighty-one diagrams that the communicators were to talk about. They were to communicate the concepts depicted by the diagrams. One of the group members was to be the transmitter, and the other two were to try either to interpret whatever the transmitting person said, or to actually question him about the designs. The two receivers could work either in competition, with each being ignorant of what the other was finding out, or cooperatively, with each letting the other know immediately about any partial solutions he was discovering. In the latter mode, the receivers were tutoring each other. To increase the control over the conditions of communication, the task was mechanized. Each student sat at a console that displayed the eighty-one designs, and was not allowed to communicate outside the prescribed channels. After the transmitting person was chosen, the two receivers decided whether they would compete or cooperate, and this decision was adhered to throughout the communication process.

If the receivers had decided upon the selective mode of playing, then they dialed the transmitter (who was then acting as the teacher) for information. If they had decided upon the receptive mode, then they observed the information that was dialed to them by the transmitter. A time limit was imposed, during which they had to arrive at the correct concept, which had been chosen by the transmitter. When either receiver believed he had arrived at the correct solution, he encoded his answer on a panel and then punched a final-decision button, which sent his answer to the transmitter. The receivers were then informed as to the correctness of their solutions.

The apparatus can be set up so as to establish control over time requirements, the availability of relevant information, the incidence of extraneous disturbances, the amount of information allowed to flow between the group members, and the degree of encouragement provided for varying the roles and patterns of communications. This control can be exerted directly, by the issuing of directives and also by interference with the necessary channels of communication (because the learners must use only those channels provided by the apparatus). The group may also be manipulated as to the extent of control assigned to each member as a reward for efficient learning. The pace of instruction may be altered, by variations in the time limits and also by variations in the difficulty of the content. Increasing time pressure is likely to reduce the range of behavior patterns, so that only the very essential operations are carried out. In some situations this is desirable, because it results in inducing the learner to discriminate between important operations and nonessential ones.

However, if the learner under time pressure is not able to make such distinctions, he becomes ever more frustrated, until he may finally stop responding. A broader range of behaviors is shown by those who are stressed by a sense of failure. This kind of anxious student is likely to cast about for all sorts of alternatives that look promising, provided that he has the time. Generally, says Lewis, it should be known that the student has the means for dealing with stress before the experimenter decides to introduce it.

The degree of control exerted by the overall controller, as well as the kind of control, depends not only on objectives for the group, but also on those of the controller for each member. The group needs feedback as to the progress both of the group and of each member. Is a group member being consistently overridden, so that his decisions, usually poor choices, are disregarded? Is one group member so outstanding that his decisions always prevail? In these cases, the controller may decide to limit the efficiency of the group in solving the problem, in order to increase the efficiency of one member or to limit the participation of the member who does it all. A skilled group leader attempts to do just this in the usual group discussion, but his control efforts are not nearly so effective. He cannot, for example, simply block the communication of a group member by punching a button. The controller may also perturb the communication channels linking him with the receivers. This increases the difficulty for the receivers and tends to convert concept-learning skill from deductive to inductive. It also tends to produce stress, so that members will look more critically at strategies that they had previously taken for granted.

The apparent implications of this approach are so numerous as to preclude discussion here. But the many variations on the experimental setup provide possibilities for years of fruitful effort. Group sizes, problem difficulty levels, degrees of perturbation of communication, competition versus cooperation, monetary reward for individual versus group success—all lend themselves well to this method of precision control. Lewis adds that the accumulation of data of this nature is of the form appropriate to the specification of an optimal design for a computer-controlled classroom.

References

1. Anderson, Robert H., *Teaching in a World of Change*. New York, Harcourt, Brace & World, Inc., 1966.
2. Bair, Medill, and Richard G. Woodward, *Team Teaching in Action*. Boston, Houghton Mifflin Company, 1964.
3. Beggs, David W. (ed.), *Team Teaching: Bold New Venture*. Indianapolis, Ind., Unified College Press, 1964.
4. Bicak, Laddie J., "Achievement in Eighth Grade Science by Heterogeneous and Homogeneous Classes," *A Cross-section of Educational Research*, Edwin Wandt (ed.). New York, David McKay Company, Inc., 1965.
5. Borg, Walter R., *Ability Grouping in the Public Schools*. Madison, Wis., Dembar Educational Research Services, Inc., 1966.
6. Chase, Francis S., "More and Better Teachers," *Saturday Review* (September 12, 1953), 16–17.
7. Clark, Donald H. (ed.), *The Psychology of Education: Current Issues and Research*. New York, The Free Press, 1967.
8. Clinchy, Evans (ed.), *Profiles of Significant Schools—Schools for Team Teaching*. New York, Educational Facilities Laboratories, 1961.
9. Cunningham, Luvern C., "Team Teaching: Where do We Stand?" *Administrator's Notebook*, Midwest Administration Center, University of Chicago, Vol. 8, No. 8 (April 1960).
10. Duncan, C. P., "Recent Research on Human Problem Solving," *Psychol. Bull.*, Vol. 56, 397–429.
11. Ekstrom, R. B., "Experimental Studies of Homogeneous Grouping: A Critical Review," *School Review*, Vol. 69, No. 2 (Summer 1961).
12. English, Horace B., and Ava C. English, *A Comprehensive Dictionary of Psychological and Psychoanalytical Terms*. New York, David McKay Company, Inc., 1964.

13. Fox, D. J., and I. Lorge, "The Relative Quality of Decisions Written by Individuals and by Groups as the Available Time for Problem Solving is Increased," *Jl. Soc. Psychol.*, Vol. 57, 227–242.

14. Gnagey, William J., *Controlling Classroom Misbehavior*. Washington, D.C., National Education Association, 1965.

15. Hall, E. J., Jane S. Mouton, and R. R. Blake, "Group Problem Solving Effectiveness Under Conditions of Polling Versus Interaction," *Jl. Soc. Psychol.*, Vol. 59, 147–157.

16. Hoppe, R. A., "Memorizing by Individuals and Groups," *Jl. Abn. Soc. Psychol.*, Vol. 65, 64–67.

17. Hudgins, B. B., "Effects of Group Experience on Individual Problem Solving," *Jl. Educ. Psychol.*, Vol. 51, 37–42.

18. Klausmeier, Herbert J., and William Goodwin, *Learning and Human Abilities*. New York, Harper & Row, Publishers, 1966.

19. ——, C. W. Harris, and W. Wiersma, *Strategies of Learning and Efficiency of Concept Attainment by Individuals and Groups*, U.S. Office of Educ. Coop. Res. Proj. No. 1442. University of Wisconsin, 1964.

20. Kounin, Jacob S., Wallace Friesen, and A. Evangeline Norton, "Managing Emotionally Disturbed Children in Regular Classrooms," *Jl. Educ. Psychol.*, Vol. 57 (February 1966), 1–13.

21. Lewin, Kurt, "Group Decisions and Social Change," *Readings in Social Psychology*, E. Maccoby, T. M. Newcomb, and E. L. Hartley (eds.). New York, Holt, Rinehart and Winston, Inc., 1958.

22. Lewis, B. N., "The Adaptive Control of Small Groups," *Programming, '63*, a bulletin produced by the Research Unit, Department of Education, Sheffield University, England, 1963.

23. Lorge, I., and H. Solomon, "Group and Individual Performance in Problem Solving Related to Previous Exposure to Problem, Level of Aspiration, and Group Size," *Behav. Sci.*, Vol. 5, 28–38.

24. Mitnick, L. L., and E. McGinnies, "Influencing Ethnocentrism in Small Discussion Groups Through a Film Communication," *Jl. Abn. Soc. Psychol.*, Vol. 56, 82–90.

25. Noel, Alice, "Effectiveness of an Academically Oriented Teaching Program with Crippled Children," *Except. Ch.* (January 1966).

26. Shaplin, Judson T., and Henry F. Olds, Jr. (eds.), *Team Teaching*. New York, Harper & Row, Publishers, 1964.

27. Stover, G. Franklin, "The Freshman Program in General Education for 1940–41," Troy State Teacher College *Bulletin*, 28 (October 1941), p. 8.

28. Terman, Lewis M., et al., *Genetic Studies of Genius, I: Mental and Physical Traits of a Thousand Gifted Children*. Stanford University, Calif., Stanford University Press, 1925.

29. Trump, J. Lloyd, *Focus on Change: Guide to Better Schools*. Chicago, Rand McNally & Company, 1966.

30. Tuckman, J., and I. Lorge, "Individual Ability as a Determinant of Group Superiority," *Hum. Relat.*, Vol. 15, 45–51.

31. Walther, R. E., *Handling Behavior Problems*, booklet prepared by U.S. Industries, Educational Science Division, Silver Springs, Md.
32. Washburne, Carleton W., and Sidney P. Marland, Jr., *Winnetka: The History and Significance of an Educational Experiment.* Englewood Cliffs, N.J., Prentice-Hall, Inc., 1963.

7

The Self and Teaching

He is not the best teacher who does the most for his pupil, but rather he who enables the child to do most for himself.

Daniel Putnam, 1891

SELF-AWARENESS FACILITATES
TEACHING PRACTICES

The minimal requirements for teacher preparation may ensure, up to a point, that teachers will be employed who understand at least something about the learning processes and about well-accepted teaching techniques, and who have had some experience, direct or vicarious, with children. It may also be assumed that this employable teacher knows a subject-matter area reasonably well. Unfortunately, not all who have been considered employable according to these criteria can perform well in the classroom. The teacher's attitudes, and his awareness of the influences that self may have upon teaching practices, may act either to enhance or to impair his effectiveness. Not only does the awareness of self influence day-to-day teaching practices, but a teacher's more general life orientations may be quite influential in formulating his philosophy. For example, if he places a great deal of value upon the inner direction of planning, teaching, and evaluation, he will not proceed as he would if he prefers to draw heavily upon systematic directives provided at least in part by more objective considerations. Obviously, there is no one-to-one ratio between the major attitudinal positions of a teacher and his daily activities. However, there are psychologists who believe that an understanding of such mediating factors as self-respect, self-esteem, self-image, self-actualization, and the ideal self are at least of equal importance for teacher performance as are the commonly accepted standards. William Menninger (1953) said that teachers not only need self-understanding, but that it is their *obligation* to implement the search for personal implications in teaching. The search for self is essentially a search for meaning. Where meaning is absent, or minimal, in one's work, the self is not likely to be involved. Teaching then becomes a mere formality.

Menninger suggested that people are responsive to two kinds of needs—those demanded by the environment, and those imposed by the self. These two types of needs are not always consonant; in fact, there are frequent struggles between them. To further complicate the picture, there are conflicts within each of the two classes of needs. Depending upon his long-established patterns, an individual may attempt to resolve the struggle by a *flight reaction*, getting away from the painful field of the conflict, or by a *fight reaction*, lashing out at the person or situation that furnishes the opposition, or he may respond by working out a *constructive compromise*. Many of the struggles between the demands of self and environment are unavoidable. The point is that teachers may become effective if they can peer into their own inner workings and recognize the part being played by the self. The extent to which a teacher can increase the number of times he makes constructive use (determines and carries out more accurately the appropriate reaction—flight, fight, or compromise) and decrease the destructive use of self factors will determine one aspect of his teaching effectiveness. Menninger's suggestion for increasing self-knowledge is first to gain recognition of the mental mechanisms of *introjection, identification, sublimation, compensation, rationalization,* and *conversion.* These mechanisms from the psychiatric school may be examined in greater depth in books on personality theory, therapy with a psychoanalytic orientation, or sources on emotion and motivation. Briefly, their practical meanings follow.

Introjection. This is an internalizing process, in which one gradually adopts the attitudes and ideas of others, after observing their acceptance and practice by others.

Identification. When an individual tries to be like those for whom he has strong emotional attachments, he identifies with them.

Sublimation. The use of constructive outlets for destructive impulses. Sublimation is associated with sound mental health.

Compensation. One compensates by developing an ability that is substituted for an area of deficiency. For example, a poor athlete becomes an excellent student, or one who is socially incompetent becomes a bookworm.

Rationalization. Locating and using acceptable excuses for unacceptable behavior is rationalization. For example, one may really believe he has postponed an important meeting because something else important came up.

Projection. A person who projects is not recognizing that disapproved behavior is his own. Instead, he blames his own wishes and faults on other people, because he cannot admit that he is guilty of them.

Displacement. One may have certain feelings toward a person, but may express them toward someone (or something) else. For example, a teacher may be aroused to anger by a principal but fears replying to him, so he vents his anger on his pupils.

Conversion. When people are emotionally upset, they may become physically upset as a result. An anxiety-ridden person may become physically paralyzed, unable to function until the cause of the anxiety is removed.

Once a teacher knows the meaning of these mechanisms and can see them in operation both in himself and in others, he is in possession of a means for self-improvement. He can understand his own actions better, and can use his observations of other selves in operation advantageously. Menninger says that the first step is the realization that improvement is possible, and that this step should be followed by the use of self-searching questions. Changing oneself is one solution; changing one's environment is another; and a third, the most satisfactory, is changing both self and environment. Recognition that good mental health does not consist of being free of problems is useful. Everyone has problems, and something can be done about most of them. Recognition that life's satisfactions are not provided by the golden moments furnished by the environment, but largely by the ingenuity and self-sufficiency of the individual is also important. Menninger gives this advice to teachers: do something out of the ordinary once in a while; make a serious effort to discover ways of accomplishing your major task in life better; recreate and refresh yourself; develop the art of friendliness; and take a good look at your life goals as you mature. You are mature emotionally to the extent that you:

Find greater satisfaction in giving than in receiving.
Form satisfying and permanent loyalties in give-and-take relationships.
Use your leisure creatively.
Contribute to the improvement of your home, school, community, nation
and world.
Learn to profit from your mistakes and successes.
Are relatively free from fears, anxieties and tensions.

(Hamachek, 1965, p. 560)

These views about self-knowledge are of very little value in constructing
patterns for systematic teaching, but they serve to set the stage for ideas
that have been widely exploited by others in their attempts at improving
teaching. Although the use of self-knowledge in teaching may not at first
suggest systematic applications, Rogers, Maslow, Combs, and others have
attempted to implement the approach.

The intensely personal quality of good teaching is emphasized by Arthur
Combs, who observed that most people remember especially good teachers,
but seldom have good ones behaved alike. Each of them had his own
unique methods and techniques, his own values, and enthusiasm. The
concept pervading Combs's writings is that of the *self as instrument*. In
addition to the knowledge, techniques, and materials available to the
teacher, the self is utilized as a tool. A teacher who uses the self approach
will shift his behaviors from time to time, according to the needs of students, situations, purposes, and the methods and materials that he may
effectively utilize for the problem at hand. For a self-as-instrument approach, it is necessary that the nature of the self be known, the ways in
which it develops outlined, and the ways in which it may be changed
indicated. Combs discussed all these in his book *The Professional Education of Teachers* (1965). The concern of the chapter, from this point on,
will be with how the teacher may utilize his unique self to greatest
advantage in teaching activities.

Emphasis on the self as instrument in effective teaching is not necessarily antithetical to emphasis on the technician mode of teaching—it
subsumes the various mechanical procedures that may be involved in the
application of prescribed methods. Nor does the approach oppose an ap-
lication of a mechanistic psychology, as represented by the stimulus-
response school, except as the scope of the stimulus is enlarged to include
the personality of the teacher, whose behavior becomes a "satisfying state
of affairs." Combs, however, seems to think that a humanistic psychology
such as he advocates provides a whole new practice, which calls for new
theoretical concepts, understandings, and directions. From the new Third
Force in American psychology (personalists, humanists, self psychologists,

phenomenologists, perceptual psychologists, transactionalists, existentialists, and others), Combs selected *perceptual psychology*. In common with others in this Third Force, perceptual psychology is said to hold the point of view that people are not things to be molded but are "unique events in the process of becoming" (p. 12). According to perceptual psychology, the behavior of a teacher (or of anyone) is the result of how he sees (1) himself, (2) his situations, and (3) the interrelations of self and situation.

Perceptual psychology departs from traditional psychologies, which place the accent on competencies. The emphasis is no longer upon telling teachers how they *ought* to behave. The development of competencies is brought about by the training of teachers in the acquisition of specified behaviors—but Combs insisted that behavior should not be the goal; it is only a symptom or surface indication of causes that lie inside the individual. It follows that the *inner life* ought to be the locus of interest in preparing people in effective teaching. What an individual sees himself to be is his self-concept—"It represents the most important single influence affecting an individual's behavior" (p. 14). It is also true that the selves of pupils are extremely important, and teaching should be student centered.

The case for a student-centered approach hinges upon the fundamental motivation of every person—a need for adequacy. In striving to become as adequate as they possibly can, pupils are reaching for the same goals that teachers ought to be setting for them. Thus, the teacher is not to prescribe, mold, coerce, coax, or cajole; he is rather to facilitate, encourage, help, and be a colleague of the pupil, as well as a friend. Generally speaking, the helping relationship seems to be the central one. But it seems to be a well-nigh impossible task to determine what a helper does. Because helpers behave in so many different ways, with no especially common characteristic, it is necessary to look to conceptual organizations rather than to behaviors. Combs and Soper (1962, 1963) found that attitudes, feelings, purposes, and self-conceptions, along with the perceptions of others, could be used in differentiating between helpers and nonhelpers. (Hence they could be used to differentiate between "good" and "bad" teachers.) Attitudes, feelings, purposes, and conceptions of self and others are different in the helping kind of person than they are in the nonhelper; they are different in each type even though both may be engaging apparently in the same kind of behaviors.

The distinction between a world of public events and a private, inner world of perceptions becomes important under a perceptual view of effective teaching. If "good" teachers are characterized primarily by the nature of their private world of perceptions, then only by a better understanding of such a world can teachers better themselves. According to the research conducted by Combs and others over a period of five years prior to the publication of his book, there are five major areas that are crucial in the perceptual organization of a good teacher:

1. Rich, extensive, and available perceptions about his subject field.
2. Accurate perceptions about what people are like.
3. Perceptions of self leading to adequacy.
4. Accurate perceptions about the purpose and process of learning.
5. Personal perceptions about appropriate methods for carrying out his purposes.

(Combs, 1965, p. 20)

Combs admitted, in passing, that teachers are more likely to fail because of an inability to *transmit* their knowledge so that it makes a difference to students, rather than because of lack of knowledge. As will be seen later, he actually attributed considerable power to this directive aspect of teaching—but he insisted that each teacher must learn his own best mode of transmitting. Even the behaviorists, who disagree with much of what self theorists say, agree with them that sheer ability to transmit knowledge, the teaching role that has traditionally been strengthened by teacher training, is rapidly assuming a relatively minor position of importance. (Behaviorists stress systematic use of environmental arrangements to improve instruction, and they emphasize a broader role that includes developing various pupil abilities and attitudes.)

The well-known halo effect is a good example of Combs's tenet that the teacher's perceptions of his students will influence his behavior toward them. A student who has shown great *ability* to learn in other classrooms, or in previous semesters with the same teacher, is assumed to have great *capacity* to continue to learn well, and his teacher is likely to overlook, as temporary lapses, any evidence that this pupil is not fulfilling his apparent promise. Similarly, the pupil who is repeatedly perceived by a teacher as a low achiever may be tagged as a hopeless case. A teacher who does not trust his pupils and has little confidence in them is not likely to provide the necessary freedoms, opportunities, or encouragements that are so readily dispensed by a trusting, confident teacher. Teachers with a bias about their pupils do not deal appropriately with them.

Although an emphasis upon the importance of self in teaching might appear to suggest that good teachers are born, not made, this is certainly not the assumption of Combs. He feels that the good teacher must not only have accurate beliefs about the nature of his pupils, but also that he should be deeply committed to the point of view established by his chosen psychology. In some instances, teachers seem to have developed into the kinds of persons who have a great deal of the necessary self-knowledge and are committed to perceptual psychology. However, it is a function of teacher-training institutions to assist prospective teachers to develop such a frame of reference, because in many cases they have not yet acquired such orientations through experience. A student may learn his chosen subject matter well and also study a great deal of psychology without really acquiring a good self-concept (or an ability to perceive how his own self-concept influences his interpersonal relations). The perceptual view of effective teaching requires teacher education curricula and practices that will aid in establishing a self-as-instrument approach to teaching.

If behavior takes its direction from the purposes of the individual, then a teacher's perception of his own purposes and those of the school, the system, and society will greatly influence his behavior. Whether a teacher becomes teacher centered, or pupil centered will depend upon whether he perceives his purpose as that of bringing all pupils up to their own optimal ability levels, or that of instructing where it seems to do the most good. According to his beliefs about purposes, he will either be quite directive, structuring and delimiting according to his own superior knowledge, or he will give pupils free rein in setting up many of their own goals, and in finding their own preferred pathways to learning. Combs would also ask that teacher-education programs include aid to the student in exploring purposes (self, school, community, and nation), so that he might acquire them as personal outlooks and knowingly use them in more effective teaching.

Thus, instead of a teacher's methods reflecting the period of his education, the region of his college, or the specific school of thought of a leading educator, they would be suited to the kind of person he is. His methods would be related to the way he felt about his environment, especially about the school milieu. The general function of a teacher-education program is thus to assist each future teacher to locate the methods best suited to his purposes, his task, and the peculiar populations and problems he will meet on the job. Methods are not to be *taught* by the professor, but they are to be *discovered* by his student, the future teacher. This assumes a breadth of experience and a development of discriminations under appropriate guidance not ordinarily found in education programs.

Combs insisted that good teachers do not accept their purpose as that of controlling students, but of freeing them. They should not control, manipulate, coerce, block, or inhibit behavior. Instead, they should assist, release, and facilitate. They also tend to be concerned with larger issues than are the main run. They tend to perceive broad perspectives and future implications, rather than to be restricted to immediate perceptions. They are self-revealing rather than self-concealing, and hence are willing to air and deal with their own shortcomings and feelings. They become personally involved and are willing to interact, instead of remaining aloof or remote. Good teachers are not so concerned with achieving goals as they are with furthering processes, and they expect to encourage pupils and help them in the process of discovery. Combs said that all these characteristics describing the good teacher have been revealed by research. He suggested that seven other traits may be hypothesized as characteristic of good teachers, but that they need further validation by research:

1. Helping rather than dominating.
2. Understanding rather than condemning.
3. Accepting rather than rejecting.
4. Valuing integrity rather than violating integrity.
5. Being positive rather than negative.
6. Being open rather than closed to experience.
7. Being tolerant of ambiguity rather than intolerant.

Once it has been accepted that the discovery of purposes represents an undertaking of great importance to students, then the next step is that of determining how teachers-to-be can be aided in the discovery-making processes. One barrier to this goal has been the attempt to present principles to students and then ask them to apply those principles. Combs prefers a problems approach to this, which would help the student to derive the principles from his own experience, or from meeting important problems. It can then be predicted that when a student so educated becomes a teacher, he will be affected in positive ways by his searches for Why? What for? What is good? What works? What is important? and What do I believe?

THE PERSONAL DISCOVERY
OF WAYS TO TEACH

As did Gage, Combs has found it difficult to find general, right methods of teaching. But Combs also placed less confidence in using any kind of a model (e.g., Gage's) from which a teacher may select and use the right method at the right time. Rather, skill in teaching is "a creative act involving the effective use of one's self as instrument" (p. 98). In general, a teacher preparation institution can aid the student by providing a facilitating atmosphere, by arranging opportunities for students to become involved with pupils and with teaching, and by providing opportunities to explore, wherein he may discover appropriate teaching techniques.

Students are not likely to explore in an atmosphere in which they see too many possibilities for becoming humiliated, where they have to play it safe. But if they are to make discoveries of methods, they must take risks, be able to stick their necks out without fear, and must then have available a staff member who will support their efforts and will assist in heading off humiliations if explorations get them into hot water. They must be accepted as they are, as a starting point, so that they can accept themselves. Preconceptions should be tentatively accepted, but then they should be discussed and tested, so that they can be modified by experience, not simply rejected by instructors. A great deal of fuss is made about readiness as an important adjunct to effective learning in young children, but little has been said about the readiness of the learning teacher. Students who are learning to teach ought to be allowed to try out those techniques and methods that they are ready to practice. The students should be permitted to approach the sales counter of methods as relaxed shoppers, concentrating, if they wish, upon only a few, so that choices may readily be made without confusion. There is no one right method, so students ought not to be preoccupied with making the choice. Combs observed that good teachers are rarely concerned about methods. An expert teacher, doctor, or counselor at work thinks about problems, ideas, goals, purposes, beliefs, and understandings, and just does what his special talent suggests. These experts do not simply dig into a large bag of tricks, they ad-lib their way, adapting to events as they come up. They are adept in the use of various methods, but they make use of knowledge and understanding that is applied to whatever problems and goals they have in mind. "What he does has a quality of 'of course.' It is appropriate. It fits" (p. 102).

The good teacher will be one who has already overcome some of the barriers to exploring techniques. One such barrier, which will make the student reluctant to make his own discoveries, is the feeling that children are not to be trusted—some will automatically take the opposite of every question that the teacher answers. With this barrier in place, students will do very little experimenting with methods—they have to spend too much time, thought, and energy in protecting their own positions. Novice teachers also tend to erect another barrier, the belief that they should be careful about what they do, because if it goes wrong it may irreparably harm the fragile pupils. The teacher's influence may be great, it is true, but it is unlikely that a single traumatic event will wreak lifelong harmful effects on children—they are too tough, too resilient for that. The final barrier to exploration is the feeling that minor mistakes are of great consequence. Too much focus on correct ways of arriving at a goal may result in never reaching it. Students should be encouraged to experiment very early in their preparation for teaching, and they should continue their explorations throughout their preparations and careers.

A second major opportunity area that should be provided is that of personal involvement with pupils. The gradual approach is best, with students in training contacting pupils at every step in their education—not a single traumatic plunge at the end of the professional course. (Many colleges now offer pre-student-teaching experiences, so that students may become acquainted with children on informal and quasi-informal bases, before they try their student teaching. The move toward simulations, to be described later in this book, is also designed to provide gradual involvement with pupils, so that the consequences of decisions may be noted but not suffered.) Early involvement also helps students to determine which teaching areas appeal to them most, and which grade levels are most attractive to them. The concept also calls for an increase in supervision, with master teachers acting not as models but as colleagues who assist the novice teachers in finding their own best approaches. The supervisor-as-critic teacher is likely to focus on results, rather than on causes. Thus, the student's beliefs, feelings, and understandings in the teaching experience are not dealt with adequately—instead, the supervisor makes suggestions as to new and better things to do.

The third major opportunity area is that in which opportunities are provided for the student to explore and discover appropriate teaching techniques. The pre-student- and student-teaching experiences do provide some opportunities, but beyond this, curriculum laboratories are needed, so that equipment, supplies, and materials may be tried out. Students should be able to set up equipment and displays that can be left standing for an extended period, if desired. Each student should be self-pacing, working now leisurely, now feverishly, if need be, and he should be allowed to browse as he will. Students should be encouraged to discuss and even to argue, and the supervisor should be sensitive to their needs and be willing to share himself and his wide variety of skills. In turn, students should be permitted to criticize his methods.

ROGERIAN NOTES

Although the name of Carl Rogers is most often associated with psycho-therapy, his orientation toward the re-education of people with problems has furnished considerable impetus in studying functions of teachers. The character of his approach to therapy provides a glimpse into what seems to be quite basic to a self-development approach to teaching. Always, the avowed aim is not merely to solve problems, but to assist in the growth of the individual. Rogers (1957) differentiated his approach from others in four ways:

1. Reliance on individual drive toward growth, health, and adjustment to a greater extent than is evident in other therapies.
2. The placing of greater emphasis upon the affec-tive domain than upon the cognitive domain.
3. Stressing the importance of the immediate situa-tion, rather than dwelling upon the past.
4. Stressing therapeutic relationships as growth ex-periences.

In the school situation, Rogers had long insisted that, for problem chil-dren, making sure that they had challenging but satisfying school tasks was the greatest single potential resource for satisfactions that could be obtained in a school setting. Challenging but satisfying tasks involve setting realistic levels of aspiration, and teachers may not only be instru-mental in supplying appropriate tasks, but in assisting children toward the realistic setting of goals, both immediate and more remote. Placing each child in a group that is appropriate to the type and level of ability that he possesses is one way to increase the probability that his learning tasks will be challenging and at the same time satisfying. Another way is to establish a curriculum that is best adapted to individual problems. Thus, the teacher may also be encouraged to make use of each child's special interests and talents, and to provide individual aid in his areas of deficiency. Special attention should be paid to influencing attitudes. The teacher should recognize that each child has a need to achieve that is not limited to a select few. Each child should be provided with the op-portunity to compete, not with others in a hopeless race, but with him-self, where he can see each improvement, and where his failures are merely in relation to his own goals, so that he may try again without fear or embarrassment. All the foregoing considerations, although rational enough from a purely intellectual point of view, are aimed at providing the student with a sense of achievement.

Helping children toward emotional security by recognizing their problems and channeling their overt behavior into constructive, legitimate pursuits is also a technique that a teacher may use in helping all children as well as the problem child. For example, to increase the legitimate opportunities for the show-off is considered beneficial, and the use of school sports and dramatics is advocated. Throughout all his writings, Rogers indicates his respect for the individual and sees a closer understanding of the self as an essential element in the personality makeup of the therapist. To the extent that a teacher is a therapist, that is, a re-educator, the teacher also ought to emphasize these points.

Abraham Maslow shares with Rogers a strong feeling toward the integrity and positive movement of the self. His concept of self-actualization is widely accepted as a useful guiding principle for those who sustain a magnificent confidence in the ability of each individual to work out his own development.

Rogers not only insisted upon recognizing and abetting the integrity of the individual in the early developmental stages of his life, but believed that graduate students preparing for professional life are still so beset by psychological needs that their satisfaction ought to be given a place in their training. It may serve a useful purpose for the reader to become acquainted with Rogers's position regarding the teaching and preparation of graduate students in psychology. He stated the assumptions, that are implied by programs of graduate education:

> *Implicit Assumption #1. The student cannot be trusted to pursue his own scientific and professional learning.* (p. 171)

College teachers assume that they must assign work, that they must supervise the completion of this work, that the whole effort must be guided and then evaluated. This places the student on one side of the desk and the teacher on the other, usually.

> *Implicit Assumption #2. Ability to pass examinations is the best criterion for student selection and for judging professional promise.* (p. 173)

Rogers does not deny that examination passing is a useful tool, he simply points out that it emphasizes rote learning and mental agility, sometimes at the expense of originality of thought and scientific curiosity.

> *Implicit Assumption #3. Evaluation is education; education is evaluation.* (p. 174)

Examinations have become so important that they are a way of life for the college student. Rogers lists eleven major evaluation hurdles to be faced by the graduate student, and some of these must be taken a second time. The examinations are in addition to the many quizzes and other examinations routinely taken during the course of each semester.

> *Implicit Assumption #4. Presentation equals learning: what is presented in the lecture is what the student learns.* (p. 177)

Objectives have been carefully established (by the instructor and/or the appropriate committee), and the course proceeds as planned, smoothly, without a hitch—except that graduate students taking such a course may make the following comments:

> Worst of all, I think, is the fact that not many of the students feel that they are learning anything at all. They feel that it is just a continuation of the idiocy of undergraduate school in which huge amounts of material are thrown at you and you are expected to regurgitate most of it on a test and then supposedly you have learned something. You may indeed have gained some separated facts about psychology, but none of them can be integrated in any coherent way. (p. 177)

Fortunately, most graduate students are better able to cope with inept, one-way methods of teaching, and they do not all react as did this one. It is also fortunate that some courses produce their greatest influences after the students leave the classroom in which they were taught. Many find ways of making courses worthwhile without leaning too heavily on the teacher.

> *Implicit Assumption #5. Knowledge is the accumulation of brick upon brick of content and information.* (p. 178)

Rogers points out that this assumption violates the finding that learning occurs most effectively when it is directly related to the meaningful purposes and motives of the learner. Many college professors would insist that they do not hold this fifth assumption—that simply because they adhere to the logical and psychological construction of the systems that work best does not mean that the structure is rigid, and that it does not allow for the purposes and motives of the learner. However, Rogers's criticism appears to be aimed primarily at the requirements imposed by graduate schools in prescribing curricula, rather than at the manner in which course work is handled in any given classroom.

> *Implicit Assumption #6. The truths of psychology are known.* (p. 179)

The instructor of the class assumes that he is in possession of these truths, and the task of the student is to acquire them also. To give the student a "substantial" education, the teacher is not permitted to deviate, nor to leave too many questions open. (Again, although *the teacher* may imply a generic application, it is recognized that many graduate faculty members do permit departures from standardized packages.)

> *Implicit Assumption #7. Method is Science.* (p. 180)

If the design of an experiment is meticulous, if the procedures and statistical inspections are carefully accomplished, then the study is a successful one. Significant observations of significant phenomena is no longer the central issue. Rogers prefers a focusing on the development of the individual's creativeness, though he recognizes the importance of competence in designing, executing, and interpreting studies.

> *Implicit Assumption #8. Creative scientists develop from passive learners.* (p. 180)

There is minimal encouragement to think for oneself, and often an absence of vigorous discussion. Yet studies of the promotion of creative thinking and of constructive problem solving point up the importance of a free and easy give-and-take. The instructor who has a vested interest in his knowledge capsules may fear a too-permissive atmosphere.

> *Implicit Assumption #9. "Weeding out" a majority of the students is a satisfactory method of producing scientists and clinicians.* (p. 182)

Although it is true that there is often a careful selection of the graduate students who will be taken into the various programs, the attrition rate is too high. It is Rogers's feeling that there is an obligation on the part of the graduate school to "conserve this potentiality." The graduate school has its own law of the wild, a survival of the fittest, but it would seem not only that the graduate student is committed to his preparing for a profession, but that the graduate school also has accepted this as its commitment, once the student has been accepted. Not erecting hurdles to be jumped, but steps to be ascended, via whatever aid the school can provide, should be the aim. (This assumption by Rogers subsumes another—that the graduate school has at its disposal always an infallible instrument for determining the applicant's fitness as he enters.)

> *Implicit Assumption #10. Students are best regarded as manipulable objects, not as persons.* (p. 183)

This one seems to be a particularly sore point with Rogers, as has been evident in his several debates with B. F. Skinner. He feels that "ultra-behaviorism," as he calls it, "tends to see all individuals simply as machines, managed by reward and punishment" (p. 16). Student-faculty relations certainly need to be improved in most colleges and universities, but to be unable to implement a desirable condition is not necessarily to oppose it. Many college instructors are defensive, so that they hide behind their own evaluative functions—because they are the judges, they cannot be judged. However, a great number of teachers do try to treat their students as humans, and despite increasingly heavy workloads, find time to advise and encourage them.

But Rogers is not merely out to destroy all the old structures—he suggests alternatives. These might be called *his* assumptions. First, graduate programs for psychologists should develop psychologists who will be creative in their field. Criteria for the selection of these students should include originality, intelligence, and independence of thought, but he admits that originality and independence of thought cannot be adequately measured at present. He assumes that the best background training will be broadly based, including the humanities, arts, and sciences. Freedom and stimulation should characterize the desirable psychological climate, because it releases the students' potential for learning, developing, and making sensible educational choices. Students should be helped to understand which subject matters are relevant to their own development, and much of the learning should occur through doing. Learning should be promoted by the providing of opportunities for students to become directly involved in research problems, clinical work, and philosophical problems. Faculty roles should include that of learner, as well as teacher, in interacting with students. A student should learn to accept responsibility for his own decisions, as he makes his own choices in education. It should be assumed that once a student has been accepted for graduate work, the faculty will help him to become certified as a Ph.D. His completed research, his professional work, and other products will be proof of his competency.

PERCEPTION AND LEARNING

(1) The infant is not entirely helpless but shows from birth on steadily increasing capacities for active searching for satisfaction and for active discovery and exploration and that it enjoys these active capacities; and

(2) that the child in many ways shows a promise which altogether too often is betrayed by adult man and his society and by the growing child itself when it yields to those forces and aspects of the culture, as transmitted by parents, teachers, and peers, which are crippling to its inherent potentialities.
(Ernest G. Schachtel, 1959, p. 5)

Robert E. Bills, in his report presented at the Third Research Institute of the Association for Supervision and Curriculum Development, 1959, described some implications about teaching that had been derived from a perceptual point of view. But there are many perceptual theories, so Bills described the area from which his implications are drawn—"roughly defined by the phenomenology of Snygg and Combs, the transactionalism of Ames and others, and the client-centered framework of Rogers" (p. 55).

Generally speaking, phenomenology refers to the systematic study of immediate experience, in which the perceiver seeks to give a detailed description of the way things look to him. As Hilgard says, "The phenomenological standpoint . . . is not easy to characterize satisfactorily in a limited space" (1948, p. 253). It is a more subjective point of view than that of behaviorism, but is more naive than the introspection of Titchener, in which the perceiver had to be specially trained. Hilgard calls the observations made "natural and childlike," in referring to phenomenology.

Bills makes the primary assumption that behavior is a function of perception. One behaves according to what he "sees." This seeing does not refer, however, merely to environmental stimuli impinging upon the senses. People are self-starters, they are selectors of behavioral acts in the light of the behaver's beliefs. They are self-actualizers, making choices according to what seems to lead to the greatest enhancement of self-organizations. But if people are self-actualizers, then they are influenced to act in accordance not only with beliefs, but with values, needs, attitudes, self-concepts, and threats.

The teacher's role is one of bringing about positive change in perceptions, but if this role is accepted what are the implications for learning? Bills listed the implications:

1. To teach a person we must understand him. This is most easily accomplished by trying to see him and his world as he sees them.

2. Education must start with problems of learners that are important and need-relevant to them.

3. Since needs, values, and attitudes are such important determiners of perception, education must seek to help students know what needs, values, and attitudes are important to them and to consider these fully and in relation to each other.

4. Since personal perceptions are not readily changed through the introduction of objective evidence, education must begin with the beliefs of students and relate knowledge to their peculiar perceptions.

5. Perceptions are most readily changed through a re-examination of needs, values, attitudes, and the possible meanings of previous experience.

6. Knowledge is but one determiner of human behavior.

7. Learners learn in response to *their* needs and perceptions, not those of their teacher's.

8. Education must start where the child is and permit him to determine his own direction and pace.

9. Not specific behavior but adequacy of perception and openness to experience should be the goals of education.

(1955, p. 63)

These implications are expected to provide help in moving forward in thinking about teaching. One way to move forward is to relate the nine implications to ways of teaching that bring about positive change in perceptions. Problem solving, group dynamics, and student-centered teaching are held to be useful. If the assumptions that behavior is a function of perception and that people move toward self-actualization and strive to enhance self-organization are accepted, then the teacher should provide the necessary conditions for meeting these assumptions.

When two persons are in psychological contact (e.g., pupil and teacher), the first of them (pupil) is in a state of incongruence—he is vulnerable to learning. The second person (teacher) is congruent, and has positive feelings toward the first. Also, the teacher empathizes with the student's frame of reference, and tries to communicate his experience to the pupil. This communication is achieved to a minimal degree. These are the *interactive* conditions in the classroom, wherein the teacher brings about conditions of positive change in his perceptions.

Thus, the teacher who advocates the viewpoint of phenomenology stresses the understanding of the pupil through seeing the world through his eyes. In the learning situation, the learner remains unchanged, though his experience of the situation or task changes. His behavior is insightful, or relevant to the situation as he presently interprets it. One's perceptions could affect one's level of intelligence, and what he learns may be related to what he perceives himself capable of learning.

Herbart A. Thelen and others attempted to pull together ideas from several streams of thought: Lewin's field theory; the human development approach of Prescott, Havighurst, and Tryon; Rogers' position on the self; and group dynamics. In 1964, Thelen published "Some Classroom Quiddities for People-Oriented Teachers," and the article was reprinted in a book of readings (1967). Thelen pointed out a facet of major opposition between some behavioristic, systematic approaches and one which is based on self:

> You can condition a child to do math homework because you can identify behaviors to reward and punish. But education proceeds through covert and sneaky processes of internal reorganization of thoughts and feelings. You cannot even find the behavior to reward or punish in order to make math homework *educative*. You can train the child to make the right reply to a question, but you cannot force him ever to use the idea for any other purpose. (1967, p. 367)

And, as Carl Rogers says in agreeing with Thelen, "We occasionally have Ph.D. candidates who have been socialized or trained over the years to make acceptable responses on tests and yet cannot think up a research proposal (let alone commit themselves to it) to save their lives" (Rogers, p. 367). Thelen would have the teacher utilize the "normal" engagements of learners—speculation, selection, and resolution of inconsistency. He does so by arranging environmental inputs, however. He also pleads for a voluntary association of learners, pursuing shared goals. Classroom learning would amount to the utilization of projects. Thelen calls this a behavioral science approach for education, and it requires that teachers (1) understand the discipline of their subjects, and (2) locate inquiry appropriately within the discipline. In Thelen's words:

The two major alternatives are: (a) the discipline of the subject is confined to knowing the ideas as organized by someone else and as sampled by achievement tests (in which case everything I have said is a waste of your time and mine); and (b) the discipline of the subject is an orientation meta-theory and methods of investigation of phenomena comprehended in the corresponding field of knowledge (in which case the activity of the sociogroup is *cooperative investigation of phenomena*). If you see education as society's provision for helping people cope with the world, then, in a world of rapid change like ours, education must develop the primitive but natural capability of inquiry; if you see education as society's provision for locating each person in some segment in which he can "belong," then education must be concerned only with developing common discourse and vocabulary among groups of students sorted out in terms of the social groups to which they shall belong. Except that I would call that socialization rather than education. (pp. 376, 377)

Those who stress the importance of self-understanding in teaching also stress acceptance of an emerging self and the fostering of its development. Such considerations logically lead to a concern for self-initiated learning, based on the interests of the child. They also point toward the need to provide learning conditions that will promote creativity. Teachers of this persuasion perceive their function primarily as that of a catalyst, giving direction only where self-direction seems to be failing, and cueing and prompting occasionally, but not bestowing information and techniques. There is an emphasis upon the discovery of principles and solutions, with some help from the teacher. Although inquiry training and creativity are not self-avowed aims of self-oriented teachers in general, the logical connection is sufficiently evident to justify a brief examination of some efforts in those directions.

TEACHING PUPILS TO INQUIRE

Learning how to learn, or the development of learning sets, has been suggested as a powerful facilitator in education. It is sometimes assumed that mere question asking indicates avid curiosity, and is accompanied by an inquiring mind. But questions may be asked merely because the questioner has formed the habit—the answers are not very important, because the person who is asking may not even bother to receive them, much less to evaluate them. Just as the questions of teachers may be ordered according to logical sequences, so may the questions of pupils be, up to a point. But pupils do not ordinarily establish very meaningful taxonomies of questions. Their inquiry processes are often of a random nature, with only occasional integration of related information. Recognizing the potential value of asking questions in an orderly, purposeful manner, educators have agreed upon the desirability of critical thinking as an objective. However, the most direct means to this end apparently have not been well developed until recently. One of those interested in the development of critical inquiry via orderly processes is Massialas (1967).

If the child is to develop an inquiring mind, what are some of the ways by which he may become habituated to the most effective inquiry techniques? If it is true that Dewey (1933) spoke of how thinking ought to proceed, rather than accounting for how people really think, then to what other source may educators turn, in order to focus upon the practical aspects of question-asking–decision-making? It is easy, for example to make the error of jumping immediately into considerations of creative thinking, and thereby broaden the scope so much that the specified processes (question asking) become submerged in considerations of generalities. It is also tempting to range far afield by asking, in effect, "inquiry into what?" Although there can be no such process without content, the focus at this point will be upon question asking by students as a learning technique, and upon ways by which the teacher may systematically foster the intelligent posing of questions based upon related purposes.

The Massialas and Zevin experiments did not utilize in any direct, structured way the employment of questioning as a method of learning. Instead, various analytical episodes were presented, and students were asked to discuss the various topics. There were also discovery episodes, and the teacher asked almost as many questions as did the students. *Analysis* appeared to be aimed at developing an intellectual structure from which problems, questions, data, and knowledge could be systematically approached. Sequencing patterns and organizing data would result in understanding phenomena. Analysis, then, would impel students to develop and test general principles as they related to available information. It was assumed that students engaged in these analysis episodes had already acquired many techniques of questioning, and had moved upward on Bloom's taxonomy to at least the analysis level. *Discovery,* as an aspect of inquiry, was concerned with a somewhat different goal. Here it is expected that the beginning consists of searching for a specific solution requiring the discovery of an unknown. This unknown may be only a small piece of information, or it may be a whole set of facts. The motivational effect of discovery dissipates, of course, once the discovery has been made. Thus, discovery has a more immediate set of goals than does analysis, though both processes entail the use of logical operations. That it was not the aim of these studies to determine systematic methods of fostering the use of questions by students is shown by the functions listed for the teacher: first, he was to select an appropriate object for discussion and plan how to introduce it into the classroom, then:

1. He offers helpful hints or clues at points of impasse or stalemate (but he must be careful not to give away the story).
2. He prods students by redirecting their original questions.
3. He insists on the evidential or rational support of student assertions.
4. He creates a classroom atmosphere that invites the free flow of views and comments.
5. He legitimizes and rewards creative thought.

In promoting the inquiry process, then, a teacher is not necessarily focusing upon the *systematic* use of questions for learning—it is a specific kind of learning that is involved. Massialas defined the inquiry process as "generally the process of identifying, exploring, and validating alternatives. Involves both deductive and inductive processes as they apply to questions of fact and of value" (1967, p. 266). One difficulty in systematically directing a learning process that might be called "teaching how to inquire" is that intuitive thinking, the process of discovery and invention, does not proceed in well-defined, orderly sequences of steps, as far as is now known. At each juncture in decision making, there are not only no prescribed sets of "right" answers, but the teacher who is described as effective in promoting this critical inquiry insists that at least some minimal direction should be provided for the learner. Inquiry training may therefore be viewed as an art rather than as a science. But surely there are certain baseline behaviors for an art, and perhaps there is just enough of a science involved here for some guidelines to emerge.

Massialas listed five "opportunities" that are presented in discovery. These are the opportunities for the learner to:

1. make a leap into that part of the world which is unknown to him personally,

2. link the past with the present and the future,
3. project and speculate intelligently on the basis of limited clues on underlying principles or generalizations explaining human interactions,
4. develop and refine heuristic devices which he can use in future investigations, and
5. exhibit an imaginative understanding of the degrees and levels of probability and predictability.

(1966, p. 137)

Social studies provide an excellent subject-matter area within which inquiry may be encouraged. A modern world history course was approached via discovery, and the progress of students was described. Students were to locate the origin of poems furnished by the teacher. Inquiry proceeded via collective questioning of the teacher and some written source materials. However, the teacher's function was only to provide the rules of the game, and to question their modes of reasoning. She also helped in getting the machinery of inquiry moving again, if it seemed to become bogged down or to run out of steam. Generally, the course of events followed that suggested by the five "opportunities." The first day was spent on orientation and the organization of the materials on hand. Inertia grips students when they are somewhat averse to accepting the responsibility for determining their own course of action. They make the leap into the unknown by carefully analyzing the poems to establish a very general source, i.e., an Eastern world origin. This narrowing down of the search leads to some bits of contradictory information that they seem to be accumulating as each poem's details are analyzed. Finally, the contradictory information was reconciled, when placed within the framework of a different hypothesis, a more conclusive one, which attempted to explain the interrelationships among social, economic, and geographic factors. On the third day, the speculations on possible answers were brought out. From Oriental origin to a specified religion was to be the next step. Using the logic of "if-then" (deduction), the students searched for evidence that would be in harmony with the data furnished by all ten poems. At this point, they realized that they had insufficient information and sought out other sources. On the fourth day, the search was narrowed, because of the finding that *if* these poems were all of the specified type, *then* they could not be any other Oriental type except Japanese.

Acceptance of the five processes of discovery as "opportunities" implies that the teaching of inquiry might be somewhat reduced to orderly sequences, after all. What Massialas suggested was that the process of inquiry and discovery is very much like Dewey's description of reflective thinking. Granted that it is the task of the teacher to foster reflective thinking, however, the task becomes considerably more complicated when the complementary nature of intuitive and analytic thinking are insisted upon—because it is so difficult to define and promote intuitive thinking.

Suchman (1966, "Inquiry in the Curriculum") treated inquiry training as training in creativity. First, he attempted to explain how the child's intellectual processes are interrelated. His ideas are summarized in Verduin's *Conceptual Models in Teacher Education* (1967). Four organizers are available to the learner that will aid him in bringing meaning into a new encounter:

1. Previous encounters that have been similar in some way to the one presently being perceived.
2. Systems for bringing meaning into his dealing with environments—ways of categorizing, subsuming, ordering, and so on.
3. Data, generated in part by previous encounters and arranged according to systems already developed—data that will help in bringing meaning to the new encounter.
4. Inferences, an organizer that makes it possible to draw up generalizations, conclusions, theories, and so on.

These four organizers can be retained by the learner for long periods of time, so that they may be used in the future in bringing meaning to new encounters. If they are so retained, they are, in effect, stored, and *storage* is one facet of Suchman's model of the intellectual process.

The child not only develops systems as organizers, but is himself a system. Any system has an *intake function,* and this function of the child seeks, selects, and groups those stimuli that he is perceiving; there is also a selective relationship in connection with what the child will expose himself to and accept as an input. A system also has a *processing function,* dealing with its inputs. The child may take action to change the environment (physical or social) or he may generate new encounters from which new data may be developed.

The child as a system does not include a direct or linear relationship between input and output (action). Whatever it is that happens within the system to make the relationship nonlinear is a *control* process, a mediator. Not all that is accepted as intake is acted upon, and not all that is available as intake is accepted. These selective functions in the mediation process are due to cognitive filters. The mediation process is, for Suchman, an important one in inquiring and in all learning.

The control process is influenced by the learner's *motivation.* The motivational function dictates intake selection, retrieval from storage, and even the actions or outputs of the system—the control function therefore executes the dictates of the motivational function. Three forces make up motivation:

1. *Closure,* in which the child is impelled to reach the final solution or to understand the new encounter.
2. *Basic curiosity,* a kind of arousal or excitement about the new encounter.
3. The power to predict, control, or explain a new encounter.

Thus, the new encounter enters the intake as selected stimuli, and the mediation or the processing of these data is carried out by the control function. The various motivational forces are activated, and stored organizers (models from past experiences) are retrieved from storage. (Also, new data begin to flow into storage.) The control function decides upon the course of action—there may be an attempt to produce an effect upon the environment, or to generate new stimuli that will act as inputs, and hence more data from the encounter will be acquired.

Thus far, there is only a description of a theoretical model of information processing. How can this be used by teachers? Suchman provided an example. When a film is shown that contains new information, there will be a gap in the *cognitive maps** of students. They then search the storage to locate an organizer that can make the new phenomena mean something. They may be unable to locate matching organizers and encounters, and will therefore develop dissonance or disharmony. (A conflict of ideas occurs.) For the film's presentation to become meaningful, pupils must restructure or combine those organizers they already have. It is Suchman's viewpoint that the gap in cognitive maps is accompanied by motivation

---

*Tolman's idea that, for example, rats in a maze act in accordance with some sort of mental "maps" of the situation, and not according to automatic responding to habit.

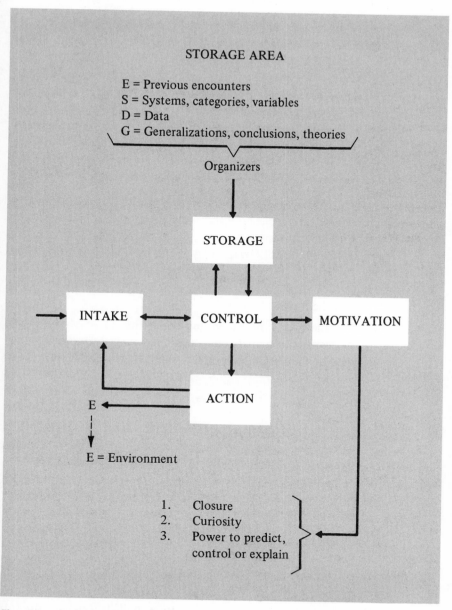

Fig. 7.1. Suchman's Theoretical Model for the Inquiry Process. This Model
is reproduced in Verduin's *Conceptual Models in Teacher
Education,* taken from an unpublished paper of Suchman.

for closure (completion). Then the control function may be either to perceive the new encounter or event in such a way that the organizers or models already available will assimilate it, or to find a way to combine the stored models so that they can create or accommodate a new model, incorporating the new meanings. For example, a boy who already plays baseball can simply alter his patterns to accommodate the learning of cricket.

When the control function has been thus exercised, pupils may begin to take action. The action may include gathering new data and generating intakes. This is done by asking questions or by analysis and examination and by testing ideas bearing on the information from the film. These forms of action make the models (organizers) in storage assist in developing new meaning. A trial-and-error process will occur, so that intake and storage will become more meaningfully matched. (Dissonance remains until a satisfactory match is made.)

Suchman presented the following suggestions or directives to teachers:

1. Create freedom to have and express ideas and to test them with data.
2. Provide a responsive environment so that (a) each is heard and understood, and (b) each learner can get the data he requires.
3. Help learners find a direction to move in, a purpose for their intellectual pursuit.

Not only must students be permitted to express their ideas, they must be provided with facilities and time in which to test them. To implement this first step is obviously quite difficult in many of today's clasrooms, but few would deny that it is an important requirement. Providing a responsive environment includes not only responsiveness by the teacher to what he perceives the student to have said, but also environmental conditions should provide for concrete, simulated, and verbal experiences, wherein students can gather data. Teacher responses should include focus—directing the cognitive and perceptual energies of students toward a focal point. He may use focusers, or media that induce students to inquire. Or he may refocus attention when it lags or comes to a halt through premature closure. At this point, questions are in order, which urge students to move to further considerations of cause-effect relations, gaining alternative viewpoints and looking at the encounter from new angles. Such questions will expose other areas that arouse new discourses, and inquiry will again proceed. Some pupils will refocus by themselves, simply for the sheer excitement of pursuing deeper meanings. Some will do so only when they have learned more about the encounter, so the teacher may need to probe, to determine how far each pupil will go on his own with a little prompting.

Suchman believed that much learning may be teacher planned, and teacher engineered. By means of language, the teacher can provide inputs to the student so that the control center can retrieve from storage the organizers needed to interpret an encounter. More interactions between student and teacher will result in bringing out other stored organizers or models. To supplement the stored models, the teacher may use graphic or schematic models on the blackboard or screen. Student restructuring with new consistent models will lead to generating new encounters, i.e., inquiry. Feedback is a necessary adjunct to the teacher's assistance. The teacher needs to know the direction in which the student is proceeding. However, Suchman insisted that the students be active—the teacher is merely helping them by sequencing and directing, but not by giving them new knowledge or ideas.

The implications for improved teacher education are rather obvious. Under many systems of teacher education, untried models are provided for the student, but they are for storage only, not for action. Because the process of inquiry can be used at any level of education, preservice teachers themselves may profitably engage in it—"There is no better way to learn about inquiry than to inquire and then analyze what has been done" (Verduin, p. 101). Four suggestions are given for the teacher who is preparing for classes to come:

(1) The preservice teacher should examine carefully what is meant by meaning and new encounters, and how to evolve these in his teaching process.

(2) Further, asking questions and responding to students are important facets of the inquiry process that should be understood and used by the preservice student.

(3) Finally, the act of focusing and refocusing on problems at hand are important operations that the student must know.

(4) The teacher education student must also have a good knowledge of the content that will be taught to enable him to develop the appropriate experiences and materials for true inquiry.

(Verduin, p. 100)

CREATIVE TEACHING

Books on creativity are more popular today than ever before. Many educators have general ideas about how to foster creativity, and many teachers who practice certain innovative techniques feel that they are teaching creatively. For a teacher to *teach* creatively in such a way as to help pupils to *live* more creatively is the hope expressed by E. Paul Torrance in the foreword to James Smith's *Setting Conditions for Creative Teaching in the Elementary School* (1966). Controlled research into factors that inhibit creativity and those that foster it has been conspicuous by its absence. But the recent acceleration of interest and research in this area has furthered the cause sufficiently for writers like Smith to attempt the formulation of systematic arrangements for creativeness. Research findings have been translated into classroom methods, and guidance is provided in identifying, understanding, and generalizing the principles that are presumably functioning in creative teaching activities.

Smith has written a series of seven books, all concerned with setting conditions for creative teaching, but the present discussion will be limited to what Torrance called "a creative synthesis of Professor Smith's rich experience in teaching children and teachers of children, a vast amount of research concerning creativity and classroom learning, and his theories of education" (Smith, 1966, p. viii). Although Smith did not wish his book to be regarded as a cookbook, he did not hesitate to specify instructional procedures for developing creativity.

He first defined creativity, or rather, described it as "sinking down taps into our past experiences and putting these selected experiences together into new patterns, new ideas or new products" (p. 4). Although definitions vary, few would reject the central idea that novelty in a pattern, an idea, or a product of the learner is what comes to mind when one is asked about creating. Without novelty, there is simply production, but no change in quality, no uniqueness, in the learner's product.

Everyone seems to know what is meant by creativity, but few pause to examine the assumptions upon which teaching for creativity rest:

1. Being creative is always better than not being creative.
2. Creative teaching is better than noncreative.
3. Pupil creativity is always a good thing—it develops potentiality and actualization, rather than frivolities and disingenuousness.

4. Something different is better than something that conforms.

5. Something new is better than the old.

6. All change is progress.

These assumptions will be evident in the discussion that follows, and once they have been accepted, a base may be established for creative production by pupils, fostered by creative teachers. To follow prescribed ways of solving a problem, of reaching a goal, or of utilizing information is not to engage in divergent thinking. To see things with a new slant, to arrive via alternative pathways, to put data together in new relationships, however, requires divergent thinking. The most general task of the teacher who would teach creatively, then, is to depart from the long-established ways. The most general provision that the teacher can make to promote creative thinking in students is to establish conditions for their divergent thinking. Smith asks the classroom teacher to observe the classroom more closely for indications of individuality in children—in their clothing, their speaking patterns, reactions to stimuli provided by the teacher, and in their ways of writing, painting, drawing—in fact, all the ways in which children depart from the usual modes. The teacher is then invited to think of ways in which these differences may be used to advantage in the classroom program. He is also asked to compare the instances in which he has required conformity with those in which he has permitted creative conditions to exist. By taking thought, the teacher ought to do at least one thing in his classroom every day, for a week, that he has never done before. This, of course, provides a model for the children, and it might even result in motivation for them to alter their routines. Because every child is born with some creative potential, it behooves the teacher to help keep that capacity alive. Dow (1959) says that worry about increasing a child's creativity is pointless—it should simply be taken for granted and utilized. For self-actualizationists, such as Maslow and Rogers, *"The mainspring of creativity appears to be the same tendency which we discover so deeply as the curative force in psychotherapy*—man's tendency to actualize himself, to become his potentialities" (Rogers, 1959, p. 72). Those factors that a teacher may use to aid in the child's development toward self-actualization would also be important in fostering creativity. Children coming from similar *psychical* environments differ in degrees and kinds of creative abilities. The *psychological* factors involved are not yet well understood, but recently a great deal of investigation has been attempted.

Smith discussed six conceptions of thinking. The first is thinking according to *traditional logic*. This refers to the use of syllogistic reasoning, using deduction. It calls into play the person's experience and experimentation to aid in induction. *Classical associationism* makes use of the ability to derive new ideas from linking them up with old ideas, and building new ones by linking up old ones in different ways. The more associations available, the more readily new ideas may be acquired. The third conception of thinking is that of *Gestalt formulations of productive thinking*. A problem situation arises, and its structure is incomplete. A number of steps are taken, which completes the structure. Each of these steps is taken while surveying the whole situation. One of the steps consists of grouping, reorganization, and structurization—dividing wholes into smaller parts that are also wholes. Another is a search for interdependent relations, such as the relatedness of form and size. The third step is to locate the functional meaning of parts. However, sometimes there is a creative process (e.g., in art or music) in which the problem's complete structure is not the starting point. Instead, the creator experiences a desire to express the interrelatedness of form and size. A fourth way of viewing thinking is that of *psychoanalytic conceptions*. Conflict may produce neurosis or it may produce creativity. The person who creates has a greater mobility between the preconscious (almost conscious) material and conscious expression than does the person who must intellectualize his thinking, according to Kubie (1958). One aspect of the creative person is his childlike imagination. The fifth theory is that of *dynamic perception*. There are opposing tendencies; one is to remain securely established in a closed world, and the other is to remain open toward the world. When the latter tendency triumphs over the former, then the individual is creative (Schachtel, 1959). Rugg's *theory of the transliminal chamber* (1963) is the sixth way of conceptualizing creativity. Creative energy is contained in the transliminal mind, a continuum somewhere between the conscious and the unconscious levels of functioning. On this continuum is located a critical point, at which the individual experiences flashes of insight, and from this creativity results. It is not an all-or-nothing situation, for each person may be at a different point along the conscious-unconscious continuum. This means that for the less inhibited, there is greater likelihood that materials in the preconscious will become conscious so that a creative act may be performed.

In order to induce first steps toward creative procedures, Smith assigns tasks to the classroom teacher, who is asked to notice those occasions when he is restricting the children's ability to use teaching assistance in a variety of ways. The teacher is then urged to get out of the rut. Can testing be made more creative? Does praise of an individual or of unique products influence increased individual production? If the weakness of underachievers is related to a lack of means for meeting certain needs, can the teacher think of ways for them to use what creativeness they may have to help them meet the needs that have not been satisfied? In order to make lessons in workbooks and textbooks more exciting, more honest, and more productive for children, the teacher should select those that exemplify creative thinking and ask children whether they like a story or film—is it because of the creative elements or for other reasons?

Smith then went on to discuss the relationships between intelligence and creativity, social-emotional nature and creativity, and the process of creativity. Most relevant to the present, however, is the treatment of the nurture of creativity:

> Educational engineers are needed to help bridge the gap (between research and application), but in general such specialists do not yet exist. The soundest approach at present is to admit that not much is known by anyone about the necessary bridging activities, and to set forth without delay to discover how to develop them ourselves. We must learn how to translate research findings so they become suitable and applicable, ready to be installed in classrooms. (Taylor, 1964, p. 5)

There have been several outstanding educational engineers who have tried to bridge the gap between what is known via research and the application of principles to classroom methodology. Mearns, Cole, Applegate, and Zirbes are prominent among them. Smith devoted at least half his book to reporting his interpretations of research and providing illustrations of its applicatons. Although he feels that a new methodology will emerge, he insists that creative teaching is already a method. But to have a method may sometimes suggest that there is a specific "how-to." To teach creatively does not mean that there should be no method at all—it means that a creative teacher must establish patterns of his own. It does not necessarily mean that the teacher should do away entirely with lesson plans, for example, only that these should be used in flexible ways, according to the perceived needs of teacher and students. "But creativity in children can only be developed when teacher training institutions spend a major portion of their time helping teachers to be creative themselves" (Smith, 1966, p. 103).

To be creative does not mean that a teacher need not be systematic. The teacher-training program may lead to some blocks to creative teaching, and the field experience itself may include some barriers:

1. *Lack of intelligence.*
2. *Conformity.*
3. *Overplanning.*
4. *Planning the same for all children.*
5. *Closed questions.*
6. *Abuse of gimmicks.* (The Montessori blocks are considered a gimmick, but are not used abusively unless used uncreatively.)
7. *Overuse of textbooks.*

George Stoddard (1959) has commented on the overuse of textbooks. He opined that too many textbooks are far removed from original sources, so that they present only fragments that do not conform to the logic of the intellectual discipline nor to the psychological needs of the learner. Because the textbooks are so formless, they are not likely to be very exciting to pupils. The textbook should have a new role, a deeper one, not necessarily a major one, in relation to the whole school day. It should provide an introduction that induces the student to ask key questions and find answers for them. It should be the kind of book that sends the learner to original readings, experiments, or experiences that would otherwise not have occurred to him. This textbook should be seen as a map, a ticket, or a guidebook—it is not creative, but it can show the way to creativeness.

If creativeness cannot really be taught, can the teacher at least set conditions for creative teaching? Smith says that once creative teaching makes its appearance, it can be made to reappear by the use of techniques designed to produce the reappearance of any behavior. However, it does not appear automatically; the conditions must be present. Setting the conditions for creativity will reinforce it. Five categories of conditions for creativity are intellectual, physical, social-emotional, psychological, and educational. Each of these conditions is selected according to its ability to encourage techniques or environmental stimuli that are likely to evoke original behavior, unusual responses, and a continuing flow of ideas. In general, all conditions may be seen as either natural or contrived, and examples of both occur in each of the five categories.

Intellectual Conditions for Creativity

Six suggestions are presented for setting the intellectual conditions:

1. Opportunities should be provided for acquiring knowledge and skills through convergent thinking. There must be a storehouse of knowledge first, for divergent thinking to occur.

2. Many situations must be provided in which learning and skill may be applied to divergent thinking. An intellectual fund is not to be acquired for its own sake, but for solving problems.

3. A large number of open-ended learning situations should be developed. Answers are not predictable, the teacher simply helps pupils move into experiences, helps them to perceive problems, and then lets them go on their own. Both slow and bright children will come up with their own answers.

4. Situations, questions, and discussions should be planned so that they will stimulate all children to think much of the time. Simple question-answer, stimulus-response modes will not accomplish this stimulus function. When one pupil is reciting, the rest should also be thinking of solutions.

5. All areas of the curriculum may be used in providing content and situations. Sometimes pupils will need merely to incubate the problem, mulling it over for a while, and then sudden insights may emerge.

6. Teaching may proceed in order to develop certain specific skills that are needed in the process of creating—ability to think deductively, to see relationships, to pass judgment and make decisions, to think critically as well as creatively, to develop associations, to defer judgment, to abstract and construct symbols, adapt, modify, magnify, minify, rearrange, reverse, classify, and contrast.

Physical Conditions

The teacher has at his disposal various ways of arranging the contents of the classroom. It may be designed to have centers, areas that are specifically designed for certain activities. An art center, a music center, a science center, and so on may be established. There may also be a construction center, with a workbench and tools. A word center or vocabulary center can be provided, wherein interesting sources of language may be enjoyed. A research center is valuable, containing encyclopedias, references, atlases, globes, almanacs, maps, and perhaps even a radio or a television set. Finally, there should be a library—an exchange center for books. Seats should be movable. The entire aspect of the room should be attractive, with a judicious use of color and good lighting.

Availability of Materials

Materials should not only be plentiful and of as wide a variety as possible, but they should be easily accessible to pupils. Some materials, of course, must be for restricted use, if they produce too much noise or confusion. Any necessary rules on the use of materials should be reasonable and explained to the pupils, and then they should be consistently enforced.

Organization of the Class

An autocratic classroom does not foster creativity. In the creative classroom, the children and the teacher plan together. When carrying out plans that they themselves helped to develop, children are less likely to get out of hand when the teacher has to leave temporarily. Although the departmentalized middle school and homogeneous grouping are ideas that are still being advocated in many areas, it is the contention of creative teachers that implementation of these ideas leads to inhibition of creativity. Time periods spent with each teacher are too short, and development of the creative process does not have time to be brought about.

Social-Emotional Conditions

Smith lists thirteen conditions that are conducive to an improved social-emotional atmosphere as a means of fostering creativity:

(1) rewarding varied kinds of talents and creative achievements;

(2) helping children recognize the value of their creative talents;

(3) developing creative acceptance of realistic limitations in a problem situation;

(4) being sensitive to the needs of children, stressing

and praising differences, uniqueness and originality rather than likeness and commonness;

(5) accepting "silly" ideas as a sign of creative thinking;

(6) helping all children to accept the creative child;

(7) developing an atmosphere that is permissive to
the extent that children are free to experiment,
explore and make mistakes;

(8) developing an appreciation for creativity in the
classroom;

(9) avoiding the equation of difference with mental
illness and delinquency;

(10) modifying the misplaced emphasis on (differences
in) sex roles;

(11) helping highly creative children become less ob-
jectionable;

(12) helping to reduce the isolation of highly creative
children; and

(13) helping highly creative children cope with anxieties and fears.

(Smith, p. 130)

Psychological Conditions

The classroom should be physically hygienic—this is obvious. But it
should also be mentally hygienic, a point often overlooked by those who
use repressive practices. Fostering definite, good self-concepts, with an
absence of neurotic conflicts (brought on by classroom procedures) are
demanded of the creative teacher.

A permissive atmosphere, not one in which license prevails, nor yet in
which there is too much control, is also necessary. Here, the teacher builds
what Smith calls an "air of expectancy," so that pupils know they are
expected to explore, experiment, try new ideas, and each be himself.
Providing for a number of success experiences gives a pupil feelings of
security, so that he will be more likely to move further into the exploratory situation.

The motivational preference is that of tension reduction. A positive
tension is produced in each child, so that needs are acquired that result
in constructive outcomes. A negative tension, one created out of excessive
threat or fear, is likely to result in emotional attitudes that inhibit creative production.

The teacher's attitude must be one of understanding of the creative
child and the creative process. A teacher can be quite influential merely by

the manner in which he speaks to children. Even his nonverbal behavior may be expressive of attitudes and lack of sensitivity for the relationships that should obtain in his classroom. Creative teachers presumably develop creative children. And teachers who have not been very creative may increase their own facility in utilizing the novel by simply participating in some of the activities suggested for the youngsters—it is never quite too late. Order should be maintained in the classroom, but for an organizational purpose, not for so-called discipline. The creative child should be helped toward self-discipline. Early lessons in independence can further the maturity of the child and help him develop self-discipline. The child must be helped toward a stage wherein he is not merely obedient to orders at all times, but has developed responsibility for his own conduct and, to some extent, for that of others.

Educational Conditions

Smith treated educational conditions from the viewpoint of a developmentalist, and more specifically, he has a concern with the developmental tasks of the child. He believes that there must be a readiness for creativity, just as there are other well-known states of readiness that do not merely emerge automatically, but can be nurtured. Creative expression may exist at immature stages, but each stage is a necessary step toward the next. In general, the stages for the developing child follow those of conceptual development—from the concrete to the more abstract. However, on the face of it, creative expression *seems* to move in the opposite direction— materials that might contribute to the construction of a creative product are gathered together with no apparent purpose in mind, and these are later interpreted as concrete components of a novel contribution. However, Smith maintains that the child is merely using whatever is at hand to refine the process of creative communication. When a child is given art materials, such as paints, brushes, paper, and structural components, he learns to manipulate them, to try out various arrangements. He then explores various ways in which they can be employed, and with increased familiarity he achieves aesthetic enjoyment as he becomes productive. However, if the tools he is using are too difficult for him to use, he may shift to others, or he may simply repeat stereotyped, inept responses. Here, the teacher can use prompts effectively. He may say "Would you like a smaller brush?" "Maybe you need thinner paper for that." "Is there a better way to fasten it?" "Is that the only combination that works?"

Smith felt that what the child expresses are subjects that are provided by his interests and needs. How successful the teacher is in promoting the creative process will be determined more by the child's feelings toward it than by what he produces. Positive feelings may be squelched, or even turned to negative ones, if the teacher forces him into situations for which he has not reached the stage of readiness. As Robert Havighurst put it, the child's "teachable moment" may not have been reached.

Principles Basic to Creative Teaching

The following principles comprise a summary taken from Smith's *Setting Conditions for Creative Teaching*. In creative teaching:

1. Something new, different, or unique results.
2. Divergent thinking processes are stressed.
3. Motivational tensions are a prerequisite to the creative process. The process serves as a tension-relieving agent.
4. Open-ended situations are utilized.
5. There comes a time when the teacher withdraws and children face the unknown themselves.
6. The outcomes are unpredictable.
7. Conditions are set which make possible preconscious thinking.
8. Students are encouraged to generate and develop their own ideas.
9. Differences, uniqueness, individuality, originality are stressed and rewarded.
10. The process is as important as the product.
11. Certain conditions must be set to permit creativity to appear.
12. Teaching is "success" rather than "failure" oriented.
13. Provision is made to learn knowledge and skills, but provision is also made to apply these in new problem-solving situations.
14. Self-initiated learning is encouraged.
15. Skills of constructive criticism and evaluation skills are developed.
16. Ideas and objects are manipulated and explored.
17. Democratic processes are employed.
18. Methods are used which are unique to the development of creativity.

(Smith, pp. 157–162)

The last principle in this list requires special implementation. Taylor (1964) summarized methods used by Parnes Instructor's Manual (1963) and Osborn (1963): deferred judgment should be developed; blocks to creativity should be removed; brainstorming should be applied; creative evaluation should be made; questions should be asked as prompts; analytic techniques should be applied; aid in sensitization to problems should be given; problems should be carefully defined; broad problems should be narrowed; and an incubation period should be provided.

For those who wish to delve further into the as yet wide-open field of nurturing creativity, the little book by George F. Kneller (1965) will be extremely useful. *The Art and Science of Creativity* contains chapters on "Meanings," "Theories," "The Act," "The Person," and "Education and the Seed." And in this book, Kneller summarizes the positions of Sinnott, Whitehead, the Gestaltists, the psychoanalysts, Schachtel's drive orientation, Rogers' self-realization, J. P. Guilford's factor analysis, and an integration of several outlooks into a single theory by A. H. Koestler.

"Openness to experience," "permissive conditions," "minimal structuring" and the like are concepts that are not limited to discussions of self in teaching; they are also emphasized as one looks at teaching as an art. The next chapter presents some considerations important to an art of teaching.

References

1. Anderson, Harold E. (ed.), *Creativity and Its Cultivation*. Harper & Row, Publishers, 1959.
2. Bills, Robert E., "Believing and Behaving: Perception and Learning," *Learning More About Learning*. Association for Supervision and Curriculum Development, National Education Association, 1959.
3. Bruner, Jerome S., "The Act of Discovery," *Harvard Educational Review*, Vol. 31, No. 1, Winter 1961, 21–32.
4. Combs, Arthur, *The Professional Education of Teachers: A Perceptual View of Teacher Preparation*. Boston, Allyn and Bacon, Inc., 1965.
5. ———, and D. W. Soper, "The Helping Relationship as Described by 'Good' and 'Poor' Teachers," *Jl. Tchr. Educ.*, Vol. 14, 14, 64–68.
6. Dewey, John, *How We Think: A Restatement of the Relation of Reflective Thinking in the Education Process*. Boston, D. C. Heath and Company, 1933.

7. Dow, A. B., "An Architect's Views on Creativity," *Creativity and Its Cultivation*, Harold Anderson (ed.). New York, Harper and Bros., 1959.
8. Getzels, J. W., "Creative Thinking, Problem-Solving and Instruction," *Theories of Learning and Instruction*. The NSSE Yearbook, 1964.
9. ——, and Philip W. Jackson, *Creativity and Intelligence*. New York, John Wiley & Sons, Inc., 1962.
10. Ghiselin, Brewster (ed.), *The Creative Process: A Symposium*. New York, A Mentor Book, The New American Library, 1952.
11. Hamachek, Don E., *The Self in Growth, Teaching, and Learning*. Englewood Cliffs, N.J., Prentice-Hall, Inc., 1965.
12. Havighurst, Robert, *Developmental Tasks and Education*. New York, David McKay Company, Inc., 1966.
13. Hilgard, Ernest, *Theories of Learning*. New York, Appleton-Century-Crofts, 1948.
14. Hullfish, H. Gordon, and Philip G. Smith, *Reflective Thinking: The Method of Education*. New York, Dodd, Mead & Company, 1961.
15. Jersild, Arthur T., *When Teachers Face Themselves*. New York, Teachers College, Columbia University Press, 1955.
16. Kneller, George F., *The Art and Science of Creativity*. New York, Holt, Rinehart and Winston, Inc., 1965.
17. Koestler, A. H., *The Act of Creation*. New York, The Macmillan Company, 1964.
18. Kubie, Lawrence S., *Neurotic Distortion of the Creative Process*. Lawrence, Kans., University of Kansas Press, 1958.
19. Lynch, W. W., "Person Perception: Its Role and Working Climate," *Indiana University School of Education Bulletin*, Vol. 37, 1–37.
20. Maslow, Abraham H., "Cognition of Being in the Peak Experiences," *Jl. Genet. Psychol.*, Vol. 94, 43–66.
21. Massialas, Byron, and C. Benjamin Cox, *Inquiry in the Social Studies*. New York, McGraw-Hill, Inc., 1966.
22. ——, and Jack Zevin, *Creative Encounters in the Classroom—Teaching and Learning Through Discovery*. New York, John Wiley & Sons, Inc., 1967.
23. Mearns, Hughes, *Creative Power: The Education of Youth in the Creative Arts*. New York, Dover Publications, Inc., 1958.
24. Menninger, William C., "Self-understanding for Teachers," *NEA Journal*, Vol. 42, September, 331–333.
25. Miehl, Alice, *Creativity in Teaching: Invitations and Instances*. Belmont, Calif., Wadsworth Publishing Company, 1961.
26. Osborn, Alex F., *Applied Imagination*. New York, Charles Scribner's Sons, 1963.
27. Parnes, Sidney J., *Instructor's Manual for Semester Courses in Creative Problem-Solving*, rev. ed. Buffalo, N.Y., Creative Education Foundation, 1963.
28. ——, *Student Workbook for Creative Problem-Solving Courses and Institutes*, rev. ed. Buffalo, N.Y., State University of New York, Bookstore, 1963.

29. Rogers, Carl, "Current Assumptions in Graduate Education: A Passionate Statement," *Freedom to Learn.* Columbus, Ohio, Charles E. Merrill Publishing Company, 1969, 169–187.

30. ———, "The Necessary and Sufficient Conditions of Therapeutic Personality Change," *Jl. Consult. Psychol.*, Vol. 21, April, 95–103.

31. ———, "Toward a Theory of Creativity," *A Source Book for Creative Thinking*, Sidney J. Parnes and Harold F. Harding (eds.). New York, Charles Scribner's Sons, 1962.

32. Rugg, Harold, *Imagination: An Inquiry Into the Sources and Conditions That Stimulate Creativity.* New York, Harper & Row, Publishers, 1963.

33. Schachtel, Ernest G., *Metamorphosis.* New York, Basic Books, 1959.

34. Smith, James, *Setting Conditions for Creative Teaching in the Elementary School.* Boston, Allyn and Bacon, Inc., 1966.

35. Snygg, Donald, "The Need for a Phenomenological System of Psychology," *Psychol. Rev.*, Vol. 48, 404–424.

36. ———, and Arthur W. Combs, *Individual Behavior.* New York, Harper & Row, Publishers, 1949.

37. Soper, D. W., and A. W. Combs, "The Helping Relationship as Seen by Teachers and Therapists," *Jl. Consult. Psychol.*, Vol. 26, 288.

38. Stoddard, George, "Creativity in Education," *Creativity and Its Cultivation*, Harold Anderson (ed.). New York, Harper and Brothers, 1959.

39. Suchman, J. R., *Developing Inquiry.* Chicago, Science Research Associates, 1966.

40. ———, *The Elementary School Training Program in Scientific Inquiry* (USOE Title VII Proj. No. 216.) Urbana, Ill., University of Illinois, January 1964.

41. ———, "In Pursuit of Meaning," *The Instructor*, Vol. 75 (September 1965).

42. ———, "Inquiry Development Program in Physical Science." Chicago, Science Research Associates (a kit).

43. ———, "Inquiry in the Curriculum," *The Instructor*, Vol. 75 (January 1966).

44. ———, "The Role of the Teacher," *The Instructor*, Vol. 75 (December 1965).

45. Taylor, Calvin, *Creativity: Progress and Potential.* New York, McGraw-Hill, Inc., 1964.

46. Thelen, Herbart A., "Classroom Quiddities for Teachers," *Readings in Human Development*, Harold W. Bernard and Wesley C. Huckins (eds.). Boston, Allyn and Bacon, Inc., 1967.

47. Torrance, E. Paul, "Education and Creativity," *Creativity: Progress and Potential*, Calvin Taylor (ed.). New York, McGraw-Hill, Inc., 1964.

48. ———, *Guiding Creative Talent.* Englewood Cliffs, N.J., Prentice-Hall, Inc., 1962.

49. ———, *Rewarding Creative Behavior.* Englewood Cliffs, N.J., Prentice-Hall, Inc., 1965.

50. Verduin, John R., Jr., *Conceptual Models in Teacher Education: An Approach to Teaching and Learning.* Washington, D.C., American Association of Colleges for Teacher Education, 1967.

8

Teaching as an Art

Whether for good or for ill, many sincere people have long believed that teaching is an art, that teachers are born not made, and that a teacher either has it or he hasn't. "Methods" courses have been storm centers of controversy, partly because they presumably can not promote growth in teaching ability, and partly because they usually amount to little more than discussions of trivia, rather than being attempts to study instructional processes systematically. This is one implication of the meaning of art, a hodge-podge, often a random set of procedures that defy orderly description, and that range from inept fumbling to inspired and inspiring aids to learning.

But there is another school of thought about art in teaching. It maintains that art represents a kind of pinnacle, to be achieved after science has provided a minimal common base. This is the orientation that admits that science is necessary, so that most teachers may acquire the basics and thereby reach the lowest acceptable level of proficiency. Others will go beyond this, however—those who not only utilize the tools provided by science, but will explore new forms and teach creatively, uniquely, and

199

with what the mathematicians might call "elegant solutions." The relationship is well expressed by Silberman (1966):

> To be sure, teaching—like the practice of medicine—is very much an art, which is to say, it calls for the exercise of talent and creativity. But like medicine, it is also—or should be—a science, for it involves a repertoire of techniques, procedures and skills that can be systematically studied and described, and therefore transmitted and improved. The great teacher, like the great doctor, is the one who adds creativity and inspiration to that basic repertoire. (p. 19)

Contrariwise, Gilbert Highet (1950) represents those who believe that an art of teaching and a science of teaching are incompatible. Excellence in teaching is not merely the practice of an art that has its base in scientific procedures and has moved beyond. He likens scientific teaching to inducing a chemical reaction and feels that teaching more nearly resembles the processes involved in painting a picture or composing music. The use of formulas will spoil the work of both teacher and pupils. Science prides itself on the ability of its findings to withstand *public* scrutiny, on the repeatability of its procedures, and even on its reaction to constructive criticism. But George G. Stern (1963) says, "The art of teaching lies . . . in the communication and projection of an essentially *private* experience" (p. 398).

Despite Highet's apparent antithesis to some methods and aims of science, however, he is not averse to applying systematic explorations in order to determine the generalities or principles for teaching well; in fact, he calls his book "a book on the methods of teaching" (p. vii). Perhaps the discussion of creativity might have been more appropriately assigned to this chapter, for virtually every writer who treats on the art of teaching also has much to say about its creative component. But the confessedly creative teacher is likely to view teaching as both a science and an art. He will take the new knowledge, skills, and materials provided by the science in education and find new and practical ways to put them to use in the classroom. He creates the optimum conditions for learning in his own way, with his own resources and materials, with his group of children, and creates his own work of art.

Highet is also in agreement with Smith (1966) that creative teaching may be carried out in connection with the lower levels of learning—Smith says that creative teaching may be found at any level from nursery school through college. The necessary methods, materials, and new approaches to teaching acts, and the techniques and devices for measuring developing creativity are not yet at hand. But the possibility exists for creativity in teaching for every teacher. This possibility is not likely to be realized, however, so long as the usual approach in teacher training prevails. Trainees are taught what is supposedly known about teaching (which really amounts, sometimes, to teaching about what is *not* known). For example, they may not learn well the difference between *research in methodology* and *opinion about methodology*. To bring about the necessary changes in the teaching population, both those who are now teaching and those who are preparing ought to develop creative concepts. Too often there is insufficient matching of creativity in the cooperating teacher and the student teacher. Smith feels that teachers who are to develop creativity must be concerned with its conditions, with a multiplicity of skills, with problem-solving approaches, and with open-ended experiences in each curriculum area. A desirable physical, emotional, social, and intellectual environment sets the conditions for creativity. When several skills are taught simultaneously, preferably through demonstration and in meaningful situations (multiple associations), children are more likely to utilize these skills creatively. Facts must necessarily be learned, but they are given added meaning when they can be used in problem-solving situations. Learning should move toward divergent and open-ended ways of creative problem solving. The breadth and scope of these suggestions has led opponents to point out that too little is actually specified. However, a few, such as Highet, Smith, and Torrance, have attempted to specify and to elaborate in order to make the art of teaching amenable to being teachable.

HIGHET'S ART OF TEACHING

Chapter III of Gilbert Highet's *The Art of Teaching* deals with the teacher's methods, and his concern is most pertinent at this point. How does the teacher prepare? How does he communicate? How is the impression made by his communications fixed, given a permanence so as not to be merely fleeting?

Preparation

The trouble with the preparation stage of some teachers is that they are too shortsighted. They may plan well for a period of a day or two, or even for a week, but beyond that the semester lies only dimly ahead. Two types of teachers tend to exhibit this shortsightedness about preparation —the first loves certain details of his subject matter so well that he gets mired down in them, revels in them, and even inspires his students about them—but he never permits his students a glimpse of the whole forest because they are so delightedly examining the individual trees! Some subject matters are never really appreciated unless certain entire segments have been examined at least as an overview. The second type of teacher is simply inept. He plays it by ear to such an extent that he never really knows where he and his class are headed. He may suddenly awaken to the realization that the semester is nearly over, and he has not quite gotten off the ground. Whichever type of teacher the shortsighted one is, he usually fails to aid student learning by establishing a sense of purpose. The teacher's own example, making clear his foresight and coordination, helps pupils learn that accumulation and planning are evidences of strength.

Planning may be shared with the class, explaining, reminding, and summarizing in connection with the plans. The degree to which pupils may themselves share in planning depends on their degree of maturity, and Highet feels that pupils are more likely to make short-range plans than long-term ones. In order to reduce the tedium involved when pupils are simply told that their assignment is to cover a given number of pages in a textbook, it is suggested that a summary be provided before the subject matter is covered. The summary may be in the form of a concise outline, it can consist of a short talk by the teacher about things to come, or it may simply be a list of main headings. It will also help clarify the path that learning should follow if teachers occasionally pause to probe for significance, and to help pupils establish connecting links that relate the various discussions and bits and pieces of information that they pick up. Occasional pauses for reflection—to relish what has been found out, to form a gel—may make a joyous experience out of what would otherwise become an act of drudgery. (Piaget applied the term *assimilation* to the behavior of the young child as he takes in and incorporates what he perceives in terms of what he knows and understands. It has been recently noted that older persons take more time in the assimilation of novel ideas, not necessarily because they are slow witted, but because they have accumulated a greater background of knowledge into which new knowledge must be assimilated.)

Highet provides a number of case studies to illustrate his points, and poses illustrations in connection with specific subject matters. For example, if the objective is to instill a taste for music, this objective might be accomplished by requiring students to read the score of all Beethoven symphonies and to transpose several pages three times a week for a year. They might also be asked to develop Beethoven's idea of the symphony without having discussed the themes) and so on. This way of "teaching" would certainly impose high standards, and some students would remember some of Beethoven's symphonies and acquire some skill in transposing, but many would also acquire a distaste for music. There is a more pleasant prospect. First, reduce the amount of reading and increase the quantity of explanatory lectures and discussions. The teaching would also be varied so as to minimize boredom. Finally, the subject matter would be handled in such a way as to be conceived of as an intellectual and artistic whole, not merely a lot of unfamiliar words to be translated and scanned. The teacher who adopted this improved manner of teaching would also need to resist the tendency to become too superficial. What is desired is a balance between being too thorough—overdeveloping the few points covered—on the one hand, and being overly conscientious about a multitude of details on the other to the point of superficiality. Awareness of the dangers of either extreme position will help the teacher to escape or avoid them.

Highet mentions another reason for lack of adequate planning by teachers. Many become ditherers, sometimes because the nature of their jobs is not demanding in the sense that they must accurately account for expenditures and returns. (It may also be true that many persons seek out a profession in which they are not so accountable.) The plea here is for the utilization of willpower on the part of teachers, to tidy up their working habits so that they may prepare their course work and stick to a plan they have worked out. It is much simpler, and easier, just to face the class and start talking. However, for most, the questions ought to be raised: "Is this useful to my students?" "Is it likely to be clear to them in the absence of illustrations?" "Is it something that they can be reasonably expected to know?" If no stage is set, if the class gets no introduction to the remarks that the teacher is making, then the seeming disorganization of content will be discouraging to many pupils.

Suppose the inital preparation has been carefully worked out. Does this careful preparation then provide a file that may be used semester after semester, obviating further preparation? As Highet says "The monotony of selling insurance is its essence. Monotony in teaching is a fault" (p. 91). Teachers, for their own development as well as for the benefits to their pupils, should keep abreast of new discoveries and ideas related to their subjects. Very few subject matters remain inalterable, and even those that change very little may be approached in different ways and can be related to other fields. (Some that are relatively stable, in this sense, are mathematics and the inorganic sciences.) But how is the teacher to keep up? One suggestion, an obvious one, is that the literature, which virtually deluges the teacher, provides valuable sources, in the form of both books and periodicals. The word *sources* is emphasized, because the original is usually preferable to an interpretation.

Communication

Communication is the stage in which the teacher conveys his knowledge to his pupils. Even a poor scholar may benefit students if he can put across ideas well, but an excellent one may help them little if he cannot communicate. The first method of communicating mentioned by Highet is *lecturing*. Its purpose is to maintain a steady flow of information to pupils. However, he also includes under lecturing the use of working models and demonstrations. The second method is the *tutorial* system. The teacher talks very little and questions a lot so that the pupils will talk more. Questions function to make pupils conscious of their own ignorance and to guide them toward probing deeper into the topics taught. The third method involves the preparation of a lesson by the pupils so that they may listen intelligently to the teacher and then respond to the examining launched by the teacher and aimed at determining how well the material has been assimilated. "This is the standard way of teaching languages, literature, history and geography, and the descriptive sciences like botany" (p. 99).

Highet sees the three methods as having equal value, each one exerting its own particular force in differing situations. He therefore discusses the advantages and applications of each. Delivery is the most important aspect of public speaking, and it is also essential in school lecturing. (Clarity, optimal speed, change of pace, variations in volume, the well-considered use of pauses—all are topics that have been discussed at length elsewhere, so they will not be elaborated upon here.) How much of the lecture ought to be dictated, so that the hearers may copy, and how much should be merely talk? Common sense should come to the aid of the speaker: if he considers something important enough for the students to transcribe, then he should deliver at a pace that makes note taking possible. He should then make a clear distinction between the parts of the lecture that he expects the listeners to take down and those that merely serve to explain, illustrate, and suggest arguments. His voice, manner, and gestures will convey this. The lecturer must have planned his lecture not only as a series of utterances, but as a delivery plus its surroundings and situation.

Should lecture notes be sketchy or lengthy and detailed? A very skillful, well-informed speaker may be able to inspire his listeners with only a few written cues to aid him. However, if he does not deliver his ideas in any recognizable sequence, then listeners may follow only with difficulty, and note taking will be well nigh impossible. At the other extreme is the lecturer who merely reads from a book or prepared paper and seems to lose touch with his audience and reads to himself; the class or audience is just an undifferentiated mass.

Highet believes that an effective lecture ought to be given with the use of notes, but that they should be supplemented more or less informally. Salient points should be delivered slowly enough to allow listeners to copy them, and the connecting argument should be presented conversationally and more quickly than the main points.

> But the main danger in lecturing on this plan is not that one's notes will be sketchy. It is that, if one establishes real rapport with the class, one will become so interested in talking to them that one fails to make them remember what one is talking about. For unless a lecture leaves in the minds of the class a lasting result—a new interpretation of facts, a technique of experiment, a chain of argument—it is only a display of learning or of acting. They must be interested. Yes; and also they must be taught. (p. 117)

The voice can be used as a means of punctuating the lecture. Pauses; variations in speed, force, and incision; and the appropriate use of gestures —all tend to enrich the delivery and to avoid the danger of monotony and boredom. If a blackboard or an overhead projector is used to supplement the lecture, it should contain only the salient points, with each called to the attention of listeners, and then the lecturer should expand, explain, and qualify without returning to the board until the next point of importance is to be presented. Handouts serve a similar purpose. Highet believes that instructional television can be used as a lecture form that should be carefully worked out in advance to combine a personal interest provided by the teacher's voice, face, and personality with the illustrations and demonstrations picked up and transmitted by different cameras, and with key phrases displayed so as to capture and hold the audience's attention.

The second method of communicating, the *tutorial*, is viewed as the least common and the most thorough way to teach. Its essence is the critical method and the positive purpose. The critical method consists of conversation that leads to the exposing of areas of the pupil's ignorance. The positive purpose is to steer the pupil toward those truths known by the teacher, or by the sources at his command. The system is difficult because it requires background knowledge, alertness, good humor, earnestness, and the submerging of self-interests in the interest of truth. The great disadvantage of the system is that it requires the expenditure of a great deal of time and money—it is less expensive to teach groups, using only a few teachers, and it takes less time. The tutorial method also takes a great deal of energy because of the constant questioning, answering, attacking, and defending, and because of the directing of efforts toward a constructive end. It is also difficult to shift from an intense tutorial session to some other mode of intellectual pursuit. However, the drain on the teacher is largely compensated for by the results obtained. The tutor establishes a relationship with the pupil that is so close as to predispose students to emulate the tutor. If the tutor actually plays down his own originality and does not use it with full power, he may meet this situation before it becomes harmful.

> Very few of its products will write, as Logan Pearsal Smith does in his autobiography, that it is "an intolerable waste of fine material" for first-class brains to be employed on tutoring half-baked youths when they might have been making their own mark in the world. But that is a proof of the success of the tutorial method. For, as I said, it is based on the principle that *education is the art of drawing out what is already within the pupil's mind.* (italics added—p. 125)

In the tutorial method, the student learns from

1. Doing his work alone.
2. Observing the mistakes he has made and defending himself on points wherein he believes he is right.
3. Examining his completed, corrected work and comparing it with his first efforts.

Highet referred to these steps as *creation, criticism,* and *appreciation of wholeness.* The tutor at his best integrates all three into a larger system.

The tutorial system is used at Oxford and Cambridge and has been tried at Harvard. Graduate schools use a quasi-tutorial system in which professors tutor graduate students on theses and in seminars, wherein, in a sense, each member of the small group acts as both pupil and tutor. Occasionally, in elementary schools. pupils from higher grades are called in to help pupils in lower grades, but technically this is hardly tutoring, which in depth and value has been symbolized in this country in the oft-quoted phrase "a pine bench, with Mark Hopkins at one end of it and me at the other, is good enough for me!" (James A. Garfield, speech, Dec. 28, 1871).

The third method of communicating, and the most common one, is that of classroom work. It consists mostly of repetition, discussion, recitation, and memory work. The teacher gives assignments, asks questions, and then explains, fills in gaps, points out, requires practice and repetition, and uses various means to ensure that students have done the assigned work. But the teacher's real job is that of *helping* pupils learn, not *making* them learn.

Written examinations are the most popular means of determining whether pupils have prepared, and/or have profited by classroom attendance. Highet said that machinelike examination systems, exemplified by the "objective" question, are merely of convenience for the teacher. "A test entirely composed of such questions must fatally alter the student's attitude to the work he is doing: because he must, for the purposes of the test, see it as a congeries of unrelated little facts." (p. 135). The student has his attention shifted away from broader questions and from a sense of structure toward atomic facts that can be learned without real knowledge and real education. (This concept assumes, of course, that testing itself is a powerful teaching device, or a shaper of attitudes.) The suggestion is that some form of essay examination should be used and that it should be scored by several judges who have definite criteria established. As to the frequency of testing, Highet did not believe in daily testing—once a week is enough. However, each pupil's skills should be noted each day via some kind of probing. If deficiencies are uncovered, something can be done about them, and positive, creative effort can be encouraged. One should simply assume that the class has tried to learn the facts, then develop discussions that will more completely integrate the new ideas, make them more vivid, and reveal their significance in relation to other ideas.

A problem should be written down, probably on the blackboard. Then partial solutions should be recorded as suggested by class members. Finally, students should be helped to understand the solution by arranging the problem and its solution in a clear, logical scheme. These are not merely helpful directives to the teacher, but they will tend to rub off on pupils, so that they too will begin to organize their thinking in this way. "They will jump the gap between memorizing and creative thinking" (p. 146).

Highet spoke of competition as being a natural instinct in the young. Because vigorous competition can be observed in playing, and in the activities of adults, it is so generally practiced as to be natural. The Jesuits, in the sixteenth and seventeenth centuries, made good use of competition. Pupil-to-pupil and group-to-group competitions produced some astonishing feats of memory. (We are not told what happened to the losers, or whether there were any admitted to the competition or even to the schooling who might have been overwhelmed by the competition.) Competition seems to be seen as a stimulus for those who can compete zestfully.

The force of tradition may work for the teacher, but it is difficult to control, analyze, or activate. Many great men have been products of great schools. How can tradition be used to make ordinary boys into outstanding men? Highet mentioned five possibilities:

1. *Encouragement.* The students who enter a school that has produced famous men may realize that the wise expenditure of their own faculties could result in their achieving distinguished careers themselves.

2. *A range of possibilities.* The student learns, via tradition, about who the leaders of men are and about the various ways of achieving prominence, and he is furnished with models that he may wish either to emulate or reject, but that are likely to provide him with accurate, not distorted, examples.

3. *A sense of order.* Human living should be a matter of organization, yet many persons are never really aware of the significance of a sense of order. Tradition can induce a sense of order. As a contrast to well-ordered schools, Highet's description of "ordinary schools" fits a great many that may be visited today.

In ordinary schools, however, this sense of order is much harder to attain. Each generation seems to live for itself alone. Time, which is one of the essential frames of human life, scarcely exists. The organization of the school itself, and of the educational and political system to which it belongs, does not mean very much to the pupils. It looks, not like a way to help them to live better, but like a clumsy device to keep them from living as they want to. At best, going to school is only a channel to "getting a job." At worst, it is a trap. (p. 156)

4. A school with a tradition of the desirable sort being described by Highet teaches *responsibility*. A school designed like a factory receives its students, stamps them, and then spews them out. It is unlikely that any strong sense of responsibility will be produced. Mind and character need the nourishment furnished by the school, and a school with tradition is more likely to furnish the necessary nourishment. This is not to say that all schools with old traditions will provide the best environments. Traditional schools also harbor some teachers who ought to be in other kinds of institutions.

5. *Challenge* is also furnished by a school with tradition. The models furnished by the great men who have preceded them are apt to bring out the best that is in students. The present generation may profit not only from the successes but from the failures of great men. To err may be human, but it is not always necessary to repeat the failures of others to learn from them. Nor is it required that successes achieved come in unbroken succession. Not dutiful imitation, then, but progress through successful rivalry with the past is the possibility provided by challenge in a traditional school.

Along with tradition and competition, *punishment* may act as a stimulus. The punishment may range from reproof following a behavioral error to more severe forms. A useful kind of punishment is to require the repetition, correctly, of work that has been poorly done. Another useful form of punishment is to withhold privileges. A single instance of making the punishment follow as a natural consequence of the crime may serve to change an individual remarkably, perhaps permanently. A child who has repeatedly disrupted the class may be forbidden to go on a desired field trip because he kept the rest of the class from learning about the subject-matter area of the trip.

Bringing in the parents may also be punishing, or it may result in reproof by the parents. Where a sense of order and responsibility already exists in the home, appeals to the parents may be made with some success. For other situations, it may actually be dangerous to let parents know of a misbehavior for they may loyally support the teacher by administering more punishment at home that may be extremely severe. The other extreme is one in which the parents encourage defiance of the teacher. Mere failure to learn, of course, ought not to be punished; such a condition calls for remedial teaching.

Fixing the Impression

Although communications make up a great deal of the semester or term activities, they do not represent the final process. Some teachers not only cover less than originally intended, but they do not leave time for reviewing and fixing the impressions that presumably have been made. Poor planning and inadequate command of the material may be causes of this failure. If a teacher is unable to recognize that the topic still is novel to pupils, so that they are still rather hazy about it, then he is likely to enable them to fix only a few impressions correctly. Good teachers are remembered because their pupils *remember* what was taught by them.

How does the impression become fixed? First, the teacher should *review*, not only re-covering the ground, but filling in gaps that will make the content more meaningful. Give the class increased time for *questioning* the teacher. *Offer help* before it is asked. (Use this sparingly with the very young, who are simply acquiring basics.) Highet admits that the three ways of fixing the impression may be somewhat artificial, and that a good teacher with a good class will hardly need to plan course completion in this way. Rather, he will explain briefly what he is doing, go over it with the students, and discuss the overview, with the students, of some of the areas that may be explored. Teaching then becomes a part of a joint enterprise, engaged in by friendly human beings who enjoy thinking.

MENTAL HEALTH AND CREATIVITY—INLOW

Such cooperation of a group of friendly humans is stressed by Inlow (1966), who developed the theme that each individual can move toward his own self-actualization even if he has rather limited capacities. The extent to which an individual achieves up to his own creative potential determines how creative he is. Creativity may therefore be expressed at various points along many dimensions, or along one, or not at all. (Inlow's idea of creativity is not necessarily related to a concrete product—it is concerned with one's capacity to relate to others with sensitivity, to think divergently, and to use imagination in dealing with people and ideas.) This position places great importance on the assumption that mental˙health is closely connected with creativity. Creativity, however, is capable of operating from a narrower base in the totality of life (as is testified to by the significant contributions of well-known creative artists who were maladjusted), whereas mental health spans life's entirety. If mental health and creativity are viewed as reciprocal, mutually dependent and mutually supportive, the attributes of a mentally healthy person are also found in descriptions of the creative individual:

1. relatively independent
2. attuned to reality
3. stands behind his actions
4. accepts himself
5. emergent
6. flexible
7. uncompartmentalized
8. relates well to others
9. basically satisfied
10. devoid of debilitating guilt
11. both present- and future-oriented
12. high tolerative level for frustration

(p. 71)

Thus, Inlow viewed education's role in creativity as an active, supportive one that ought to provide not only a narrow support of the few maladjusted students who happen also to be creative, but that ought also to foster mental health and creativity in all. Inlow felt that permissiveness, the allowance of room for doubt and error, and intensive rather than extensive treatments of subjects would characterize the creative teacher.

SCIENCE AND ART IN TEACHING

B. F. Skinner is one of the foremost men of science engaged in investigating learning and has also been one of the most vocal critics of teaching. He seems inclined to look upon teaching as an art and criticizes the present practice of that art in one of his early articles, which introduced the general public to the possibilities presented by programmed learning and teaching machines. In "The Science of Learning and the Art of Teaching" (1954, 1968), Skinner pointed out three notable shortcomings in teaching as usually practiced:

1. Educational control, until recently, has been aversive—the child acted to avoid or escape punishment, not because of frequent reinforcement.

2. The contingencies of reinforcement provided by the teacher were not adequately arranged—too much time elapsed between response and reinforcement. Too many other responses are reinforced meanwhile.

3. Skillful programs, moving via a series of successive approximation to the final behavior desired, have been conspicuously absent.

Thus, reinforcement was too sparingly used, poorly timed, and unsystematically applied.

Recent technological advances, however, have made the systematic use of reinforcement more likely, simply because the teacher can relegate many reinforcements to other arranging mechanisms. Automated devices and programs have increased the availability of reinforcers to students, reaching down to strengthen the responses of many who had seldom been reinforced before. How does all this effect the *art* of teaching? This talk of machines and programs sounds more like science. The teacher needs answers to questions such as: "What behavior is to be set up? What responses are available in embarking upon a program of progressive approximation which will lead to the final form of the behavior? How can reinforcements be most efficiently scheduled to maintain the behavior in strength?" (1968, p. 19). Do these sound like the questions that might be asked by those interested in teaching as an art? They do, if art is not thought of as a catch-as-catch-can, play-it-by-ear procedure, based upon minimal preparation, but rather as a scientifically based series of intelligently planned instructional situations made effective by means of the most advanced aids, techniques, strategies, and methods possible.

Skinner says that reinforcements are available in the material to be learned. For instance, when children play with toys, games, and objects, these acts may feed back significant changes in the environment that are relatively free of aversive properties, and that are likely to provide reinforcement. Wise use of even a small amount of reinforcement may be very effective—"The sheer control of nature is itself reinforcing" (1968, p. 20). But in case the nature of the task or the play is *not* very reinforcing, it may be furthered by other reinforcers. Competition is reinforcing to successful competitors but not to all children, especially not to those who compete poorly or to those who have high anxiety about competitive situations. The good will and affection of the teacher is usually sought by pupils and can be quite reinforcing to them.

As to how reinforcements can be made contingent upon the learning of the desired behavior, there are two major considerations.

1. If the desired behavior is broken up into a large number of small steps toward that behavior, and each step is reinforced, then progress is likely. The likelihood of failing and subsequent aversive feedback is reduced by the use of small steps, and the frequency of reinforcement is increased. (Teachers can now practice the art of providing frequent reinforcement as never before, using the various machines and programs to be discussed later in this book.)

2. Behavior can be maintained in strength by the utilizing of the knowledge of schedules of reinforcement.

Skinner's experiments have shown that once a given bit of behavior has been learned, it may then be maintained by intermittent, occasional reinforcement. Thus, automated or programmed means might be used to establish certain learnings, according to the suggestion in (1), and then the teacher could provide intermittent praise and other reinforcers to enable the student to retain what was learned. Teachers cannot effectively provide the frequency of reinforcing contingencies necessary in novel learning without help, however:

> We have every reason to expect, therefore, that the most effective control of human learning will require instrumental aid. The simple fact is that, as a mere reinforcing mechanism, the teacher is out of date. This would be true even if a single teacher devoted all her time to a single child, but her inadequacy is multiplied many-fold when she must serve as a reinforcing device to many children at once. If the teacher is to take advantage of recent

advances in the study of learning, she must have the help of mechanical devices. (1968, p. 22)

With this help, the teacher can exercise other functions than saying, "Right," or "Wrong." The help given by new instruments consists of their ability to improve the relations between the teacher and the pupil, as well as in its chore work. The teacher need no longer carry out the merely mechanical functions—he may function according to those factors that make him distinctively human; he may increase and improve his intellectual, cultural, and emotional contacts.

Science, by its insistent search for the relevant variables that influence learning, can provide some minimal bases for teachers. Not all the reports are as pessimistic as the Stephens book (1967) and the Coleman report (1966). N. L. Gage, for example, in a recent article, "Can Science Contribute to the Art of Teaching?" (1968), concluded that research has provided some dimensions that may be accepted as general. Ryans (1960) found that observers rated teachers "good" according to three teacher-behavior patterns:

1. Warm, understanding, and friendly—rather than aloof, egocentric, and restricted.
2. Responsible, businesslike, and systematic—rather than evading, unplanned, and slipshod.
3. Stimulating and imaginative—rather than dull and routine.

And Gage felt it safe to assume that a reasonable use of the guided discovery method, or indirectness, in teaching is desirable. Of course teachers should acquire a good intellectual grasp of what they are to teach. Skinner's suggestions concerning the three Ryans criteria may be readily found in the discussions of Ryans and Gage. In order to exercise the warm, friendly, and understanding facets of his personality, a teacher needs to be freed of routine custodial and clerical work. Being responsible, businesslike, and systematic is easier, when media and programs are available to improve instructional efficiency. Being stimulating and releasing the imagination are most likely when learning proceeds easily and without pressure. As to whether science can contribute to the art of teaching, Gage concluded; "The faith persists that educationally significant differences can be consistently produced in the future as new intellectual and material resources are brought to bear on educational problems" (1968, p. 403).

SYSTEMATIZING CREATIVE
PROBLEM-SOLVING—SYNECTICS

The viewpoint that creativity can only be stimulated and not subjected to orderly procedures without restricting its freedom is losing ground. The new *Journal of Creative Behavior* includes, among other forward-looking ideas, a description of a set of procedures called *synectics*. It is generally assumed that most normal persons have on days, times during which they are not only more productive, but they think with greater clarity, and, occasionally, with originality. Synectics, as a discipline, attempts to teach people to imitate such on days whenever they desire. Certain operational mechanisms are brought to bear so that one need not wait for their fortuitous occurrence.

Synectics, then, is a structured approach to creative problem-solving. The purpose of the methodology is to provide the individual with a repeatable procedure which will increase the probability of his success and hasten his arrival at an innovative solution. (Prince, 1967, p. 4)

A strange situation or a strange concept is likely to be perceived as threatening to varying degrees, and a human being, ordinarily a conservative organism, is likely to force whatever is strange into some acceptable pattern. Or he may restructure his own cognitions in such a way as to accommodate a strange pattern. This form of adaptation to the strange in one's environment utilizes analysis, generalization, and a comparing process called *analogy* or *model seeking*. In thinking via analogy, one may ask, "What in my knowledge or experience is analogous (similar to) this?" An analysis of the strange data into parts and significant patterns makes it possible to locate a comparable model from individual experience. Once this analysis is accomplished, the strangeness takes on the aspects of familiarity.

Synectics applies two opposite techniques. The first, as in the above description, is to make the strange familiar via analysis, generalization, and analogy. The second technique is to make the familiar strange, to be perceived in some distorted fashion, so that it is upended, transposed, seen from an unusual angle. Thus, the familiar becomes fertile ground for novelty, and a fresh appreciation is gained of what had heretofore been merely accepted as a matter of fact.

The conscious production of on periods is begun by the construction of a flow chart, a means of diagramming the mechanisms of synectics.

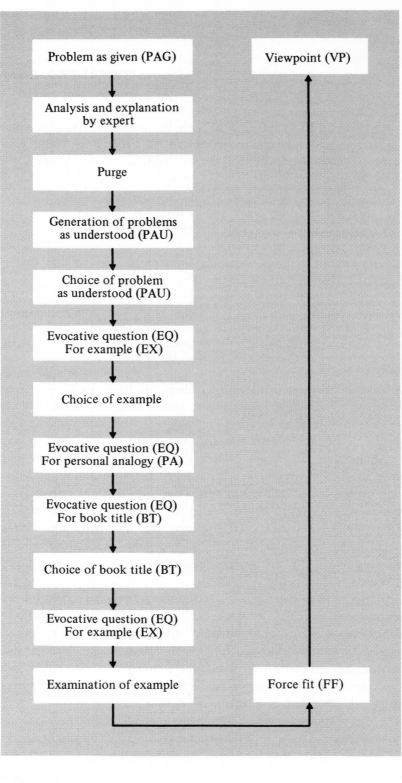

Then group sessions are arranged. But the function of the group leader is quite different from that of the usual head of a group. He is simply a person who tries to keep the problem (or production) within the guidelines provided by the flow chart. He does not act as a judge of the contributions made by each group member, nor does he act as a mediator between contributions that are in disagreement. However, he is supposed to help generate, develop, and use analogies efficiently. His will be the decision to use or not to use certain analogies. He uses evocative questions, which bridge the gap between analysis and analogy. The synectics flow chart is reproduced in Figure 8.1.

The Problem as Given (PAG)

The problem to be solved may have been furnished from an outside source, and it may have arisen in the group. At any rate as it is originally expressed, unaltered, it is designated as the problem as given.

Analysis

In order to make the strange problem familiar, an expert in the problem area explains it. The explanation should be given with enough detail so that the problem may be understood by all in the group. However, because the expert is to remain a member of the group, he need not try to make everyone as knowledgeable about the problem as he is.

Purge

Immediate solutions of various sorts are usually suggested by group members. It seems to be constructive to encourage people to air their immediate solutions. If the solutions are poor the expert will be in a position to explain why they won't work, and each member will thereby understand the problem better.

Problem as Understood (PAU)

After the PAG has been explained and the purge has occurred, each participant then writes a statement of the problem as he now sees it

Fig. 8.1. Synectics Flow Chart. (From George M. Prince, "The Operational Mechanism of Synectics," *Journal of Creative Behavior*, Vol. 2, No. 1, Winter 1968.)

or describes a goal he believes would be a desirable one. The participants are encouraged to suggest anything they can imagine, even if it violates laws they know hold true.

Evocative Question (EQ)

An evocative question requires an answer that is in the form of an analogy or a metaphor. Three different kinds of analogy are therefore produced. The first, *Example,* is the Direct Analogy, in which the actual comparison of parallel facts, knowledge, or technology is described. The participant who is answering searches his experiences and knowledge for something that is like the subject at hand or that has some familiar relationship to it. *Personal Analogy* is used when a member says something like "If I were he . . ." When the problem is people-oriented rather than technical, role playing serves as a rudimentary aid. The participant identifies himself with a hypothetical person in a given situation and speculates on how he would feel and act. However, identification is carried to the extreme in Synectics. One's identification may be with a purely nonhuman entity that is important to the problem, and one therefore invests this entity with his own vitality. He speculates on how this thing would "feel" and act in the problem situation. This is a valuable tool for making the familiar strange. A *Book Title* (Symbolic Analogy) is a statement of the implications of a key word from the Problem as Understood, or which has some connection with the problem, and the statement is made in a highly compressed, almost poetic form. The key word is selected and then one of the group members is asked for the essence of its meaning. Subjective meaning is stressed, so that the person responding empathizes or feels for the important connotations of the word as it appears to him. Next, he tries to put these feelings into one or two words. Such words are more useful if they are quite general and all-encompassing, because they are to be used in suggesting areas for speculation. A few Book Titles, for example, could be *Ratchet, Viscosity, Hesitant Displacement,* and *Balanced Confusion.* It may be difficult for the reader to make the connections between the analogy and its subject in some of these titles, and this is principally because each title or Symbolic Analogy is based on someone else's view of the key word and its implications. But a Book Title should require some psychological strain for its understanding. It may even need to be surprising, or to embrace an apparent paradox, in order for it to become *strange* enough to be useful. *Involuntary Willingness* as a title involves a paradox that must be resolved, and its resolution brings out insights.

Examination

A selected Example (a parallel from personal experience) is factually examined to produce both descriptive facts about the Example and super facts, statements that are speculative and strange.

Force Fit

Analogical mechanisms are actually the heart of synectics, and these are force fitted to the problem at hand. The problem is stretched and pulled and refocused so that it is seen in a new way. It is a deliberate attempt to find relevance in apparent irrelevance. If one analogy merely leads to another and to still another, then potentially fruitful possibilities will be cast aside. New contexts are suggested by a Force Fit, so that the raw material for new lines of speculation is provided.

Viewpoint

Synectics gathers its strength from its locating strange angles from which to view the familiar facts of a problem. During the Examination, a useful but strange Example may emerge that suggests many different potential solutions or viewpoints. The usual problem-solving procedure is aimed at seeking solutions, whereas synectics seeks new lines of speculation. These new lines then lead to potential solutions by means of the Force Fit. The odd angle, the novel viewpoint gives the problem solver a different place to stand and exercise emerging powers.

Excursion

Excursion is a term describing the Synectics procedure as it moves from the choice of Problem as Understood through the Force Fit, or the point where the analogies are fitted into the problem, even though this stretching may appear to be so distorting as not to be useful. If no new Viewpoint has been developed, then the procedure, beginning with the Problem as Understood, must be begun again. This time around (new Excursion), there may be new Examples located for an original Evocative Question, or for a new one. The Force Fit itself may uncover a new aspect of the problem, so that a new Problem as Understood can be stated.

In a typical Synectics session, someone who already knows a great deal about a given problem area may present a problem that has not yet been successfully dealt with by his associates or by anyone working at his speciality. Such a problem requires creative problem-solving, because the usual procedures in problem solving have not resulted in a satisfactory solution. Prince provided this example:

Problem as Given. How can the oil saturation in an underground reservoir be determined? The expert fills in some details about difficulties in solving this problem, that is, he makes an *Analysis.* He explains that it is quite difficult to obtain a sample from the reservoir that will be truly representative of the reservoir. A drill pipe may be lowered with a hollow bit on it, so as to cut out a piece of the rock in the reservoir. This core is then brought to the surface and a guess is made as to how representative it is of the oil reservoir. Even if the core has been chosen at just the spot that will make it representative of the entire reservoir, the fact that it is brought from a great depth, has been under great pressure, and must be brought up through six or seven thousand feet of muddy water with the pressure now released, makes the core considerably different from what it was when it was thousands of feet below ground. But it is necessary that oilmen be able to estimate how much oil is in a core as it was when below ground, so that they can form a more accurate opinion as to how much oil reserve lies in the reservoir beneath them.

After this Analysis, no Purges were made for this session. Two different understandings of the problem (PAU's) were presented:

1. We need to determine how to make the reservoir rock tell us the true amount of oil saturation. The leader did not consider this understanding of the problem to have as much value as the second.
2. How can we make the oil tell how crowded it is in the reservoir rock? (Crowdedness has to do with the degree of saturation.)

After choosing the second PAU, the leader then asked the group to put the problem out of their minds. The leader's next step was to provide an Evocative Question that called for an Example of a crowded situation in some other field. He asked for an Example from Biology, and several suggestions of crowding in Biology were given. The leader finally decided that a virus culture gave a good Example of crowding. Now the group members were to try to put themselves into the place of a virus

—to actually feel like one. The leader asked how they felt, at this Personal Analogy stage. They discussed how they felt, and the leader then asked for a Symbolic Analogy or Book Title—a key expression that compresses the feelings of individuals who are making the Personal Analogy. After several offerings, the leader suggested they try one offered that was titled *Compulsive Indifference.*

The Evocative Question for this paradox asked for an Example from nature of compulsive indifference. Someone suggested *cat.* After some discussion about cats, the leader asked how the idea of a cat could be used to help have the oil tell how crowded (the degree of saturation) it was in the original reservoir rock. This was the Force Fit phase. A group member said that a cat that is crowded loses its indifference and goes into a rage. The leader interpreted this as meaning that the oil could be crowded a little in some way, and then it would tell how crowded it was. More discussion ensued, and the leader asked how the oil could be calmed down. Now the expert stepped in and said that the oil needed to be stroked—to be chilled—to be cooled down. The leader replied that the oil could even be frozen, and the expert added that liquid nitrogen could be pumped into the reservoir to freeze the sample. Then, as the sample was brought up, it would be kept cold, retaining its original oil saturation. The expert decided that this was a new and worthwhile way to view the problem, so it was written up as a Viewpoint.

It is not expected that every Synectics session will result in excellent solutions. However, the central idea, that of departing from the usual ways of attacking the problem (because they have not yielded satisfactory results) and then relating the new and the known, has a long history. Highly creative individuals have proceeded in a similar manner. The contribution of Synectics, however, is that it makes it possible for individuals to systematically explore their thinking, without waiting for fortuitous occasions and/or thought patterns to occur.

References

1. Anderson, Robert H., *Teaching in a World of Change.* New York, Harcourt, Brace & World, Inc., 1966.
2. Coleman, J. S., et al., *Equality of Educational Opportunity.* Washington,

D.C., U.S. Dept. of Health, Education and Welfare, 1966. (Govt. Printing Office, Supt. Documents, Cat. #FS5-238:38001.)

3. Gage, N. L., "Can Science Contribute to the Art of Teaching?" *Phi Delta Kappan*, XLIX (March 1968), 399–403.

4. Highet, Gilbert, *The Art of Teaching*. New York, Alfred A. Knopf, Inc., 1950.

5. Inlow, Gail M., *The Emergent in Curriculum*. New York, John Wiley & Sons, Inc., 1966.

6. Prince, George M., "The Operational Mechanism of Synectics," *Jl. Creat. Behav.*, Vol. 2, No. 1 (Winter 1967), 1–13.

7. Ryans, D. G., "Characteristics of Teachers," Washington, D.C., American Council on Education, 1960.

8. Silberman, Charles F., "Teaching—Art or Science?" *Educational Technology*, Vol. VI (September 30, 1966), 19.

9. Skinner, B. F., "The Science of Learning and the Art of Teaching," *Current Trends in Psychology and the Behavioral Sciences*. Pittsburgh, Pa., University of Pittsburgh Press, 1954. (Also, *Technology of Teaching*. New York, Appleton-Century-Crofts, 1968.)

10. Smith, James A., *Setting Conditions for Creative Teaching in the Elementary School*. Boston, Allyn and Bacon, Inc., 1966.

11. Stephens, J. M., *The Process of Schooling*. New York, Holt, Rinehart and Winston, Inc., 1967.

12. Stern, George G., "Measuring Noncognitive Variables in Research on Teaching," *Handbook of Research on Teaching*, N. L. Gage (ed.). Chicago, Rand McNally & Company, 1963.

13. Torrance, E. P., *Guiding Creative Talent*. Englewood Cliffs, N.J., Prentice-Hall, Inc., 1962.

9

Technology and Teaching

THE MEANINGS OF *EDUCATIONAL TECHNOLOGY*

Educational technology is one of the catch phrases of the present time. It may be used as a scare technique for some, and as the promise of a panacea for others. Many people have a vague idea that it means something that has to do with machines, but beyond that their knowledge is limited. The January 15, 1968, issue of *Educational Technology* was devoted entirely to discussions of what *educational technology* means. Ely's definition is in the language of communication theory:

Educational technology is that branch of educational theory and practice concerned primarily with the design and use of messages which control the learning process. It undertakes (a) the study of the unique and relative strengths and weaknesses of both pictorial and non-representational messages which may be employed in the learning process for any purpose; and (b) the structuring and systematizing of messages by men and instruments in an educational environment. These undertakings include the planning, production, selection, management, and utilization of both components and entire instructional systems. Its practical goal is the efficient utilization of every method and medium of communication which can contribute to the development of the learner's full potential. (1968, p. 1)

This definition and the discussion that follows it represent Ely's view that educational technology has not simply been borrowed from other fields, but includes its own utilization of systematically organized principles. Although learning theory contributes to this technology, as do communications theory and system analysis, it is a special technology, a branch of education. The educational technologist is uniquely qualified to work with the teacher in the formulation of plans that will result in optimal learning. Ely admits that there are those who would prefer to use the term *facilitate* where he has used *control* in connection with the learning process, but he insists that the substitution would make the definition of *educational technology* more ambiguous. If design procedures are to be definitely specified, then the learning process must be controlled by the messages that are designed and used for that purpose.

Where does educational technology fit into the art-versus-science debate? It may be seen as a mediator, necessary for blending the science of learning with the art of teaching. When Skinner states that no teacher can provide the frequency of reinforcers or the necessary contingencies for optimal learning (and that a teacher needs machine aid for the job), he is in agreement with this view of the mediating role.

A Broader Meaning and
One That Is More Limited

Science and technology cannot very well be considered separately in education. If technology is to serve a blending function for a science of learning and an art of teaching, it may also be seen as an attempt to apply the science of education. Silverman (1968) called this viewpoint "constructive educational technology." Constructive educational technology is the basic educational application, dealing with

(1) the analysis of instructional problems;

(2) the selection or construction of measuring instruments needed to evaluate instructional outcomes; and

(3) the construction or selection of techniques or devices to produce the desired instructional outcomes. (p. 3)

Technology, defined in the constructive sense, is not a means that shapes the ends—it concentrates on the analysis, selection, and construction of whatever is necessary to meet educational needs. This kind of technology is also self-modifying, because it is responsive to developing needs. Inventive modifications and combinations of techniques emerge.

A second viewpoint on educational technology is called "relative technology" by Silverman. This is a borrowing, applying technology that merely deals with procedures and devices—it gathers materials. Obviously this second view is a more restricted one, for the technology here does not develop its own techniques and principles; it performs a rather simple service function in education.

Constructive technology has not yet been fully established as a discipline in its own right, a discipline that would find its place between the science of learning and applications in teaching problems. A constructive technologist would possess the characteristics of a behavioral scientist, an individual trained in some aspects of engineering as well as in education.

Unfortunately, many educators still cling to the tendency to define technology as the use of machines. As Silverman indicated, there must be an understanding of technology in the constructive sense—but Heinich (1968) calls for a commitment to the technological *process*. In a very broad sense, technology refers to the *systematic* application of knowledge to practical tasks, and the usual case is that this organized knowledge has been contributed by science. There must, therefore, be a systematic analysis of kinds of knowledge, and its relevance and its power in providing solutions in education. If machines happen to be useful in bringing about adequate applications, then machines are to be used—otherwise, the term *machine* need not be generally applied to discussions about technology. The instructional factor in education is of primary interest at the moment:

> As technology applies to instruction (the area of education which more specifically concerns me), any move toward analysis of curriculum into specific objectives and then devising means of achieving them is a step in the direction of technology. (Heinich, p. 4)

The Instructional Designer

Glaser (1968) predicts that educational technology will become a unique occupational speciality, dealing with instructional designs. Persons engaged in this speciality will be concerned with the production of educational procedures, with the materials to be used in instruction, and with systems. Specialists will be involved in research and development stemming from the knowledge provided by behavioral science, and the outcomes of their efforts will be fed back to the behavioral scientists.

In the early stages of experimentation, technologist and behaviorist were embodied in the same person. The discoverer was also the man who followed with applications of his discovery. Launor Carter (1966) found that in fifty-five of sixty-three research and development events, the person conceiving of the idea also was involved in carrying it out. But this instructional designer isn't likely to consist of a single individual —a team is more probable. There may be a specialist who prepares designs for teacher practices; another team member may deal with language and linguistics; yet another will be a specialist in computer systems, and so on. Because the era of carefully designed systems is only now emerging, a great deal of the projection is based on speculation, but Glaser has stated that the function of an instructional designer includes:

> Analysis of the subject matter area, with the specification of necessary performance competencies.
> a. What are the properties of the content?
> b. What is the nature of the responses the learner must make (memorizing, concept learning, application of principles, problem solving and so on)? And what kinds of students are to be learning—what background information do they have; what sets have been established; what aptitudes do they possess; and to what extent does what they already know act to facilitate or interfere with the new tasks?
> c. What teaching procedures and materials should be constructed? How can this be based upon known motivational effects, and upon abilities of learners to maintain and extend their competence in the knowledge or skill to be taught?
> d. How can the design provide for the evaluation of the competence and kind of knowledge achieved? (1968)

The instructional designer seems likely to occupy a position somewhere between that of teacher and that of student, a technologist whose status is somewhat analogous to that of the medical technologist who operates as a go-between for the physician and his patient.

The major concern of educational technology, then, is implementing desirable changes in learner behavior, just as it has been the major concern of educators for a long time. The great difference seems to lie in the fact that now as never before the locus of responsibility for student learning is viewed as residing in the teacher and in the teaching agents, rather than primarily in the student. If the student does not learn, he is no longer seen as lazy, indolent, or incapacitated by mental blocks, provided, of course, that he is intact. This represents a strong, optimistic, behavioristic point of view, that merely because a student has not learned does not mean that he cannot—it means that the proper learning conditions have not been provided.

Instructional design has increasingly moved not only toward improved ways of structuring the topics to be taught, but also toward the efficient use of media. Unfortunately, to many teachers, *media* means gadgets, either too impractical to be useful in their classrooms, or too esoteric to be comprehended. They fail to recognize that educational technology is a "science of the practical," to apply Humphrey's (1968) terminology. This practical science application extends not only directly to the media of instruction, but to the design of school buildings and complete learning systems. This extension is included in the definition provided by Unwin (1968):

> Educational Technology is concerned with the application of modern skills and techniques to requirements of education and training. This includes the facilitation of learning by manipulation of media and methods, and the control of environment in so far as this reflects on learning. (p. 12)

And he provided a timely warning when he said that if a technology is to function successfully in education, it should be simple and convenient; it should capture and maintain interest; and it should communicate well. Picture the teacher surrounded by electronic marvels, unable to determine which button to punch, which lever to throw, when to turn what on, and what each warning light signifies! Picture also the one who does know all these things, but who punches and throws, doing so simply because the controls are available. And pity the poor student, confronted by a response console, speaker-headset switch, audio-video selector, dial access and microphone, who is so bewildered by it all that he makes more engineering errors than subject matter errors! Fortunately, neither teachers nor students are quite faced with such problems, but the lesson to be learned from this is that facilitators ought to be simply operated.

What directions are to be taken, in the development of new media? Unwin made some predictions:

> Specifically, I expect to see cheaper and better multipurpose copying/transparency making machines; accelerating rationalization of video/audio software; the disappearance of the "teaching machine"; advances in micro-storage and information retrieval which will tend to keep CAI and DAIR out on a research limb; immense efforts to improve and indeed to under-

stand motivation, and in this connection I hazard a guess that Academic Gaming will be a notable growth area.

A final forecast: in five years time many of today's prophecies will still be prophecies. (p. 13)

Locke (1968) is another who is wary of the poorly considered distribution of "loose collections of related materials." Media should be designed and applied as components in a complete system, with each medium performing its particular function. And because it is not only important to teach children efficiently, but to provide for individual differences, each task or objective should be approached with alternative media that will accommodate differences in ability, experience, motivation, style, and rate of learning. Programmed instruction, for example, has already shown that different learning characteristics do match better with some kinds of media than with others.

Silvern (1968) said that whatever the definition of educational technology, education itself is a processing of information and an acquisition, identification, analysis, sorting, storage, retrieval, and transmission of information between teachers and learners. This means that education is a system and that sometimes books and hardware-software elements are included in that system. However, the typical educational environment does not evidence an awareness and a knowledge of the system as a cybernetic model. The application of cybernetics to education is a relatively recent development and is likely to make a tremendous impact. If educators move, not in the direction of analyzing the present situation and then applying patches, but with system objectives and the creation of a system designed to achieve those objectives, then education's face will achieve a new look.

Cybernetics

Guilbaud (1960) traced the meanings of cybernetics from the Greek *kybernētikē* through its acquisition, loss, and reinstatement of the connotation *governor*. By the time it had begun to be publicized, cybernetics had been interpreted as procedures dealing with thinking machines, robots, and so on. However, cybernetics is not now considered to be merely concerned with a theory of machines. The central association is that of self-guidance or self-regulation. The self-guidance of mechanisms, of people who guide machines, and of societies—each of these has been associated with cybernetics. Cybernetics has something in common with educational technology in that it acts as a mediator, borrowing from sciences, such as electronics, neurology, and sociology, in order to be applied in other fields, such as education. The principle of self-regulation includes the influence of the activated device's output applied in such a way as to guide the further action of the device. The term *servo-mechanism* is now rather commonly used to indicate a guiding influence that comes from the output of a device. For example, a thermostat opens or closes its contacts to regulate a heating system—the system heats, producing effects upon the air temperature, and this temperature in turn affects the thermostat, which shuts off the heat when it reaches a predetermined level. In humans, feedback, in the form of knowledge of the results of acting upon or in response to the environment, acts to regulate behavior.

Cybernetics and Education

One of the implications of cybernetics is that models may be constructed that may be useful in examining the ways in which humans think. "The analogy between a machine solving problems which human beings solve when they think is used to provide a model for what a man is doing when he is described as thinking" (Sluckin, 1960). Machines and humans obviously have a great many differences, but they are at least alike in that they are self-regulating.

Smith and Smith (1966) attempted to bridge the gap between experimental psychology in learning and applications in teaching. They see cybernetics as furnishing a general theory of behavior organization, one that differs from the usual type of learning theory. Each individual is a feedback system, originating activities that will detect and control environmental stimulus characteristics. Research conducted under this point of view is therefore concerned with how intrinsic control is established, and therefore with closed-loop sensory feedback mechanisms that mediate between the learner and his environment. This differs from most learning theory approaches in that the concern is not with external events as they occur in appropriate relationships in time, but with the nature of the feedback-control processes available to the learner. Maturation and learning are often viewed as separate entities or processes, but the cybernetics approach assumes that maturation and learning involve *interrelated* feedback mechanisms, and these mechanisms act to integrate, differentiate, and change responses. Thus, there is considerable emphasis upon somatic behavior as a regulator.

The preceding remarks require considerable explanation, and one way of clarifying the applications in education is to accept the cybernetics point of view as it applies to developmental psychology. Behavior may be specialized and integrated in different ways at different periods of development, and it may occur during different phases of adaptive and meaningful learning.

> A cybernetic approach to educational designs assumes at the outset that education is the applied science of human learning. It recognizes that learning proceeds in a developmental context wherein its course is defined not only by the general features of human design but also by the developmental progress of the particular individual. (p. 454)

Most educators are now familiar with the term *feedback*. The usual meaning is that of a process occurring in a closed-loop system—the individual gains knowledge of the results of his behaviors, or he undergoes some sensory consequence. By some means, something of the output of the individual is conveyed back to his input, that is, to his perceptions, or to his means of registering experience. B. F. Skinner's ideas in the psychology of reinforcement emphasize the importance of the effects of one's own behaviors upon learning, and hence they spotlight the importance of accurate and relatively immediate feedback. (The more immediate the feedback, the lower the probalility that other inputs may intervene and interfere with the learning.) Conventional psychologies of learning suggest that learning is defined by external events that occur in appropriate time relationships. According to cybernetics theory, learning and other aspects of behavior organization are primarily determined by the nature of the feedback-control processes that are available to the behaving person. To view humans as having at their disposal certain processes by which feedback is regulated is to view them as closed-loop systems. Ordinarily, learning theories do not consider human learning as occurring in a closed-loop system, but in an open-loop one. If the human does operate in a closed-loop system and is self-regulating, then two broad training principles are implied:

1. The individual at all ages should be aided in gaining control over his own actions in relation to the environment and over the environment.
2. The teaching of specific skills or knowledge must be adapted to the phase of adjustment of the feedback-control mechanisms.

These principles differ slightly from those of Skinner in terminology, but it may be that they do not differ in intent. It is not difficult to find adherents to the first principle, because teachers everywhere are admonished to aid the individual in his quest for self-control and for an ability to adjust to the environment as well as to adjust it. Developmentalists all subscribe to fitting the task to the stage of development, as is proposed by the second principle. But when a stage is described in terms of the phase of adjustment of the feedback-control mechanisms, then breaks between cyberneticists and traditionalists appear. And there is something that raises the hackles of certain "humanists" when the term *human engineering* makes the scene. But the human use of machines and the subsequent influence of machines upon humans has been gradually accepted, and along with it must come an acceptance of human engineering. Human engineering is concerned with educational design, and Smith and Smith see educational design as referring to "the effectiveness of teaching tools, symbol design, and the rules of language as organizing devices for feedback control; we refer to the operational procedures of manipulating information and symbols in the schooling process" (p. 467).

The study of humans as tool users is an old one. What cybernetics adds is the investigation of intrinsic relationships in the varying of the different sensory properties of feedback. One may vary these properties by displacing, delaying, distorting, and intensifying the feedback properties. Tampering with the usual modes of feedback imposes unusual conditions. The early Skinnerian experiments also made possible contingencies that were not ordinarily met with in the learner's life, and this suggests that a great deal of the failure of humans to learn may be brought about by a dearth of naturally facilitative conditions. If such conditions do not arise in the natural course of events, then the individual may fail to learn certain things. Cyberneticists feel that investigations of humans as tool users, and of the extension of tool using, are but a first step in the right direction.

Spotlighting the area called human engineering began as the need arose for humans to adjust technological design to human design, so that man-machine interactions might be facilitated. With the human viewed as a feedback-regulated control system, the control loop ought to have incorporated into it any instrument or symbolic device or rule that is necessary for activation in learning. These instruments, devices, or rules should be adjusted to human capabilities, in order to bring about the greatest efficiency. This leads to the implication, developmentally, that because humans change, develop, and grow, then educational design must also be adjusted to the needs of these changing conditions. Human engineering efforts are now being directed at maximizing the usefulness of man-machine *interfaces* (points of communications contact between machine and man) in such a way that the capabilities of both man and machine are optimally tapped. After appropriate job descriptions and task analyses, tasks are then relegated to either man or machine, depending upon which can carry out the tasks most efficiently, while meeting the necessary criteria of quality and quantity. Cybernetics and human engineering meet the systems approach at this point.

Feedback is closely analyzed by cyberneticists, and the process as they view it is something more than the provision of the knowledge of results. Two general kinds of feedback are described. The first, *dynamic* feedback, is provided by the senses. Every person acquires his data about the world outside his skin through the senses. Dynamic feedback may indicate accuracy or appropriateness of performance. In some cases, where there is no means of comparing with an extrinsic standard, there may be no dynamic feedback or error signal that will be useful in controlling behavior. In a sense, this is to say that the learner may occasionally receive feedback but has no means for evaluating it. The second type of feedback is called *static* knowledge of success, and it uses the built-in, intrinsic standards of the individual—but it has no provisions for the extrinsic measurement of accuracy. Hence, in most, if not all, tasks, the inclusion of dynamic feedback, with accompanying extrinsic standards for comparisons, is preferable to the use of static feedback, though the latter is often necessary. The preceding points indicate the inadequacy of treating *feedback* simply as a synonym for the *knowledge of results*. The statement about efficient learners is also supported—that they seem to have built-in means for feedback, in addition to the usual provisions for model answers and other extrinsic standards.

Skinner saw clearly that humans are systems whose behaviors are regulated in accordance with an awareness of the effects of those behaviors. Cyberneticists (Smith and Smith) have carried the idea farther in saying that disturbances in the regularity and stability of feedback are called *perturbances*. Some perturbances are not only present but necessary. It may therefore be concluded that *it is important for educators to know how to systematically control feedback perturbation*. Feedback opportunities ought to be provided throughout a broad range of functioning. For example, for some learnings visual feedback alone may not be as effective as the visual with audible aids added. Visual plus audible feedback may also be occasionally supplemented with psychomotor feedback. The context in which feedback processes are occurring may also be manipulated by teachers. There may be too much feedback, so that there is a kind of clutter, and it is too difficult for the individual to discriminate and process that which is most relevant. Feedback may also be meager and weak. In such cases, a teacher's function might be to strengthen it by using cues and prompts, and by focusing.

In addition to the necessity for establishing in the learner feedback controls of different sensory modes and combinations of these occurring in different settings, teachers ought to intentionally perturb feedback. This may be accomplished by the provision of a wide variety of sensory experiences and reinforcements for reacting in diverse ways, not always in the specified patterns of responses that are regarded as the only correct ones possible. It is suggested that pupils be prepared to meet emergency conditions that will place unusual excitements and stresses upon them, by being given carefully controlled learning experiences that induce excitement and stress. Models and simulated or derived experiences are useful, but there are obviously some learnings that consist of general aspects of education, and that cannot be simulated. The best way of training for general education is to provide opportunities for a diversity of sensory experience, and then to reinforce for diverse responses—providing a wide range of experiences builds the ability to apply responses throughout a broad range of situations. The viewpoint extends so far as to include learning in varying group structures, as well as in varying sensorimotor contexts, and even under conditions of stress.

Diversity in opportunities also implies a wide selection of educational materials and techniques, even beyond what machine teaching and self-instructional programs have already provided.

The concept of transfer has been treated rather extensively in the experimental and applied literature. Providing a variety of perturbed feedbacks has the effect of helping the learner to extend his knowledge, understanding, and control of the environment, because he must respond to it in diverse ways. With increased breadth of experience, the individual acquires more and more adaptive response patterns and establishes stable symbolic meanings.

In areas of social learning, it is especially important that diverse contexts be provided. For example, if speech happens to be learned primarily in a social setting that contains only one or two persons, then the transfer value is limited, and the speech that is learned tends to become specialized in relation to that particular social context. It has been speculated that textbooks, audio-visual aids, lectures, field trips, discussions, laboratory sessions, self-instructional programs, and tests ought all to be furnished to enhance the learner's control of knowledge and skill. Cybernetics theory supports the speculation. However, little is known about the controlled introduction of various levels of stress. It is at least an important recognition that the possibilities are worthy of investigation. Some of the effects of anxiety have been studied but not often from the viewpoint of cybernetics. A fact presented in many contexts and under various levels of stress becomes a response controlled under many patterns of feedback. Thus, information may be stored in the memory under many different classifications and it may be retrieved under many different kinds of conditions.

The teacher's function involves not only providing a wide range of experiences, but aiding in the establishment of feedback controls. The teacher helps set up intrinsic standards in the learner by providing extrinsic signals judiciously. This means that these signals are to be applied at optimal intervals, in just the right amounts, and then gradually reduced or faded. With this kind of assistance, the learner develops his body of symbolic knowledge, organized in such a way as to make possible the setting of his own standards for accuracy, logic, and consistency. The probability is high that there will be an increasing dependency on machines in systems that include man-machine interactions. Not only will this extension of tools act to shape the future skills demanded of man, it will also tend to shape much of the feedback that he must learn to control. One of the difficulties that may have to be coped with is that it is often much easier to learn direct control than automated control. Because the controls are not directly sensed, that is, there is a delay timewise, or there is a displacement spatially, a lag in feedback is introduced, or an adjustment must be made in the feedback when automated controls are applied. The machine is acting as an intermediary between certain outcomes of behavior and the individual's perceptions. Humans are remarkably adaptable, so that, for instance, they can even learn to reverse an upside-down world, after wearing special glasses that turn the images over. But although people can learn to adapt to feedback delays after a time, they can disturb accurate performance, especially if they are variable rather than fixed—as might be the case when it is necessary to enter a complex system that includes a variety of man-machine interactions.

THE NEW MEDIA

One way of providing for a variety of sensory experiences in different settings is to utilize media. A media specialist is often supposed to be a projectionist or operator of various machines—or he may be thought of as a dispenser of aids, such as films, filmstrips, disk recordings, and tapes. Sometimes he is expected to have something to do with educational television. But the study of media as facilitators in teaching is not limited to a study of machines or even to man-machine interactions. (In fact, man himself acts as a medium, in his role of teacher.) Furthermore, an important issue seems to be whether a teacher can and does adequately use those media that are available, as well as employ them for the development of new techniques and approaches. Williams (1966) defined media as

> all the aids for transmitting information and learning via the senses, such as printed materials including books and programmed devices of instruction; the graphic arts including transparent slides, pictures, charts, filmstrips, and video tapes; audio materials including tapes, recorders, radio and language laboratory equipment; and combination audiovisual materials including the sound motion picture and television. (p. 355)

He also classified these visual and/or audio stimuli:

> Visual Stimuli Inputs
>   Pictorial
>   Print
> Audio Stimuli Inputs
>   Verbal
>   Nonverbal

Williams and others feel that the optimal use of media should not be confined merely to the transmission and subsequent testing for knowledge and skills. Instructional media should also foster creativity. The use of models, for example, can be a very constructive utilization of a medium, and can lead to creative efforts by both pupils and teachers. Williams presented a model of a transmission system developed to evoke creativity through the use of a wide variety of instructional media.

All of the *programmer* section includes transmitting media, which are outside the body. All the *receiver* section includes the organs, which are inside the body. The transmitting function scans its array of symbols and constructs a chain of signs, forming a message. The message can take the form of a single input, as in the case of words. Or, it can assume the form of combinations of inputs, as in the case of pictures and accompanying narration.

The message is encoded at the programmer end and decoded at the receiver end. At the programmer end, the message may be either producer-designed (a film is made, for example, by someone other than the teacher)

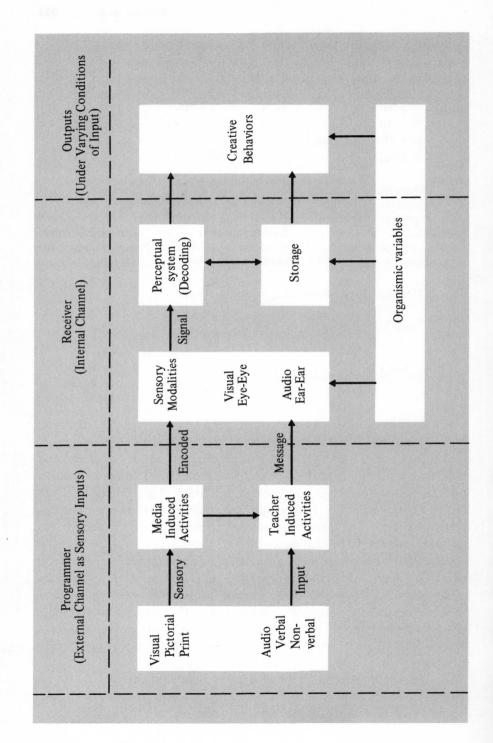

or teacher-elicited. Also, some messages may be encoded by the producer but modified by the teacher.

The receiver (pupil) must already have acquired some understanding of the components of the message; for example, he must have established a meaning in common with the producer's meaning for each. (The correspondence is seldom exact.) The decoding or the understanding of the message, whether pictorial or auditory, requires that the learner or receiver perceives them accurately and then assigns the proper relationships. However, if, along with the desired communication, the receiver also perceives unrelated, interfering (noise) inputs, he will lose some of the desired information. To combat noise interferences, it is common for transmitting systems to send an excess of stimuli—redundancy, or presentation of the same information via different types of sensory inputs. An audio narration supplements a visual presentation, and this may be done by the presenting of the audio along with the visual, or by the following of one with the other. Because it may be the way the message is transmitted that determines its value, inputs need to be carefully arranged for specified purposes in learning. A model of the sort presented by Williams is called a *general model of information theory.*

Williams's Five Categories of Media and Creativity

Williams has listed 112 tenable ideas about media and creativity from *The Proceedings of the Sixth Utah Creativity Research Conference.* Because no attempt was made at fully classifying the ideas, the five major categories under which they appear are listed here, with an accompanying discussion of the ideas.

1. *Individual Differences.* Instructional media should be programmed by being geared to the intellectual level of the intended audience. For those who do not perform well in verbal activities (usually those of relatively low IQ), media need to be especially developed. Such individual differences as sex, intelligence level, grade level, reading comprehension, creativeness, and amount and type of deprivation should have some de-

Fig. 9.1. Information Transmission System for Evoking Creativity Through the Design or Use of Instructional Media. (From Frank E. Williams's model in Frank E. Williams and Calvin W. Taylor, *Instructional Media and Creativity.* New York, John Wiley & Sons, Inc., 1966.)

termination in the design of media. Media should also be designed to take into account a shift from adjustment to development; that is, showing how failures or mistakes pay off, and illustrating the effects of discontent, anxieties, and the overcoming of conflicts, as well as suggesting means for change. Self-generated activities may be suggested by instructional media that have been specifically designed for the purpose. Others may be designed primarily to encourage independent thinking, realistic goal-setting, and the posing of self-discovered problems. Media may be developed to provide more feedback for self-evaluation at different stages of the creative process. (Guilford's model for problem solving illustrates this.) The earlier a teacher can discover the differences in his pupils the better, and a media device that would show which learning skills have been well developed in certain children by the time they enter school might also show how he should build onto these skills. Pupils also carry into the classroom various attitudes toward the information that they already possess. Those attitudes that are positive in nature may be strengthened by media constructed with that end in view. Instructional media that depict change and adaptation in nature and that parallel these changes to human applications would be valuable in meeting the educational goal of learning how to change and of adapting to change. A series of films that would present or extend the learner's range of emotional responses through dramatizations would enable the child to achieve emotional enrichment vicariously. Finally, media ought to be developed around the objective of influencing people and events to modify man's environment, as contrasted to adjusting to the environment.

2. *Multiple Approaches.* Different kinds of instructional media could be designed that would be used not only for pupil instruction, but for the pre-instruction of teachers. Older materials may also be converted to be fitted into the productive divergent-thinking model. Large numbers of creative problem-solving types of visual aids, such as transparencies, mock-up boards, and programmed learning devices should be developed. Flexibility may be provided by pupils' choosing for themselves ways in which they will use the information presented by media—encourage their using the information in committees, in groups, or independently. A main (trunk) film may be used to present an overview of a subject that brings out questions for a large group, along with shorter satellite films for individual use in which terms are defined, issues are clarified, and questions answered. Trunk films may also be designed around the noncontroversial issues of a subject, with satellite films that present several controversial issues arising out of the

subject—teachers may select those issues that are safe to use within their particular community or setting.

3. *Independence of Thought: Creativity.* In promoting independence of thought, instructional media may be used for presenting modes of search and inquiry. From the modeling approach, media may be designed that depict creative persons making works of art of their own lives. Principles of creative thinking may be presented via media showing the utilization of analogies, similes, paradoxes, metaphors, attribute listing, deferring judgment, check listing, and so on. Media may be designed that point out the main value systems of creative individuals, such as aesthetic values, including the elegance of products, and the theoretical values of functionality and practicality. It is ordinarily considered most useful to provide immediate feedback, but delayed feedback may be useful in the design of instructional media devices for evoking creative behaviors. Media may also present planned gaps in a field, so that the learner must deal with unknowns as well as knowns. Rigid thinking and functional fixity in the design of things are opposed to creative thinking. Hence, media that present rigidities and fixed functions for objects, and in which questions are posed that ask why certain aspects have not been changed and how they ought to be changed, should promote flexible thinking. Media that show man in the process of creation and how he reaches into the unknowns and the unconscious will facilitate the development of creativity. Instructional media have been used for promoting creativity in the past, so a sketching out of that history is also suggested, along with the story of how media have been used for creating. Filmstrips may be produced that present samples of tests of creativity, and that present instructions on how to think creatively and provide drill in following those instructions. The theme "nothing new under the sun" may be exemplified via media, and then followed up by the showing of the importance of associating and combining items of past knowledge to create something new.

Three kinds of creativity may be demonstrated by the use of a series of short films:

1. Show sequences of groups of people and interaction processes dealing with *social creativity*.
2. Present an autobiographical sketch of a person revealing his own relationship to himself, demonstrating *personal creativity*.

3. Develop a highly original idea translated into the creation of a novel product, demonstrating *productive creativity*.

But creative persons, too, have to overcome anxieties in their early lives, and they have conflicts and uncertainties. Instructional media should be developed that show how people have overcome such problems, or, in some cases, have used the very problem situations as springboards to creativity. Media might also show idiosyncracies of creative people living the creative way of life, rather than a conventional way, and the nature and psychology of creative thinking skills should be presented. This would lead to the design of a medium for comparing or contrasting creative thinking in the areas of science with the aesthetic areas, such as music, writing, and the visual arts. The first area might be portrayed as one in which problem solving is paramount, whereas the second deals with problems of expression in artistic form. The psychology of creativity would also suggest that materials should also include sepcial efforts to develop transformation and evaluation—imaginative interrelations with knowledge and decision-making functions. Career-type media (films or filmstrips) may be developed, showing creative people in the work world, noting the kinds of things that contribute to creative success on the job. Media with a negative viewpoint may also be used effectively for showing the most effective ways to stifle or hinder creativity.

A teasing out technique may be used, in which creative responses emerge —"What does this color (or sound, or image) make you feel like?" Creativity may also be teased out by open-ended questions. Perplexing social problems with no solutions may be presented via instructional media. A film or learning program may be stopped at some crucial point to permit students to create and design continuing inputs or information that will bring the film or program to a conclusion. Tape recordings or eight-millimeter film clips may be developed that depict the creative process occurring in a classroom situation. Students may then analyze these to reinforce their learning and their realization of how the creative process develops or unfolds. A silent film or filmstrip may be presented with an opportunity to guess what is occurring and what people are saying.

4. *Teacher Preparation.* Those who produce media and those who use them must understand the various types of creativity in order to know which type is being developed by each medium. They should locate and observe very creative teachers, and then produce instructional-media de-

vices that are based upon those creative methods and procedures. These empirically based media may then be used in teacher in-service training programs. Research evidence concerning when and how teachers reinforce creative behaviors may also aid in the design of media. (The consequences of failure to reinforce creative behavior may also be depicted profitably.) Films with spliced-in questions (Churchill Films, Inc., Los Angeles) should be used more often.

Instructional media should be developed that give information about the creative process and that could be used by teachers solely to motivate and orient students before taking up a new subject for study. An animated film or filmstrip may be developed for viewing humans as processors of information, linking the creative process to information theory (Guilford problem-solving model), i.e., committing and coding information to storage, and retrieving information in some form or connection other than that in which it was learned and stored. A media device for teacher training that would be quite useful would be one that showed a wide repertoire of teaching styles, with varied opportunities for students to learn in different ways in a self-contained classroom. Films that present problems requiring open-ended answers may be used as lead activities for teachers in in-service training and for discussion groups and parent-teacher meetings.

5. *The Teaching Purposes of Media.* Media devices that deal with generalized problem-solving skills, such as those involved in preparation, incubation, illumination, ideation, and verification, are designed to increase problem-solving ability. Films may be developed that show the beginning and the outcome of an event, so that students may be required to create the intervening steps—this can be tied in with sequences that compare people looking at where information might take them and with people who are judging that information's correctness, or where it has taken them before. Questions may also be posed that cannot be answered authoritatively, so that students and teachers may work them out together. Students may also be shown situations for which they may develop their own hypotheses. The use of models for solving analogous situations may also be illustrated audio-visually. Film may be designed that will take children to the forefront of science, giving them a feeling of participation in the process of innovation and adventure.

The preceding ideas about media are by no means all that Williams has reported from the creativity research conference, but they are representative of each of the five categories.

One is tempted to say that the place for media is wherever they work effectively. However, the obvious parallel with using a cannon to kill a mosquito is evident—just because something works well does not mean that it is always the best means, or that it is even necessary at all. Lagrone (1964) stated that once a learning process has been selected, and a structural basis for a body of knowledge has been established, then the use of new media is at least partially resolved. He and his associates suggest that a special, unique value of new media in teacher preparation lies in their ability to correct or minimize "some of the persistent problems of time, distance and numbers" (p. 12). Closed-circuit television, video-tape recorders, and eight-millimeter film are examples of media that provide teachers with closer glimpses of the real referents that are necessary for perception. The new media are being used with increasing effectiveness by practicing teachers, as they widen the scope of sensory experiences made available to pupils. One does not simply acquire an overhead projector, for example, and then seek out ways of using it. As a tool, it has its applications, and when a teacher perceives that a tool is indicated as the best available means for fulfilling a necessary function, then it is used. Schultz (1965), in his *The Teacher and Overhead Projection*, for example, showed that merely to know how to turn on, focus, and adjust the projector, or even to be able to prepare transparencies, must be supplemented by a knowledge of the use of the projector for instruction.

TROW—ENVIRONMENTAL
CONTROL—THE NEW MEDIA

When does an innovation become a medium? Trow (1963) implied that when media escape from the adjunct category, then they are to be considered new media. An occasional teaching aid, then, is simply an innovation for a while, but it becomes a medium when it is regularly used as a principle means in instruction. For example, the language laboratory (or, in the broader sense, the sound laboratory) has passed out of the experimental stage in which only a few well-favored schools tested the effectiveness of this audio-lingual approach. Now, it is an accepted part of instruction in foreign languages. Trow listed ten advantages summarized by Hutchinson (1961) of a good language laboratory:

1. It provides active simultaneous participation of all students.
2. A variety of native voices are heard by the student, and they never tire of making repetitions.
3. Individual differences are provided for; lessons are adapted to student needs, and self-pacing is possible.
4. The teacher is freed from tedious drilling routines.
5. The teacher may correct students without interrupting others.
6. All students have equal hearing conditions.
7. Inhibitions and distractions are reduced because of privacy.
8. Facilities are available for group testing of listening and speaking skills.
9. Audio and visual materials may be coordinated.
10. Teachers are aided in improving their audio-lingual proficiency.

(Trow, p. 72)

As provisions for teaching reading and writing skills are added to the repertoire of the language laboratory, it will actually become a complex teaching machine. The *use* of language is emphasized, not merely discussions about it. This emphasis tends to bring about the following student behaviors:

Get set: Readiness for the lessons being studied is assured by testing and previous progress, and often aided by preliminary warming up, perhaps including music or pictures from the country that uses the language being studied.

Listen: Language sounds (phonemes) are presented separately, in words, and in sentences.

Discriminate: Differences that make a difference in the new language are emphasized, e.g., Spanish-speaking students learning English may confuse *bet* and *bit*; Japanese students, *lamb* and *ram*, English-speaking students, the Spanish *r*, and so on.

Respond: Practice follows in imitating or echoing the foreign sounds, since practically all of them are different from the English sounds. Verbal instruction can reduce the trial-and-error process here as in other motor skills. Echoing includes practice in intonation, the pitch changes in spoken sentences.

Drill: Responses are repeated over and over in different contexts.

Practice patterns: Lexical meanings are introduced by inserting them in different parts or "slots" of stock sentences.

Correct through feedback: Throughout, the student compares his pronunciation with that of the recorded voice of the native speaker and, through successive approximations, he relatively quickly acquires the correct pronunciation.

Drill more: The student repeats sounds, words, passages and questions.

Reinforce: Improved and strengthened responses are established as a result of immediate correction, and the attendant satisfaction increases motivation.

Test: Each response is a test, but cleverly designed paper-and-pencil tests reveal the progress each student is actually making.

Progress: The student proceeds at his own rate. If he is absent, on his return he begins where he left off.

Habituate: Review experiences and continuing effort help the student to make his responses automatic so that he no longer has to think about them but only about what he is saying.

(Trow, pp. 74, 75)

Trow considered media as means for increasing the effectiveness of environmental control over learning behavior, so he included a consideration of radio and television. He mentioned a number of cities, such as New York, Philadelphia, and Flint, Michigan, that broadcast regular educational radio programs. Skornia (1962) reported that there is often a tendency to confuse attraction and interest with impact, when it is felt that communication through more than one sense (as in TV) is "better" than communication through only one (as in radio). "Dispersal rather than concentration sometimes characterizes multi-sensory effects—whereas education requires concentration and focusing more often than not" (p. 355). Because radio tends to be a medium used on a one-to-one basis, it is closer to reading as a learning device, or to programmed instruction, than is any other medium currently being used.

Radio

At first, as radio began performing an educational function, there was the hope that it would not lapse into the use of a backlog of materials, to be used merely because they had been used before and had been available. Now, at last, there would be a live, dynamic medium. But the advent of the extensive use of records and tapes dashed that hope. Accumulations from the old media poured out through the new. However, there are some indications that radio is once again being seriously considered as a truly educational medium. Radio's influence can be altered by a change in the sequencing of its offerings and those of printed materials. When the material is first heard, then read, the effect is more pronounced than if this sequence is reversed. It has also been found that a slow rate of delivery of the spoken word may tend to reduce concentration in listeners. And it is not difficult to double the rate of comprehension of spoken words.

Recently, educational use of radio, especially in the FM bands, has found more powerful applications. "Educasting" permits student feedback or talkback to the teacher. WFIL-FM, Philadelphia, broadcasts on a frequency to be picked up only by students who have the special radio receiver, and students can interact with the teacher via this radio. Radio's effectiveness as an educational medium had been limited by the inability of the students to question the teacher and to respond in other ways that the teacher might hear and react to. Now, FM radio will be furnishing instruction that is aided by two-way communication. Other stations, in Philadelphia, Binghamton, New Haven, Fresno, and Altoona, will also be Educasting. (The franchise holder is Triangle Stations, 320 Park Avenue, New York, New York 10022.)

Television

Television as an instructional medium has far outstripped radio in popularity. Occasionally, the regular commercial channels present formal educational programs, and there are also more than fifty channels that have been designated for educational use. The latter require either special provisions on regular receivers or sets designed solely for ultra-high-frequency reception. MPATI, the Midwest Program in Airborn Television Instruction, beamed video taped lessons from an airplane cruising at twenty-three thousand feet over Montpelier, Indiana. Booster stations are unnecessary, because pupils within a radius of two hundred miles can receive the programs directly. Lessons are telecast for elementary, secondary, and college-level students. Besides the obvious advantage to students in having instruction available that is not otherwise open to them, there is the added advantage to teachers in being able to watch skilled teachers perform.

In 1962, the Institute for Communication Research at Stanford University produced a report and summary of major studies on the problems and potential of educational television, a U.S. Office of Education project. It was pointed out that there are functions of this medium that it performs superlativley, and, in fact, it provides opportunities that would otherwise be closed to some students. For example, many students may simultaneously view a microscope slide; and activities that might be upset by direct observation by a large number of students may be viewed without disturbance to the observed. There are disadvantages, of course, and there are misuses, because the one-way communication is not adaptable to the conducting of a seminar and is not usually designed to give specific, direct personal help.

In its usual application, ETV is not expected to stand on its own, but to be combined wth a total learning situation, one in which students are strongly motivated. It may also serve to motivate, and to provide background and demonstrations that will guide and sharpen reading skills. It can foster independent learning and provide new insights, and induce the excitement of discovery.

Asheim (1962) summarized the arguments of a panel of experts, and presented some of the major objections to ETV:

1. Television lessons are fragmentary representations, and do not become a part of the continuing process which gives value to teaching.
2. The personal relationship established by a pupil's knowing his teacher and being known by him is not established.
3. If educational television lends itself to being nothing more than information-acquisition, this is not enough.
4. Talk-back systems have not been used successfully enough—the larger the audience, the less successful they are.
5. Students are reluctant to use the talk-back, and sometimes, the better the student, the less likely it is that he will use the microphone for asking questions.
6. It is very difficult to adapt lessons to the different needs of various schools and of different teaching situations.
7. Television is essentially a fixed-rate presentation device. It makes no provisions for differences in rates of learning.
8. Teacher attitudes may vary, depending to some extent upon whether television is being used at the teacher's request, or the teacher has been told to use it.
9. Standards of production do not compare favorably with commercial efforts.
10. Kinescopes and tapes are likely to be used and re-used in unimaginative fashion—the system should not be used merely as a projector of films.

(pp. 18–20)

Other experts felt that these questions were not unanswerable. Asheim added five "incontrovertible strengths:"

1. Sharing the good teacher.
2. Provision of demonstrations, etc., in areas where certain facilities are not available.
3. Superiority in providing close-up views.
4. Catalytic action in bringing together groups across country and across other traditional lines—triggering of cooperation.
5. Freeing the teacher for more individual work with students.

(pp. 21, 22)

Carpenter and Greenhill, in the same report and summary wrote on "Facilities for Instructional Television" (pp. 286–332). Of primary interest here is their discussion of the teaching-learning cycle and the role of television. The teaching-learning cycle is

1. Organized units of information or content.
2. Information made available on a medium for television origination and distribution.
3. Organized information displayed in one or more modes.
4. Instruction perceived by the persons who are expected to learn and who expect to do so.
5. Learner reactions to presented materials.
6. Learning taking place.
7. Learning being assessed by the learners and others.
8. Reviews, practice sessions, summaries, and reinforcements.

Television does not instruct, but is used by instructors for the transmission and display of information. However, when adequate talkback facilities or some other kind of feedback of student responses have been developed, then educational television may also be used as a programmed instruction device, and perhaps even for some inquiry training. Closed-circuit television is finding increased application. Schools and departments of education are supplementing student-teaching observations with CCTV. When a television camera is available in a classroom, student teachers may be seated in a group at a remote point, viewing a television screen. The advantages are at least twofold: students do not disrupt classroom activities by being present in appreciable numbers for observations; and discussions of teaching techniques may be carried on in full voice.

Overhead Projector; Slide Projector; Filmstrips

The various projectors do not require the transmission of information from a remote point to the classroom, and so have the advantage of local control. The use of a screen that may be viewed by every pupil in the room permits group observation, where once each may have had to await his turn to view pictures, graphs, and diagrams. Teachers may now wield oil pens on transparencies while sitting at their desks facing the class, instead of drawing or writing on the blackboard with their backs to the class, often making it difficult to hear their remarks. Flannel boards, magnetic chalk boards, maps, globes, charts, graphs, models, and various sorts of simulation devices also perform the function of enabling more than one or two pupils at a time to view demonstrations. The addition of motion, via films or television, is sometimes not only an unnecessary adjunct, but may even distract from the focal points of interest.

Bisson (1968) has suggested that increased effectiveness of filmstrips may be obtained by the requiring of active responding. Because of the manner in which filmstrips are sequenced, they furnish natural breaks, or points at which cues may be inserted, calling for student rseponses. This amounts to more than the usual discussion that ensued when older filmstrips or slides were used, because not enough students actually responded. It is expected that filmstrips, even older ones, may acquire greater teaching power if the procedures applied call for controlled responses from each viewer, provided that these responses lead to the desired terminal behavior intended by the filmstrip. As in so many innovative procedures, this educator's insistence is upon first specifying the objectives: What kind of response? Recognition? Recall? Constructed? He also found it important to determine filmstrip procedures by testing the entering behaviors of students. For example, whereas the response required of a student who enters at one level might be simply to recognize correct statements about what has been viewed, another might be asked to analyze a sequence.

Bisson provided an example of how active responding might be induced. A picture is presented, and the student consults a sheet containing questions and directions. He reads a question related to the picture, and then writes in his response on that cue sheet. The sheet contains the correct answer, so that the student gets immediate feedback. It also tells him when to move the filmstrip to the next picture. The method could also be applied to the use of slide projectors and to the overhead projector.

MULTIMEDIA APPROACHES

Phillips (1967) believes, as did Woodruff, that educators may tend to find uses for such media as happen to be available, rather than to plan for their inclusion according to the objectives as determined by the teacher. The curriculum, in a broader sense, may also be affected by the media selected. Cooperative efforts among teachers will be required to bring about a reorganization of the curriculum, and a new look at the quality and quantity to be included. Where team teaching is employed, the small-group sessions and individual instruction will spotlight the desirability of using a number of media. Audio-tapes, eight-millimeter film loops (single-concept, short films), sixteen-millimeter films, video tapes, various charts, and even dial-access systems are becoming available. (In dial access, the student dials as he would in using a telephone, in order to listen to selected tapes.) The use of a multimedia system for instruction would require curriculum revision, perhaps rather frequently, so that there would be less disparity between the old and the new. It would also impose upon the instructor a more urgent necessity for keeping up with the latest findings in his field. Figure 9. 2. shows the position occupied by various media in a multimedia system.

A Multimedia Programmer
and Classroom Communicator

One of the major advantages of programmed instruction, whether via textbook or machine, is that it requires each student to respond frequently; in fact, each student, before the program has been completed, will have responded (almost) as frequently as every other student. (In the case of branching programs, the poorer student will have responded more times than the good student.) The Edex Multimedia System provides each student with a responder or student station, whereby he uses push buttons to indicate his choice of answers to a stimulus item. The stimulus item (often but not always a question) may be presented orally by the teacher or by an audio tape, or by written handouts, or it may appear on a screen illuminated by a slide projector, filmstrip, or movie projector. Teachers

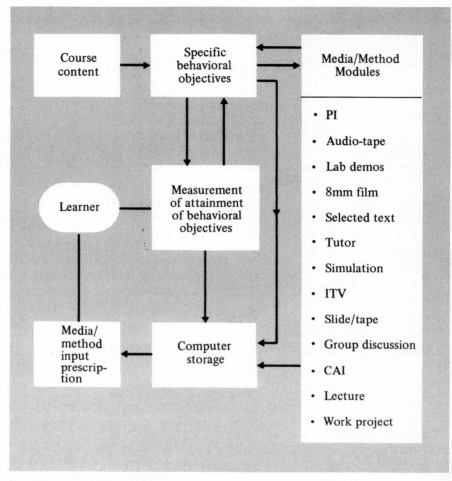

Fig. 9.2. Model for a single course instructional system. (From Robert M. Morgan and David S. Bushnell, "Vocational Training and Curriculum Design," *Educational Technology*, June 15, 1967.)

need not guess whether the rest of the class is responding while they are listening to the oral responses of one student, because a console on the teacher's desk indicates which button has been depressed by each student for each item. The teacher receives relatively immediate feedback concerning areas of student weaknesses and can elect to reteach, revise, supplement, change pace, review, or shift to small-group work or to individualized self-instruction with supervision. The student may also receive rapid feedback as the screen or loudspeaker furnishes correct answers, and additional elaboration, if needed, immediately following upon his responses. A printed record of the entire class session may also be made available to the teacher. As an aid to self-evaluation and to the overall teaching effort as it is occurring, four meters are mounted on the console, with each meter showing what percentage of the class is responding to a given answer choice. If meter A, for example, gives a reading of 10 per cent, this means that 10 per cent of the students punched button A. If button A corresponds to the correct answer, then only 10 per cent of the class answered correctly. If all students, or nearly all, selected that button, then the item either had been taught very well, or it was a trivial one, easily answered. Occasionally, a teacher could use alternatives that are of equal correctness, and he would simply dial so as to assign equal credit for those answers. As an instructional aid, this classroom communicator section of the Edex Teaching System has many strong points, but it may also be used as a quick-scoring testing device, using either multiple-choice or true-false items.

The multimedia programmer section of the Edex uses an ordinary audio tape for recording both the audio portion of programs and the control pulses. The audio portion operates simply as a tape recorder of the conventional type. Control pulses are recorded on the same type by a push-button arrangement on the console, and there are also some ready-made programs now available. A programmed tape can control the presentations of a thirty-five-millimeter automatic filmstrip projector, an eight-millimeter motion picture projector, an automatic slide projector, and a sixteen-millimeter motion picture projector. Variable pacing, fixed pacing, student-controlled pacing, or manual pacing by the teacher may all be utilized. A teacher may use a full automatic mode, merely turning on the console and letting it control an entire learning unit, including his recorded lecture and cumulative scoring of responses, or he may usurp the function at any time. He may wish to interrupt to make comments and explanatory remarks, or to provide enrichment and raise additional questions. He may wish to exercise his function as a master teacher, using many of the facilities of the Edex, then shift to small-group discussions and individual self-instruction, in a manner somewhat similar to team teaching. (In the case of classes not too large, for example, two classes could be combined, and the teachers would practice cooperative instruction.)

With increased effectiveness in utilizing media to implement educational goals, preparations for a changing role of the teacher must be instituted. Teachers will become tutors, managers of quite efficient dispensers of information, and decision makers at a much higher level than is presently the case. If greater individualization in instruction is an outcome, and there is a strengthening of the relationship between the teacher and each pupil, then the teacher, and each pupil, becomes very definitely a component in a system.

> The main thing is to create direct and easily accessible communication lines between the goal definitions of the curricula and the various media combinations and teacher contributions which facilitate the pupils' learning activities. All links in the chain must fit into each other, and stand up to the demands made: if a pupil does not learn what is required of him, it is the fault of the system, not of the pupil. (Eskil Bjorklund, 1968, p. 13)

The conclusion of the above quotation is interesting because of its assignment of the responsibility for learning to *the system*. Today, many schools pride themselves on having progressed from the stage in which a child's failure to learn is not the fault of the child. They have embraced the school of thought that says that the teacher is at fault when the child does not learn well. But apparently they must take the further step toward fixing greater responsibility upon the system, rather than only upon the teacher.

As the child loses responsibility for the rate at which he learns, does he assume other responsibilities? Certainly new life styles will be emerging, at home, in the community, and at the school. The educational innovations, the increased use of new media, will undoubtedly bring pupil and teacher into closer, more understanding relationships. It is to be expected that individual needs will be more fully provided for as they are more fully understood. But with the increased understanding and the analysis of each individual will come a considerable loss of privacy. Will privacy also become less valued? Perhaps the development of social competence will entail a tendency to reduce the need for privacy.

A BEHAVIORAL MODEL FOR TEACHING—REESE

Frequent note has been taken of the insistence by most learning theorists and educationists that learning and teaching are not simply opposite sides of the same coin. Among those who have noted the inferences that may be drawn from learning to aid in teaching, the common agreement seems to be that only isolated principles, some taken from one theoretical position and some from another, have found any really helpful application. But Reese (1966) has constructed a table that might be considered a framework upon which a quite workable system of teaching might be based. In fact, although the table is titled "A Behavioral Model for Learning," it provides what may be interpreted as directives for teachers (or therapists, or others interested in educating either remedially or developmentally). Reese stated that the table is "an attempt to specify a general procedure for operant conditioning" (applying measures of behavioral control) (p. 49). By developing some of the details that are implied by Reese's general model, it is possible to specify one approach to classroom teaching. Specifics are made possible by some of the recent systematic developments such as those provided by Mager (1962), Bloom (1956), Bandura (1963), Skinner (1953, 1968), and others. Reese's model appears in the following discussion.

Specifying the Final Performance (Terminal Behavior)

Although the classroom instructor does not have the precise control of relevant variables that is often available to the laboratory experimenter, he may still specify objectives more precisely than is usually the case. Bloom's *Taxonomy of Educational Objectives* (1956), along with Mager's (1962) or Walbesser's (1967) suggestions as to the structuring of statements of objectives, ought to greatly facilitate specifying terminal behaviors, both as to levels of complexity and standards of acceptability of performance under given conditions. Although arguments may be advanced against the application of specific objectives as the *only* goals, still the careful statement of educational objectives is unquestionably an aid to both instruction and evaluation.

> When he knows what behavior he wants to teach and how he will evaluate the student's performance, then—and only then—can the instructor decide what procedures he should follow to accomplish his objective: to produce the desired behavior. (Reese, p. 50)

Bloom's *Taxonomy*, as well as Sanders's questions, which may be based upon it, are discussed elsewhere in this book, and the importance of examining the rationale for objectives is also emphasized.

Determining the Operant Level or Current Baseline

After the teacher has specified where the learners are going, then he may determine where the learners must start. Because this is one aspect of teaching according to individual differences, the requirement is evident that a careful evaluation must be made, not only of each child's *ability* level, but of possible prerequisites that may be necessary as later, more advanced levels of the new content are reached. Before a teacher presents a pupil with a unit of programmed instruction, for example, he may wish to give the pupil a test for prerequisites, in order to determine the point at which he should enter the program and what kind of program best fits his needs. If the program is not in the form of a complete book but is segmented, so much the better—the pupil may then start with Segment One, Two, or even Five, as his present baseline or level of functioning may indicate. (Sometimes the pupil is also given the test for terminal performance, so that when he takes it again after the instructional period, his degree of progress may be more accurately assessed. If the pupil does not have the prerequisite abilities, then the teacher would be well advised to arrange for their acquisition before he begins the unit of instruction, or, if that is not feasible, to establish some means of developing these abilities concurrently with the unit of instruction.

Structuring a Favorable Situation

What kind of a situation is a favorable one? It is one in which the probability of competing behavior is reduced to a minimum. In such a situation, *discriminative stimuli* are provided for the desired behavior, and discriminative stimuli for competing behaviors are absent. (Discriminative stimuli are those that are occasions upon which responses are followed by reinforcement. Hence, for a favorable situation stimuli that may have been reinforced for other competing behaviors, but not for the one to be learned, ought to be removed. Only the distracting or competing stimuli must be removed, however—many learners respond better when certain other behaviors accompany the one to be learned. For example, for many of today's youth, a loudly playing radio or record player is not a competing stimulus, and moving about the room is not competitive with memorizing a poem. However, some learning settings are simply incompatible with learning of the sort the teacher desires—learning the Morse code is not likely to proceed favorably near an open window outside of which a trip hammer is operating. The many how-to-study manuals (or sections in educational psychology books) now available suggest good study habits and include tips about how to structure a favorable situation. Although the same conditions are not always disrupting or favorable to every individual, there are some suggestions that are generally applicable. Lighting should be adequate, without any point sources or unusually brilliant or moving sources. Seating arrangements should be comfortable but not so relaxing as to dull consciousness. Influences suggestive of studying may help, such as the presence of others who are intently studying, and it is usually found that specificity of cues aids in concentration—the same chair, always used for study only; a desk or other place for study materials, which is seldom used for any other purpose; and even a time and place allocated to specified learning experiences. Teachers can determine what the competing stimuli and behaviors are and arrange conditions for their reduction. They may even be able to establish a smoothly operating schedule for study, so that each learner, each learning session, is not unduly interrupted.

In cases where competing behaviors arise within the learner so that they are quite disruptive to him and to others, it is often desirable to deal with that behavior, to reduce it, before attempting to establish other favorable conditions. If more than one kind of behavior incompatible with desirable learning is present, it is usually best to deal with the most disruptive first. Although punishment is not a recommended procedure, it is sometimes necessary to forcibly remove an extremely aggressive child from the presence of others. With reduced opportunities for behavior incompatible with the desired learnings, the latter will proceed more easily.

Establishing Motivation

The characteristics of use of an adequate reinforcer include: (1) provisions for its presentation immediately following the desired response; (2) repeated presentation without the producing of satiation; and (3) availability in an adequate amount. The effect of presenting a reinforcer (one form of which is called a *reward*) is to strengthen the response that it follows—that is, to make that response increase its probability of occurrence. If an object or event is one that is reinforced because it represents a number of other reinforcers, it is a *generalized reinforcer*. For a reinforcer to be available immediately following the desired response, it must either be present when the act is performed, or it must be represented by something at that time. A common way of providing the representative function is through a generalized reinforcer, such as tokens that may be later exchanged for something else. Tickets, paper money, marbles, gold stars, and so on may all serve as temporary reinforcers that accumulate and may be cashed in for something valuable. Notice, however, that they actually are cumulative—none may be canceled out by an average, as is done in the accumulation of grades. If the semester grade is to act as a generalized reinforcer, then the assignment grades, quiz grades, and so on should simply add up to the semester grade, not be averaged toward it. The child would then save up his A's until enough were accumulated to be worth an A semester grade. (The drawback under most systems is that some pupils would spend years trying to accumulate enough good grades to equal one good semester grade. One solution has been suggested by programmed instruction. If the content to be learned is broken up into small enough steps and they are logically arranged, then it will be possible for each student to acquire his A's, albeit much smaller ones in value, but he will eventually achieve the final A.) At any rate, a generalized reinforcer may represent a variety of reinforcers, and one way to postpone satiation (and hence continue motivation) is to present a variety of reinforcers or generalized reinforcers that represent that variety. Reese illustrated this point by listing the reinforcers that were available in exchange for tokens in a study by Ayllon and Azrin (1965). The reinforcers were those available to patients in a psychiatric ward, but with sufficient care and patience a teacher might also list a great many reinforcers in the classroom, which could be purchased by students with their accumulated tokens. An advantage in using tokens, or generalized reinforcers, is that they can be dispensed very soon after the desired response, so that undesired responses do not intervene and become reinforced instead.

One technique that is used in motivating subjects experimentally is to establish a state of deprivation so that the subject responds in order to receive reinforcers that will reduce the state of deprivation. Teachers have always faced the problem of making pupils feel that they need more knowledge and skills than they have, and that they need those that the school wishes to develop. In the hospital situation described by Reese, a patient who would not eat in a beautiful, harmonious setting was moved into a setting that was not at all attractive. Furthermore, attendants who had cheerfully attempted conversation with her withheld their remarks. However, when she could be induced to approximate eating, they talked with her, and the greater the effort she made, the more they re-established this reinforcer. Similarly, they strengthened eating behavior by permitting her to listen to the radio or watch television after her eating showed improvement. (Eating behavior was instrumental in making listening behavior possible.) Each of the known reinforcers that was used was made contingent upon eating. Going for walks, receiving visitors, receiving mail—all were made contingent upon her improvement in eating. However, after she left the hospital, controls over the contingencies of reinforcement would no longer be possible. Hence self-control had to be gradually established.

Teachers are not likely to take drastic steps, certainly not so drastic as those that had to be taken in the above account in order to save the patient from starvation. Many teachers have a knack for locating reinforcers, however, and are skilled in dispensing them. They know, for example, that reinforcers ought to be presented a little at a time, not all in one big piece. They know that if reinforcers are given automatically, whether the learner has produced the desired response or not, then he will not try very hard to produce that response—the reinforcer must depend upon the response. Skilled teachers also know that whereas some responses are to be strengthened or learned, others ought to be weakened or unlearned. The strength of such behaviors may be decreased by the withholding of the reinforcers that maintain them. The difficulty in this task is twofold; determining the nature of the reinforcers and withholding them. Sometimes a teacher unwittingly reinforces what he wishes to extinguish. For example, he may give sympathy and attention to behavior that is sustained by sympathy and attention. Chronic complainers are reinforced for complaining by those who listen patiently.

Adaptation

Some children will find the school situation new and strange to them. All children will eventually be placed in some kind of novel situation that may seem threatening, and that will result in uneasiness, if not in pronounced anxiety. It is sometimes necessary to provide an adaptation phase in learning, so that the learner becomes accustomed or adapted to the stimuli, and the novel conditions acquire discriminative properties that may be associated with reinforcers already accepted. A child who is promoted to a new grade faces many strange conditions. The teacher is new, the subject matter is new, procedures are different, perhaps, and many of his classmates are at first unknown to him. The child who enters a classroom via transfer from another school or even another community faces even more changes. Teachers who wish to facilitate the adaptation phase will help such a child to locate "old friends," such as books he has used before, familiar skills that may be enlarged upon, conversations in which he feels at home, and activities in which his responses may be reinforced by the cooperation and approval of peers. Similarities between the old and the new may be pointed out. Teachers who want to prepare their pupils so that they will have less difficulty in adapting to other novel situations will help them to establish behaviors controlled by a wide variety of discriminative stimuli. The important phase of adaptation may thus be facilitated via the extinction of disruptive emotional responses, the provision of many discriminative stimuli, and the establishment of appropriate reinforcers.

Shaping the Desired Behavior

Shaping is a step-by-step procedure in which the learner is reinforced for whatever response he makes in the desired direction, until that response is well established. Thereafter, he is reinforced differentially, that is to say, he receives reinforcement only for responses that are progressively improved. It is not expected that a pupil will show spontaneously novel complex behavior that is very much like the desired behavior. Even if he did, the occasions might be so long in coming that the teacher would devote a great deal of time to simply waiting for the desired responses in order to reinforce them. It is far better to start where the child is. Shaping may also be brought about by the Premack principle. The Premack principle states that the probability of occurrence of a low probability behavior may be increased by making it contingent upon a high probability behavior. When children are left to their own devices, they are likely to engage in high probability behavior. Low probability behavior is often a learning activity that a teacher would like to have them engage in. The high probability behavior may therefore be used as a reinforcer, to be permitted after the child has engaged in the desired behavior. The teacher watches for moments when pupils' activities are approximating some of the behavior that he wishes them to acquire. Soon after its occasion, he blows a whistle or rings a bell, or provides some other convenient form of signal that indicates to pupils that they may go ahead and engage in the behavior they like. At another signal, they must break and return to the low probability behavior. Eventually, the signal acquires some stimulus control, and the teacher gradually works toward longer and longer periods and more frequent occasions during which pupils behave in desirable ways.

Utilizing the Reduction of Stimulus Control: Fading

As a child gradually acquires more and more of the desired terminal behavior, he needs less and less help, or cueing. Thus, in addition to differential reinforcement for moving from level to level of proficiency, the teacher may gradually remove learning aids. Eventually, the learner is able to produce the desired response pattern unaided. Gradual cue reduction of this sort is called *fading*. Handwriting has been effectively taught by the use of this technique. The child first traces the entire letter, and his writing movements come under the control of the outline that is furnished. Little by little, portions of the letter being learned are removed (fading), so that stimulus control, little by little, is being shifted from the visual pattern furnished by the cued-in letter to the child's own psychomotor system.

Reinforcing Intermittently

In the shaping procedures previously described, the learner is reinforced for each approximation of the desired behavior—he is continuously, regularly reinforced. But experiments have shown that intermittent reinforcement, not continuous, leads to behavior that is more resistant to extinction and less likely to be forgotten or erased. One reason for this is that reinforcement provided only occasionally, instead of for every desired response, is more likely to delay the point of satiation. Another might be that the interruption of rewards that have been certain to follow leads to more doubt of their being reinstated than is the case when the interruption is only another among many. Fortunately, teachers are most likely to find it necessary to reinforce intermittently rather than continuously as a matter of practicality. Too many pupils, too many occasions for reinforcement arise, for him to reinforce continuously.

Keeping Continuous Objective Records

If records are kept of responses as they occur, corrective measures can be instituted early, when they are most likely to be effective. This relatively immediate feedback to the teacher is often unavailable, however. The use of mechanical devices such as responders, push-buttons operated by students, makes more responses visible to the teacher. The teacher's records should be as objective and free of personal feelings as possible, to free them from ambiguous interpretations. If the attitude of the teacher, his subjective orientations, and other anecdotal supplements or interpretations are considered necessary, they should be entered into the record separately from the objective measures. The table furnished by Reese appears in a summarized form below.

1. Specify the final performance (terminal behavior): (a) identify the behavior; and (b) determine how it is to be measured.

2. Determine the operant level or current baseline.

3. Structure a favorable situation: (a) provide discriminative stimuli for appropriate behavior; and

(b) remove discriminative stimuli or the opportunity for incompatible behavior.

4. Establish motivation: (a) locate reinforcers; (b) deprive (if necessary); and (c) locate and withhold reinforcers for incompatible behavior.

5. Adaptation: (a) extinguish emotional respondents; (b) provide or establish discriminative stimuli; and (c) establish reinforcers.

6. Shape the Desired Behavior: (a) reinforce successive approximations of the final performance; (b) raise the criterion for reinforcement gradually; and (c) present reinforcement immediately, contingent upon the behavior.

7. Utilize stimulus control: fading.

8. Reinforce intermittently.

9. Keep continuous objective records.

J. Lloyd Trump (1966) emphasized that there must be a focus on change, so that in the coming environment of machines and systems, people must acquire a flexible training base. (Notice that this is an application of that part of Reese's model called *adaptation*.) With a flexible grounding, people will be able to retrain and to relearn sufficiently to meet the new demands of the systems of which they are to be parts. It will no longer do to simply tell the child that the harder he works the more valuable he will become—already the jobs of many skilled hard workers have been dissolved. The future citizen, if he is to become even moderately successful, will need to develop expectations, goals, and attitudes that may shift with the times, and the shifting will be at a rate that has heretofore been incomprehensible. Something happens to the once stable values that teachers could help the child to acquire—and teachers themselves are products of an age that has not yet become really accustomed to accelerated change.

The greater the influence a man wields upon other men, the greater the responsibility he has for wisely using his influence. Yet our technologies have granted powers to men who have not yet learned how best to exert that influence—and members of this group, composed of scientists, engineers, technicians, and teachers, will frequently act as models for others who will inherit their places.

DeCarlo (1967) made some predictions about the requirements to be faced by people in the future:

1. Because they will be thinking logically and handling symbolic and abstract material, and will learn throughout their lives, rather than merely to work, the satisfaction to be obtained from work will become increasingly different from what it is today.

2. Because more people will have more leisure time, they will need to be taught to use it in a meaningful way. They will need to acquire skills in probing questions of values and meaning, and their artistic, spiritual, and intellectual experiences will be widened.

3. Social contacts will increase. Because an individual will simultaneously hold membership in many different groups, his loyalties will often be divided. He will face problems concerning his privacy, the social graces, and respect for others to a greater extent than man has had to at most times in the past.

4. Political and social institutions will change rapidly to keep pace with the expansion of life in a technological society, and men will need to know how to face these changes.

The implication is that the early preparation of the child to live in this changing world must stress basic, central values, and these values are still to be found in the conservative traditions of religion and education. The integrity of the self will be of the utmost importance. From an early age, children will need to be taught concepts of responsibility and respect for others. Sensitivity to the needs of others and empathy with their feelings during grief and joy should characterize the well-educated person. This well-educated person must also be able to become loyal and committed to large groups, at the same time maintaining his own interior freedom and integrity. Although mention of an "old, outmoded" system of instruction may appear to be out of place in a chapter on educational technology, perhaps there is something to be gained at this point by looking into the influence wielded by Maria Montessori of Italy. She had somehow acquired the aforementioned sensitivity and empathy, and then she applied it in an educational setting for which her training had not originally prepared her.

MEDIA AND MONTESSORI

Skinnerian behaviorism had not yet appeared, but Montessori insisted on a "prepared environment" that would maximize the perceptions of young children. Spontaneous autoeducation was unheard of, but Montessori felt it should be nurtured. *Readiness* and the *teachable moment* were not yet bywords, but she observed that when she was a child of two she thought as a child of two, but when she became a child of six she thought as a child of six and no longer thought as she had when a child of two (M. Standing, 1929). She therefore advocated teaching according to the stage of the child's development, or matching teaching to periods of special sensibility. She observed that the child of three to six was at a stage when the activities of the senses predominate, and hence tried to provide those senses with planned stimuli. She also saw that each stage is a preparation for the next one. Montessori preceded Piaget, but she believed in the encouragement of a "spontaneous ascent from concrete to abstract," and the "doctrine of interests" was used to develop concentration as well as to build character. Maria Montessori (1869–1952) had not been trained primarily as an educator; she was a medical doctor. However, she began teaching defective children, three to six years of age, in San Lorenzo, Italy, and results there convinced her that normal children might also respond to her methods. She felt that children between ages two and six pass through periods during which their sensibilities mature and become acute, and appropriate teaching materials (media) should be made available. Her use of media was to sharpen the senses as they became ready, rather than merely to implement cognitive learnings. The approach opposes behavioristic viewpoints in that the environment does not function to mold the individual, but to reveal him. However, the general statement that acts as a directive to teachers is similar: The nature of the growing child can best be understood by discovering talents revealed by placing him in an environment which meets his needs, and permitting him to be free in it. Being free in the environment meant being able to manipulate it, but not without direction.

Direction, in the Montessori method, is provided in ample quantities by the teacher, but direction is perceived of as being as much a function of what is excluded from the environment as of what is included. However, careful selection in the preparation of the environment tends to reduce the number of restrictions that the teacher must make. Within the limitations provided by the controlled environment, however, the child is given considerable freedom under the Montessori system. The material for development, which is now called *didactic apparatus,* is all designed to concentrate the child's attention on objects to be sensed. At first, this sensory concentration serves the function of developing and refining sense perceptions. Later, it leads to a knowledge of reading, writing, and arithmetic by a combination of sensing and recognition. The prepared environment consists of a bright, cheerful room, equipped with chairs, tables, closets, and tools that are scaled down to the child's size. The teacher is also considered a part of this environment.

The freedom granted to the children does not include freedom from maintaining order or freedom from work. It is believed that work is satisfying to children, as it is to adults. Thus, in the elementary school, the child does not merely acquire the basic skills, but he also acquires favorable attitudes toward work and is exposed to the values of his culture. Exercises in practical living give the individual practice in exercising good judgment. The child must learn to make choices among alternatives that he *knows.* If he chooses only out of curiosity, he is not really exercising a free choice. There is an insistence that the child be given the freedom to do right—not to do what is wrong. A great deal of understanding on the part of the teacher is required to determine whether the actions of a child really have good motives and serve useful purposes—otherwise, the teacher might unwittingly suppress them to the detriment of the child.

In a Montessori environment, thoroughness is emphasized, and *simple* media are used. Children are likely to be separated into three-year groups —three to six, six to nine, and nine to twelve. Within these groups, each child is allowed a great deal of flexibility. The children wash and dust, sweep and mop, and so on in some of their exercises in practical living, and thereby take care of their own classrooms. Discipline is aimed at self-mastery, taking the road somewhere between the position of an extreme discipline imposed on the child and that of almost nonexistent control. The child is prepared to meet failures by a series of successes, so the Montessori method arranges for many success opportunities.

The materials used between ages three and six look like games. Two principles of organization underlie their design: (1) they consist of pairs of elements that are to be matched; and (2) the elements can be graded according to increasing or decreasing intensity. Sound boxes, composed of twelve hollow wooden cylinders, are arranged in pairs and are filled with various materials. They make sounds, when shaken. Color tablets are also arranged in pairs. The easiest set contains the three primary color pairs, and the advanced set has eight shades of each color. These shades can be graded in intensity from lightest to darkest or from darkest to lightest.

Three- and four-year-olds are given sets of sandpaper letters mounted on a smooth surface to increase their sensory perception of these symbols, and they repeat the sound rather than the name of each letter. Later they begin to compose words, phonetically, each from his own set of letters (an easier task in the phonetic Italian language than in English). Eventually they learn to spell, before they learn to read. Similarly, the materials used in arithmetic have an appeal to the hand as well as to the eye. Gold-colored beads introduce the units, tens, hundreds, and thousands series. In geography, children use clay models along with the usual flat maps.

The Montessori system does not try to teach the child instead of the subject. The subject is taught to the child, so although the child is an active agent in learning, he is also to be provided with matter to learn. It is felt that conditions favorable to the child's social development must be provided, so that he will be free to learn, but the environment is the condition in which learning occurs, it is not the object of learning. The concept of readiness is well understood, and a child begins his learning when he shows interest; for children in Montessori schools, this may be at an early age for languages, history, geography, arithmetic, and reading. No child is diverted from the study of an acceptable subject simply because it does not seem suited to his age. These pupils tend to mature in many ways more rapidly than do others, because of an emphasis on self-control and mastery of the environment.

In 1913, Kilpatrick examined the Montessori method and dismissed it rather perfunctorily. Recently, there has been an upsurge of interest in the method and the establishment of schools throughout this country. The first of these was the Whitby School, founded in 1958 in Greenwich, Connecticut. This is currently the home of the American Montessori Society.

The first university in the United States to offer a Montessori teacher-training program was Xavier University, Cincinnati, in 1965. Since that time, the University has expanded its program. There, graduate students, as well as teachers from both public and parochial schools, are learning that the very young can acquire knowledge at a surprisingly rapid pace. The furniture and other objects in the child's environment are made appropriate to his size and to his coordination and abilities. Self-pacing is the rule, and materials are furnished for self-instruction and self-correction. Wherever children can be helped to learn by sensory-motor activities, they are encouraged to be active. From the moment the child enters the school, he is free to choose what he will do. When a group engages in singing or in playing, a child may elect to continue what he is already doing, and he is free to do so. Meanwhile, if he decides that he would like to stop working on something, he may leave it as it is, and it will be there waiting for him, undisturbed, on his return. Xavier University has not simply accepted Montessori teaching at its face value, however. It is conducting research into its advantages and disadvantages. Montessori Society groups have been established all across the country (and throughout the world). The surge of interest that began in the late nineteen-fifties was felt in colleges that had never before even mentioned Montessori methods.

How well Montessori training will succeed in producing children who will be able to sustain the necessary stable values and yet be adaptable to the future that DeCarlo foresees is unknown. The problems of life-long learning and satisfactions with work might be expected to be solved rather well. The use of leisure time and the necessity for developing skills in probing questions of values and meaning have long furnished grist for the mill of Montessori teachers. Presumably, however, the increasing social contacts and inroads on privacy will remain as insoluble for graduates of Montessori schools as for others. And the school system is yet to be designed that will adequately prepare all children for the extremely rapid changes in scientific, political, and social domains that loom over the horizon.

References

1. Asheim, Lester, "A Survey of Informed Opinion on Television's Future Place in Education," *Educational Television: The Next Ten Years.* Stanford University, Calif., Institute for Communication Research, 1962.
2. Ayllon, T., and N. H. Azrin, "The Measurement and Reinforcement of Behavior of Psychotics," *Jl. Exp. Anal. Behav.*, Vol. 8, 357–383.
3. Bandura, A., and R. H. Walters, *Social Learning and Personality Development.* New York, Holt, Rinehart and Winston, Inc., 1963.
4. Bisson, Robert F., "Filmstrips and Active Responding," *Educational Technology*, VIII (April 15, 1968), 16–17.
5. Bjorklund, Eskil, "A View from Sweden—Models for School Reform," *Educational Technology*, Vol. VIII (January 30, 1968), 10–14.
6. Bloom, Benjamin S. (ed.), and Max D. Engelhart, Edward J. Furst,

Walker H. Hill, and David R. Krathwohl, *Taxonomy of Educational Objectives: The Classification of Educational Goals, Handbook I: Cognitive Domain.* New York, David McKay Company, Inc., 1956.

7. Carpenter, C. R., and L. P. Greenhill, "Facilities for Instructional Television," *Educational Television: The Next Ten Years.* Stanford University, Calif., Institute for Communication Research, 1962.

8. Carter, Launor, "From Research to Development to Use," *Organizations for Research and Development in Education,* Robert Glaser (ed.). Bloomington, Indiana, AERA—Phi Delta Kappa, 1966.

9. Davis, John A., "Using Instructional Media in College," *Phi Delta Kappan,* XLIX (November 1967), 152–154.

10. DeCarlo, C. R., "Technology and Value Systems," *Educational Technology,* VII (March 15, 1967), 1–8.

11. *Educational Technology* (edit.), "Broadcasting System Permits Student Feedback," VI (May 30, 1966), p. 11.

12. Ely, Donald P. (ed.), "The Changing Role of the Audiovisual Process in Education: A Definition and Glossary of Related Terms," *AV Comm. Rev.,* Vol. II, No. 1 (January–February, 1963).

13. Ely, Donald P., "Educational Technology as Instructional Communication," *Educational Technology,* Vol. VIII (January 15, 1968), p. 7.

14. Fisher, D., *Montessori for Parents.* Cambridge, Mass., R. Bentley, 1965.

15. Gardner, R., "A Psychologist Looks at Montessori," *Elem. School Jl.,* Vol. 67 (November 1966), 72–83.

16. Glaser, Robert, "Educational Technology as Instructional Design," *Educational Technology,* VIII (January 15, 1968), 5–6.

17. Guilbaud, G. F., *What Is Cybernetics?* Grove Press, Inc., 1960.

18. Heinich, Robert, "Educational Technology as Technology," *Educational Technology,* VIII (January 15, 1968), p. 4.

19. Humphrey, John H., "Educational Technology—Science of the Practical," *Educational Technology,* VIII (January 15, 1968), p. 9.

20. Hutchinson, Joseph C., "Modern Foreign Languages in High School: The Language Laboratory," U.S. Office of Education Bulletin No. 23, 1961.

21. Kersh, Bert V., "The Classroom Simulator," *Audiovisual Instruction,* Vol. 6 (November 1961), 447–448.

22. Lagrone, Herbert F. (dir.), *A Proposal for the Revision of the Pre-service Professional Component of a Program of Teacher Education.* Washington, D.C., Teacher Education and Media Project (TEAM), American Association of Colleges for Teacher Education, 1964.

23. Locke, Robert W., "Educational Technology and the Educational Publisher," *Educational Technology,* Vol. VIII (January 15, 1968), 14–16.

24. Lubienska, Helene, "The Child, His Body and His Soul," *Jubilee* V (June 1957).

25. Mager, Robert, *Preparing Objectives for Programmed Instruction.* San Francisco, Fearon Publishers, 1962.

26. McLuhan, Marshall, *Understanding Media: The Extensions of Man.* New York, A Signet Book, New American Library, 1964.

27. "Montessori Teacher Training Curriculum" (edit.), *Educational Technology*, VII (July 15, 1967), 11–12.
28. Orem, R. C. (ed.), *Montessori for the Disadvantaged*. New York, G. P. Putnam's Sons, 1967.
29. Phillips, Jack, "Instructional Media and the Curriculum," *Educational Technology*, VII (November 30, 1967), 17–18.
29a. Rambusch, Nancy M., "Freedom, Order and the Child," *Jubilee* V (April 1958).
30. Reese, Ellen P., *The Analysis of Human Operant Behavior*. Dubuque, Iowa, William C. Brown Company, Publishers, 1966.
31. Riggsby, Ernest D., "Instructional Media—Essential Element in Teacher Preparation?" *Educational Technology*, VII (November 15, 1967), 18–19.
32. Schultz, Morton J., *The Teacher and Overhead Projection: A Treasury of Ideas, Uses and Techniques*. Englewood Cliffs, N.J., Prentice-Hall, Inc., 1965.
33. Silverman, Robert E., "Two Kinds of Technology," *Educational Technology* (January 15, 1968). Vol. VIII.
34. Silvern, L. C., "A Cybernetic System Model for Occupational Education," *Educational Technology*, Vol. VIII (January 30, 1968), 3–9.
35. Skinner, B. F., *Science and Human Behavior*. New York, The Macmillan Company, 1953.
36. ——, *The Technology of Teaching*. New York, Appleton-Century-Crofts, 1968.
37. Skornia, Harry J., *Educational Radio: Its Past and Its Future*. Stanford University, Calif., Institute for Communication Research, 1962.
38. Sluckin, W., *Minds and Machines*. London, Penguin Books, Inc., 1960.
39. Smith, Karl U., and Margaret Folz Smith, *Cybernetics Principles and Educational Design*. New York, Holt, Rinehart and Winston, Inc., 1966.
40. Standing, M., *The Child in the Church*. London, Sands and Company, 1929.
41. Trow, William Clark, *Teacher and Technology: New Designs for Learning*. Des Moines, Iowa, Meredith Publishing Company, 1963.
42. Trump, J. Lloyd, *Focus on Change: Guide to Better Schools*. Chicago, Rand McNally & Company, 1966.
43. Unwin, Derek, "Applying Educational Technology," *Educational Technology*, VIII (January 15, 1968), 12–13.
44. Walbesser, Robert, *Constructing Behavioral Objectives*, series of unpublished papers. College Park, Md., Bureau of Educational Research, University of Maryland, 1967.
45. Wiener, Norbert, *The Human Use of Human Beings: Cybernetics and Society*. New York, Doubleday Anchor Books, Doubleday & Company, Inc., 1954.
46. Williams, F. E., "Models, Summary Lists of Tenable Ideas and Research Areas," *Instructional Media and Creativity*, C. W. Taylor and F. E. Williams (eds.). New York, John Wiley & Sons, Inc., 1966.

10

Systems and Simulations

SIMULATIONS AND GAMES

The term *involvement* has become a favorite in popular language in recent years, so that its applications range from active interest to deep, emotional commitment and participation. *Involvement* seems to be a key term in understanding the aims of simulations. Getting students involved in experiences is supposed not only to motivate them, but to produce more rapid and meaningful learning, which is better retained and transferred. Getting students involved sometimes means that teachers are to be less directive, certainly less dominating, because a student's involvement is limited when too many restrictions are imposed upon his activities.

A second major concern of simulations has to do with the very old question about education for what is real. Educational psychology has been frequently criticized for dealing with abstract ideas, not practical, applied utilization. Simulations is an attempt to deal with real educational problems. The procedures can be used not only as a training device for those engaged in the simulations activities, but as a research tool for examining interaction patterns under a variety of decision-making requirements.

Fattu's introductory chapter to Phi Delta Kappa's *Simulation Models for Education* (1965) provides more than a mere definition:

> Simulation is a blanket term used to cover a multiude of activities, all intended to describe a complex system. Several levels may be identified: human simulation as observed in role playing, mixed man-machine simulations as observed in business and military gaming, and pure computer simulations such as studies of computer problem-solving behavior, or artificial intelligence. Man-machine simulations may range from those involving simple electrical or mechanical devices to those that involve the most sophisticated electronic computers. (pp. 6, 7)

Simulations, then, are next to the real thing, a major advantage being that the decision makers (learners) may become aware of the consequences of their decisions without suffering the real consequences. However, the consequences may also be simulated, so that the learner may follow up and attempt to take remedial action, or else try the whole series again. Simulations compress time, because the decision maker or role player can cover a great span of time, if necessary, by simply assuming that the period has elapsed. This is facilitated, of course, on the part of the system by the furnishing of results that would have been obtained had that span of time actually occurred. (When the required data are available and it may be assumed that certain tendencies noted will continue, teachers are able to extrapolate.) With the ability to compress time in this way also goes a compression of experience for the learner. He can be exposed to many more experiences in a brief period. And just as it is less tiring to think out a problem rather than to manipulate all objects and sequences that will solve the problem, it is also less tiring to pretend, to manipulate a model, than it is to carry out the activities and react to the materials and processes that the model represents. In order to preserve the near-reality of the experiences it makes possible, the model must be carefully constructed. The system to be simulated must be analyzed and the analogies upon which the model is to be based must be meticulously drawn, so that the model will yield relatively complete directions for its use.

The use of *conceptual models* involves a degree of abstraction, or of symbolic representation, but this is not the same as the use of simulations. A conceptual model may not necessarily resemble the situation it represents, whereas a simulations system must. The conceptual model is presented so the learner will improve his *understanding*, whereas the simulations model requires the learner to *enter into* the system as a part of it.

Much has been said recently about the importance of making educational objectives explicit. Too many teachers tend to teach by hit-or-miss methods that produce unreliable results. One teacher cannot, by observing, by asking, or by reading a statement of another's aims, determine just what the other teacher expects pupils to accomplish. Carefully planned simulations, especially when a computer is available, can force the teacher or other practitioner to abandon the previously intuitive or artistic bases for behavior and to make them explicit.

Fattu, in his "An Introduction to Simulation," lists the reasons for its use. When an environment cannot be duplicated exactly, then it may be made as realistic as possible. When a process is to be examined systematically, it may yield information via the developing and operating of a simulation. When a system is too difficult to manage, a simulation may suggest a way of breaking it down into subsystems. Then it may be noted how the skills and information required may be pooled. When a problem solver is confronted with a problem beyond his ability, a simulation may help him synthesize and infer a good solution. Cost may be reduced by simulating rather than by the alternative forms of experimenting or testing. Simulation may also indicate which variables in a complex operation or system are important and how they are related to each other. The amount of time compression accomplished is controllable by the simulator. Unforeseen problems arising from the introduction of innovations may be identified by simulation, and risk is minimized.

Degrees of Reality in Simulation

In a speech given at the dedication of the Systems Simulation Research Laboratory, System Development Corporation, in September, 1961, Harman listed five reference points for simulation. These points, as reported by Bushnell (1962), progressivley decrease in reality, from exact situation to very abstract representation:

1. *Identity simulation*, in which the actual system is used as the model that provides information about itself.

2. *Replication simulation* is only a step removed from the real system. An operational model of the system in its normal environment is used.

3. *Laboratory simulation*, wherein replication is attempted in the laboratory, with features of the

real system represented. People, hardware, operating procedures, mathematical functions, and probability distributions may make up this simulated system.

4. *Computer simulation* is a more abstract representation of the real system than is the laboratory simulation. "All aspects of the system are reduced to logical decision rules and operations which can be programmed for a computer. (Bushnell, p. 4)

5. *Analytical simulation* uses a mathematical model and attempts to obtain a solution by analytical means. The disadvantage of this very high degree of abstraction from the real system is that "Such a thorough mathematical description could exceed the capacities of the professional staff and of the computing equipment, or it could require an inordinate amount of time for accomplishment." (Bushnell, p. 4)

Harman's list indicates that not all simulations amount to the kind of game playing that usually comes to mind when simulation is mentioned. However, some of those who have experimented with games extensively believe that this application of simulations tends to deal more effectively with three important defects in American secondary education:

1. What students are taught has value for future application and furnishes little motivation for students oriented to the present.
2. Marking systems aid teachers in evaluation, but marking based on standards established by a single superior performer influences students to suppress their accomplishments.
3. Teachers who must both instruct and dispense rewards and punishments may become disliked by students.

These defects, according to Boocock (1966), are directly attacked by the use of simulation games. In simulations, a child may play roles that are not restricted to the future or to the classroom. He is not merely carrying out assignments, he is making decisions about how to survive in the simulated environment. However, if he makes mistakes, he does not suffer the consequences—at least not the dire ones that he might face in the real situation. Competition is not merely on an individual basis, and the student may acquire both individual and collective rewards, because he is engaged in a team effort. In fact, playing the game is itself rewarding. Motivation is provided intrinsically. Simulations require self-discipline and self-judging, because the actions of each player determine the outcomes. Students tend to become more responsible and autonomous. The teacher is freed to spend more time with students and to help meet their individual needs. Not only do student interests increase, but it is possible, by the use of carefully designed simulations, to make the experiences appear meaningful to students, not merely seem to be a game.

The University of Tennessee Simulation in the Preparation of Student Teachers

Time compression is important in training student teachers, and many representative experiences must be provided. By using sound-on-film, filmstrips, and cumulative record folders, Donald R. Cruickshank has been able to provide a realistic series of experiences for teachers-to-be. Each participant assumes the role of a newly employed teacher in "Longacre School." He or she is given an introduction to the town and to the school system via a filmstrip with an accompanying narration by the superintendent of schools. Then the school principal orients the newcomer in greater detail to the community, the school, the faculty, and the educational program. He is also provided with all the materials that a new teacher would be given—a faculty handbook, a curriculum handbook, an audio-visual catalogue, and the cumulative records of thirty-one children. The student playing this role of teacher is to become the new fifth grade teacher during the simulations exercises. From the Perceived Problems Inventory, thirty problems have been selected as significant ones in teaching, so these thirty incidents are all encountered by the learner. Ten are viewed on films, and the rest occur as the episodes in which the new teacher is role playing, or they are posed as written incidents. In this teaching environment laboratory, the student teacher is constantly asked what he or she would do, given the circumstances that appear. For example, facing the first class provides an incident. In this film, the children are reading, silently, but one boy yawns loudly, leaves his seat, spends a lot of time sharpening his pencil, making a great display of it. As he returns to his seat, he slams another boy's book shut, so that the boy shouts "Cut it out!" The teacher's voice (on film) is heard, asking the offender to get back to work. Then the boy begins to hum. Again the teacher tells him to stop and asks whether his work is finished. The boy says that it is almost done. He next grabs a neighbor's paper. At this point the film ends. Now the student-teacher is required to give:

1. A definition of the problem.
2. An identification of contributing factors.
3. The task of locating related information, to be found in the materials which have been handed out.
4. Some alternative actions which the teacher might have taken.
5. A choice of more desirable action the teacher might have taken.
6. Some implementing decisions.

(Cruikshank, 1966, p. 24)

Participation in this series of simulations is expected to increase students' skill in problem identification. The requirement of locating data and applying it to the given situation also contributes to teaching skills. The search for alternative actions has the effect of stretching student responses, so that they are not content with pat answers. And because a variety of situations is posed, each different from the example given above, the student teacher becomes vicariously involved in a variety of teaching experiences.

In general, students reported greater satisfaction and ability to cope with teaching problems and preferred the laboratory to beginning actual student teaching two weeks earlier, when given a choice. This set of experiences acted to connect theory and practice more rapidly than would have been the case had they occurred in the real life of the student teacher. It also allowed participants to meet the problems in a more relaxed manner than would have been likely had they been under the pressures of the classroom. (The *adaptation* phase of their teaching-learning design was more carefully controlled. See Reese's model, earlier in this chapter.) The simulations approach is especially valuable for use in remote regions where student teaching cannot possibly be practiced. (Science Research Associates is now offering the entire teaching simulations package.)

Kersh's Simulations

Kersh's simulations for student teachers, conducted at the Center for Teaching Research in the Oregon State System of Higher Education, also use film clips extensively. They stimulate students to enter subjectively into various situations and to make subsequent decisions based on vicarious experience. The student teacher faces a rear-projection screen that shows life-sized images. The film clips present a variety of classroom situations to which the student must react. The system is flexible because the training supervisor uses the student responses or acting out to determine which film sequence, available from three different projectors, will be shown to the student. One sequence, for example, may show the classroom going to pieces as a result of lack of firm direction by the teacher. Or the film may show pupils going to their seats, but then erupting again with new problems, just when the teacher (student teacher) is relaxing his vigilance, or when he is not managing the classroom very effectively.

COMPUTER-ASSISTED SIMULATIONS IN BEHAVIORAL DIAGNOSIS

Diagnostic skill depends on the ability to make accurate predictions or to generate relevant hypotheses and test them. Successful teachers are those who are best able to guess about behavioral patterns in students in relation to acts of teachers. Student teachers are provided with experiences that are assumed to be representative of those that they will meet when they become professionals. However, it is frequently the case that many of the important real-life experiences do not occur, or that they occur infrequently during student-teaching terms. One answer to this limited sampling has been the approach used in *microteaching,* in which student teachers demonstrate their techniques in very brief teaching sessions. They are then constructively criticized by both fellow students and by specialists skilled in noting weaknesses in classroom strategies. The microteaching approach is designed to upgrade the initiated acts of the student teacher, but it usually does not emphasize pupil reactions with the novice teacher, nor does it concentrate on the ensuing interactions.

Simulated experiences requiring decisions by student teachers, or by experienced teachers desiring to enhance their skills, can be provided by a flexible, adaptive machine, such as a computer. An obvious advantage is that no live pupils are required, and key experiences can be repeated so that the teacher may adjust his responses.

Medical schools are already experimenting with simulations in diagnosing various pathological conditions. Medical students, who for various reasons are unable to be actually present when real cases furnish symptoms, may nevertheless profit from questioning a model, in the form of a bank of statements, questions, and hypothetical cases on file in the computer. Similarly, students of teaching may gain vicarious experience of a very condensed sort, by interacting with a computer whose data bank contains statements about the kinds of critical situations and typical professional reactions that a well-trained teacher is expected to acquire.

To fill the computer's data bank with appropriate problems, questions, and corrective answers and alternatives, competent educators must first decide upon the situations that are most crucial, and that are most likely to provide difficulty for the student teacher. They must then either guess at or actually question student teachers to determine the most likely wrong answers that students will give when they are questioned by the computer. Then the descriptions of the situations, the directions and questions to be presented to the student, and the various alternatives and corrections must all be programmed for the computer. Once the computer contains its necessary materials, a student teacher may sit before the keyboard and project himself into a situation that closely simulates a real experience in the classroom—one that he might never meet in a student-teaching assignment, but that could be important for him and for his pupils later in his professional career. Corrections occur on the spot, immediately following upon errors, and the students have opportunities to correct them under nonpunitive, constructive conditions.

SIMULATIONS PROJECTS

Wynn (1964) described the use of simulations efforts in preparing students for administrative positions (principal, superintendent, business manager, and so on). A school district is simulated, using a 152-page survey of the school system as a background. Information made available to the student playing the part of the administrator included:

1. A sociological study of the faculty.
2. Personnel records.
3. Chart of class sizes.
4. School directory.
5. Achievement test results.
6. School census report.
7. Staff handbook.
8. Annotated school laws.
9. Board statement of policies and bylaws.
10. Motion picture films.
11. A slide that described the community, the system, and the school.
12. Tape recordings of school board meetings, administrative staff meetings, PTA meetings, and parent-teacher conferences.
13. Other informational bits related to the system.

(1964, p. 171)

The learner first familiarizes himself with the background material, and then assumes the job of elementary principal, or superintendent, and so on, in the make-believe system. He is presented with problem items and must make his decisions as an administrator. He writes up descriptions of his actions for each problem, and these are then discussed and compared by other students.

In teaching basic concepts of international relations, such as balance of power, sovereignty, and international law, the Lawrence (Kansas) High School used simulations. Ten hypothetical nations were interacting in mock situations closely paralleling actions often found in the actual, modern world. For example, two aggressor nations had decided to conquer a third. But the United Nations intervened when the two attacked, and the aggressors were defeated. But the nation that had received aid from the UN now felt overconfident, having what it felt was unlimited support, so it declared war on a neutral nation. But this, too, was viewed as aggression by the UN, and the attack was not supported. The attack was carried out anyway, but it failed, as the neutral nation was sustained. Two nations applied for membership in the UN, but they were not admitted. This postwar period saw imperialism in the UN leadership, so unanimity was destroyed. The UN even became militaristic, finally declaring war on one of its members. The member nation was defeated, as was another nation that supported it. The UN then formed an effective common market, and the ten-nation world became, in effect, a four-nation one.

Students' interests always are intensified with a realistic simulation, but it is quite important that the experiences met should appear meaningful to them. It should not seem to be merely a game with no human element involved. If the human feelings are lost, then decisions will be made strictly according to logic, and behaviors will become more warlike. Students may easily tend to favor strong, central decision-making processes. Teachers may find that their work increases. They must be alert at each juncture, so that they may furnish proper guidance in the form of cues and prompts to students. Teachers also need to introduce the simulations seriously and help students understand what is to be gained; otherwise, the unstructured atmosphere can promote disorder.

The essence of a workshop as a means of education is found in the commitment of participants to a search for ideas, information, and skills, according to Ramey (1968). But many workshops fail to meet their objectives when the participants are only mildly interested, if at all, in contributing actively. Video taping and simulation can supply the missing elements, providing students a basis for analysis, evaluation, and discussion of the problems that are presented on tape. Case studies often provide rich sources for discussions, but their static presentation does not involve the learner in the process of problem solving. He talks about the case and its solutions in a very objective way—in fact, he is too objective—so that he does not inject his own being into the case. Also, there are disadvantages in the usual role-playing situation. When a player faces situations requiring his spontaneous reactions, he is frequently too embarrassed to respond adequately. He may also face topical areas that are unfamiliar to him, even though he has prepared previously for the experience. And if he is able to enter into the situation, to become subjectively a part of it, it is difficult for him to revert to an objective examination of what it all means.

Ramey used video-tape recordings of student role playing. They had studied a case intensively and, to reduce embarrassment, were recorded with only the players present. Other participants were also given the cases to study, followed by a viewing of the roles as played by their fellow students. The group leader started and stopped the tape according to the perceived needs for discussion about what was being seen. Occasionally group members were invited to clarify what had just happened, to analyze some nonverbal behavior that may have appeared on the screen, or to predict the sequence of events that might be likely to happen next. They tended to inject themselves into the televised images, but they also remained sufficiently objective for discussion of the tape without considering the personalities of the sutdent actors involved.

THE TEACHING PROCESS AND MODELS

Many assumptions have been made without testing what goes on when we engage in problem solving. The use of models and the video-taped analysis of various simulation experiences is likely to improve the teaching process. Already, the learner's behavior has been described in many ways: word and referent associations, sentence comprehension, and even the decision-making model furnished by Woodruff, all of which contribute to an immensely increased understanding of the learner. For such models to be effective, they must be quite specific about the essential details of teaching; then ideas about teaching effectiveness may be tested. But specification of the structure of what is actually being taught is also necessary, for without it, simulation will merely amount to a poor imitation. (However, for a discussion of the degrees of reality in simulation, see Harman, earlier in this chapter.)

Some models can be quite specific but not very realistic. Others may provide a great deal of realism, but do not adequately specify or emphasize the most important processes and details. There are models that are proving themselves useful that are not so concrete as the several herein described. For years, colleges have offered courses designed to help doctoral candidates learn the various steps involved in collecting data and reporting its analysis and interpretation in dissertations. The student is asked to simulate most of the sections, to make up data, and then to write a "baby dissertation." Although this kind of simulation only minimally involves the student in moving through the behavioral sequences, it does require decision making and the exercise of skills that are similar to those utilized in the actual research, analysis, and reporting that are necessary in producing a real dissertation. Recently, the Automata Corporation of Richland, Washington, offered a statistical process simulator. Simulation of abstract properties and processes is not yet common, but the movement is growing. Any projection of trends or extrapolation at least implies a simulation. In the statistics simulator, statistical sampling techniques are used in estimating population characteristics, and then the actual population makeup is reconstructed for comparison.

Digital computers have received widespread publicity in their rapidly expanding roles in education, but less is known about the possibilities being uncovered by analogue computers. But the analogue computer is also a simulations device, because it uses analogies for setting up a direct relationship between some variable that is found in a problem and a physical quantity in the computer. Borko (1962) stated that

> Insofar as one can reduce complex behavioral phenomena to mathematical formulas, whether this involves predicting the behavior of tides or calculating the trajectory of a ballistic missile or rocket, one can, by indirect analogy, solve these problems on a differential analyzer. (p. 29)

Ashby described the progress made in the simulation of a brain, in a series of articles in Borko's book (pp. 452–465), and Yount and De Kock (1968), in "Simulations and the Social Studies," summarized the principles and steps necessary for organizing simulations in the classroom.

Role playing has been successfully applied to psychodrama and sociodrama, but extensive use of it in educational simulations has not yet been accepted or developed. The Yount–De Kock organizational plan seems to imply a certain amount of matching of students to the roles most nearly suited to their needs, but this is not so stated. Assigning responsibility for how hard and when a student will work to that student, and providing depth assignments for the more capable, as well as helping individual students, are all aimed at providing for individual differences. However, it would seem that another step in the right direction would be to plan simulations specifically designed for various remedial efforts, involving interests, and the affective as well as the cognitive domain of educational objectives.

OTHER APPLICATIONS OF SIMULATIONS

The Board of Cooperative Educational Services of Northwestern Westchester, New York, conducts research in computer-assisted instruction, using a games approach for teaching the principles of economics. Elementary school children are given opportunities to make decisions and peck out their answers on a keyboard. Problem situations are posed and the children act out situations as though they were real, but they can proceed at their own rates, as they pretend that they are governing an ancient citystate, for example. The problems gradually increase in complexity, until a child must react to severe crises.

In 1962, Johns Hopkins began a research project that was concerned with the use of gaming techniques in schools. James S. Coleman, James

Principles	Organization Steps
Freedom	
Eliminates typical teacher-dominated class —democratic organization replaces authoritarian organization.	Arrange classroom into activity areas. Divide students into groups.
Interaction Through Involvement	
Group to group. Individual to group. Individual to individual.	Establish point system where individuals and groups receive points representing power and intensifying interaction. Intertwine individual and group grades.
Knowledge	
Basic information necessary for understanding the unit being studied.	Organize knowledge into specific behavioral performances explained to students in beginning of game.
	Design depth assignments for more capable students.
Decision-Making	
By individuals. By groups.	Give student responsibility for deciding how hard he'll work and when he'll do his work.
	Allot sufficient class time for all students to succeed in the basic assignments. Allot sufficient class time for group meetings for group decisions.
Commitment	
Individual learning to care enough to overcome fear of consequences of his actions.	Plan culminating experience allowing students opportunities to commit themselves to action.
	Subtly plan stepping-stone experiences which move the game to the culminating experience.
Teacher Role	
Organizes. Facilitates. Acts as a resource.	Plan the game with extreme care.
	Arbitrate disputes by interpreting game rules.
	Stimulate game movement to culminating experience by using "pressure factors" to insure interaction.
	Help individual students.
	Keep out of the way—let students make own decisions.

(From David Yount and Paul De Kock, "Simulations and the Social Studies," *Innovation in the Social Studies: Teachers Speak for Themselves*, Dale L. Brubaker, ed. New York, Thomas Y. Crowell Company, 1968)

Kuethe, and Sarane S. Boocock first developed a game that simulated a national presidential election, and then they went on to study the relationship between games experiences and intellectual achievement. They also developed new games and materials. Groups such as the Job Corps and 4-H clubs are now using and evaluating the games developed at Johns Hopkins, and some of the games may now be purchased. One of these simulates a community hit by a natural disaster, in which each learner tries to reduce his own anxiety for family members while he also functions in a job that is vital to the community. From six to sixteen students may play the game, which occupies them for from two to six hours. Other games available are "Consumer," "Democracy," "Parent-Child," "Economic System," and "Life Career." Currently being developed are games attempting to simulate a slum neighborhood; various aspects of the high school and the parental and peer influences that obtain there; and a *general* game method, which may be used to teach any topic. This research effort will ultimately result in a detailed teacher's manual being written for each game, along with lesson plans, readings, and relevant materials for enrichment.

Abt Associates of Cambridge, Massachusetts, now develops games or has them developed on order. For kindergarten and elementary school, they have produced eight reading readiness exercises. For elementary social studies, there is the game of "Bushman Hunting" and "Seal Hunting." Two elementary economics games are called "Market" and "Economy." For simulations of problems of urban society, "Landfall," "Neighborhood," and "Pollution" were developed for the Wellesley, Massachusetts, public schools. At the junior and senior high school levels, Abt furnished "Empire" and "Adventuring," which simulate the arguments that arose between England and the American colonies, as well as the inner problems of each country. "Kolkhoz" simulates the operations of a collective farm in the Soviet Union. "Potlatch" aids in understanding the social and economic institutions of the Indians of the Pacific Northwest. "Mathematics" was developed especially for slow learners. College freshmen at Johnson and Wales Business College have been simulating the principles of production and distribution, using the "Manufacturing Game" produced for them by Abt Associates. "Transportation" was developed for the Department of Commerce. A regional transportation system for the Northwest Corridor is simulated, and eighty players are involved, representing different economic and political interests. For training bank employees, there is "Bankloan" and "Adam." Abt also conducts teacher-training workshops in the use of educational games, and SRA booklets on games are furnished by Abt.

The Foreign Policy Association, 345 East 46th Street, New York City, has the most recent comprehensive lists of games in social studies. SRA, Inc., Educational Games Extension Service, collects and disseminates information on the development and use of games, at 259 East Erie Street, Chicago.

The November 9, 1968, issue of *Scholastic Teacher* (both elementary and secondary editions) has a listing of games for social studies classes, language arts, and mathematics. Robert E. Allen, National Games Center, Nova University, Fort Lauderdale, Florida, provides in-service training to teachers, and has the interscholastic academic games "Olympics," and also produces films about games.

Cleo Cherryholmes, of Michigan State University, has developed "Inter-Nation Simulation," published by SRA, as well as a thirty-minute film on it. Hall Sprague and R. Garry Shirts are the directors of Project Simile, Western Behavioral Sciences Institute, 1121 Torrey Pines Road, La Jolla, California. They also issue the *Occasional Newsletter* for subscribers. Elliot Carlson is writing a full-length book on games, and a survey reported by Carlson appears in "Games in the Classroom," *Saturday Review*, April 15, 1967. E. O. Schild and Sarane S. Boocock have written *Simulation Games in Learning*, a collection of articles on the theory of simulations and on research on the value of games in learning (Sage Publications, Beverly Hills, California). Bibliographies on simulations appear in the November, 1966, issue of *American Behavioral Scientist*.

References

1. AASA (American Association of School Administrators), *The Professional Preparation of Superintendents of Schools*. Washington, D.C., AASA, 1964.
2. Abt Associates, Inc., 55 Wheeler St., Cambridge, Massachusetts 02138.
3. Ashby, W. Ross, "Simulations of a Brain," *Computer Applications in the Behavioral Sciences*, Harold Borko (ed.). Englewood Cliffs, N.J., Prentice-Hall, Inc., 1962.
4. Audiovisual Instruction, EDUCOM, April, 1967.
5. Bitzer, Donald L., "An Electronic Teaching Device," *Simulation Models for Education*, Nicholas A. Fattu and Stanley Elam (eds.). Fourth Annual Phi Delta Kappa Symposium on Educational Research, Phi Delta Kappa, 1965.

6. Bogdanoff, E., et al., "Problems and Implications of Simulation," *Simulation, An Introduction to a New Technology*, TM-499, Santa Monica, System Development Corporation, 1960.

7. Boocock, Sarane S., "Changing the Structure of Secondary Education with Simulated Environments," *Educational Technology*, VII (February 15, 1968), 3–6.

8. ——, and James S. Coleman, "Games with Simulated Environments in Learning," *Sociology of Education*, Vol. 39 (Summer 1966), 215–236.

9. ——, "The Life Career Game," *Personnel and Guidance Journal*, Vol. 46 (December 1967), 328–334.

10. ——, "Simulation Games Today," *Educational Technology*, Vol. VIII (April 30, 1968), 7–10.

11. Borko, Harold, *Computer Applications in the Behavioral Sciences*. Englewood Cliffs, N.J., Prentice-Hall, Inc., 1962.

12. Brooks, H. E., et al., "Uses of Simulation in Analysis and Training," *Simulation, an Introduction to a New Technology*, TM-499, Santa Monica, System Development Corporation, 1960.

13. Brubaker, Dale L. (ed.), *Innovation in the Social Studies: Teachers Speak for Themselves*. New York, Thomas Y. Crowell Company, 1968.

14. Bushnell, Don, and John A. Cogswell, "A Computer-Based Laboratory for Automation in School Systems." Santa Monica, Calif., System Development Corporation, March 2, 1961.

15. ——, "System Simulation: A New Technology for Education," System Development Corporation, paper prepared for presentation at American Personnel and Guidance Association Annual Convention, April 17, 1962.

16. Cherryholmes, Cleo, "Developments in Simulation of International Relations in High School Teaching," *Phi Delta Kappan*, XLVI (January 1965), 227–231.

17. Coleman, James S., "Learning Through Games," *National Education Association Journal*, Vol. 56 (January 1967), 69–70.

18. COMSPACE Corporation, Simulated Computer Console, for compressing computer functions while teaching computer programming. 2372 Linden Blvd., Brooklyn, N.Y.

19. Cruickshank, Donald R., "Simulations: New Direction in Teacher Edution," Phi Delta Kappan, 1966, 48:23–24.

20. *Educational Researcher*, "NSF, Computers and Educational Researchers," Number 6, 1968, 5–60.

21. *Educational Technology*, "New Equipment and Materials—Computerized Simulation," Vol. VIII (April 30, 1968), 18–19.

22. Fattu, Nicholas, and Stanley Elam (eds.), *Simulation Models for Education: Fourth Annual Phi Delta Kappa Symposium on Educational Research*. Bloomington, Ind., Phi Delta Kappa, Inc., 1965.

23. Harman, Harry, "Speech Systems Simulation Research Laboratory." Santa Monica, Calif., System Development Corporation, September 1961.

24. Hickey, Albert E., and John M. Newton, "Computer-Assisted Instruction

—A Survey of the Literature." Newburyport, Mass., ENTELEK, Inc., January 1967.

25. Kershaw, J. A., and R. N. McKean, "Systems Analysis and Education," RM-2473-FF. Santa Monica, Calif., The Rand Corporation, 1959.

26. Kopstein, Felix F., and Robert J. Seidel, "Computer Administered Instruction Versus Traditionally Administered Instruction: Economics," Washington, D.C., Human Resources Research Office, The George Washington University, April 1967.

27. Lackner, Michael R., "Toward a General Simulation Capability," *Simulation Models for Education: Fourth Annual Phi Delta Kappa Symposium on Education Research*, Phi Delta Kappa, Inc., 1965.

28. Ramey, James W., "Using Video Tape Simulation to Make a Workshop Work," *Phi Delta Kappan*, XLIX (May 1968), 525–527.

29. Ryans, D. G., "Education Research and Development at System Development Corporation," SP-715." Santa Monica, Calif., System Development Corporation, 1962.

30. Stansfield, David. "The Computer and Education," *Educational Technology*, VIII (May 30, 1968), 3–8.

31. Suppes, Patrick, "Computer Technology and the Future of Education," *Phi Delta Kappan*, XLIX (April 1968), 420–429.

32. Swets, John A., and Wallace Feurzig, "Computer-Aided Instruction," *Science*, Vol. 150 (October 29, 1965), 572–576.

33. Wynn, Richard, "Simulation: Terrible Reality in the Preparation of School Administrators," *Phi Delta Kappan*, Vol. XLVI (December 1964), 170–173.

34. Yount, David, and Paul De Kock, "Simulations and the Social Studies," *Innovation in the Social Studies: Teachers Speak for Themselves*, Dale L. Brubaker (ed.). New York, Thomas Y. Crowell Company, 1968.

11

Some Forward Looks in Education

COMPUTERS AND INSTRUCTION

Although they are still novel, computers have at least been considered by most educators when data processing is required. They are known to be able to store, sort, and furnish great amounts of information from their storage area at remarkable speed. The terms *software* and *hardware* are dropped in casual conversation, and it is known that some sort of recording occurs, via cards that are punched, magnetic tapes, and disks. Some high schools are fortunate enough to be able to offer computer-programming courses that actually use computers. However, many high schools and colleges still do not have computer centers. So rapidly has this area of technology grown that many teachers have had little opportunity to acquire even the terminology. There are those who share the fears of parents who insist that these electronic monsters will dehumanize children. College students may register and sign up for courses by marking in appropriate columns with soft lead pencils on cards that are fed into the computer system. Many feel that the older method, in which they simply wrote a list of courses on a sheet of paper, was better. On the other hand, there is a certain mystique of the whirring machine that seems to hypnotize some individuals so that they will spend hours finding excuses for using a computer!

Probably the best-known function of the digital computer is that of *data processing*. But this is such a general term that it covers a multitude of capabilities. What the layman is likely to mean by it is the function of recording, storing, and retrieving discrete pieces of information according to a planned arrangement. Typically, information is fed into a computer by being typed on what appears to be an electric typewriter. The typing is done in a special code or language, which then activates the machinery so that it records the data on magnetic or paper tape. The data is then available to anyone who types the correct coded "commands" on the keyboard.

Educators have long employed various information-handling processes. They have made lists of words, names, facts, and so on, arranged in alphabetical, temporal, spatial, or other logical order; and they have stored such information in files, journals, books, and libraries. They have made decisions derived from a consideration of facts, rules, principles, and recorded environmental contingencies, and they have taught how to make such decisions. Intelligent decisions ought to be made on the basis of relevant information and should be available with minimum delay when the need exists, so sorting out the information and furnishing it so that it may be acted upon is vital to the decision-making process. Most teachers and administrators must still depend upon their own memories, notes, books, and various library sources, and the mere scanning of these requires an exorbitant amount of time. None of these sources has been eliminated with the advent of computers, but for some users an awesomely efficient scanning device has been available to facilitate the finding and utilization of tremendous amounts of data, often cross-indexed, providing an extension of memory that is well-nigh beyond belief. The speedy sorting and delivery of information by an electronic computer is called *information retrieval*. Without the aid of a computer, a decision maker may sometimes spend so much time seeking out the information he needs for his decision that the time for applying it to the decision has passed before the information can be located. Other time-consuming indexing and calculating processes may have been too burdensome to be worth the effort, or even impossible to carry out within one man's or one research team's life span. Now, with computers often available to students as well as to teachers, theses, dissertations, and other research efforts are being completed that once could not have been attempted.

In a sense, a computer can carry out a self-initiated research task, and it can certainly develop problems involving combinations of factors that would not have occurred to humans, but it is actually the wisdom of the human operator that preplans the operations that the machine can perform. Humans record data in the computer's storage, and humans write up, each step of the way, what the computer is called upon to do with that information and what calculating processes it must carry out. Also, it is the need of the current users that determines whether a given plan of operation (program) is ever followed up. A major problem facing anyone who expects to use a computer as an aid to problem solving and other higher-order functioning is to determine which functions may be best left to humans or to man-machine combinations, and which ought to be assigned to machines only. It is not simply a question of which can do the job best when separate functions are considered. Sometimes a machine can carry out a function more efficiently, but the task is assigned to a man instead, because of various interactional difficulties requiring a flexibility that is not built into machines. An extremely fascinating new set of procedures called *system development* is engaged in task description, task analysis, task allocation, the interactions of components in whole systems (man may be one of these parts), and the regulation of systems by means of continuous self-evaluation and consequent self-modification. Any system, or whole with interacting parts, should be self-regulating when the need is indicated. But regulation of a system is too slow if the feedback or knowledge of its functioning is furnished too late. If feedback is delayed too much, the part of the system in which a source of malfunctioning has been detected may continue to disrupt operations without being corrected. The design of a system is involved when it must be decided as to what type of computer ought to be bought or rented, what jobs it is to be assigned to, whether it can be shared with other systems, and so on. The computer itself may often be used to indicate when and where it ought to be used. Sometimes it is quite difficult to determine whether one is about to attempt to kill a mosquito with a sledge hammer or to slay an elephant with a fly swatter. Small computers may struggle to carry out tasks that are far beyond their capacities. Huge computers, with high speed and great storage capacity, may be wasted on some operations that could be accomplished reasonably well by other means or by the use of a smaller computer.

Programs and Computer Programs

Secretaries and other office workers have indexing systems, so that they may file (store) correspondence and other data in an orderly fashion. They assign letters, numbers, and word combinations to the various headings, so that these symbols will trigger their searching processes, guiding them to the correct information when they seek it. Libraries also have their indexing systems to locate the various cues for narrowing their searches. One of the functions of a *program* is to tell the computer where to search in its storage for the information that the user wants. Symbols are arranged in a series that are plans of action, plans for carrying out a task or an investigation. (If the operator depresses one key, it may mean, for instance, that he is asking the computer to search in its file or storage for all the stored facts concerning the subject that the symbol represents. He may type another word that is a request to the computer to solve a problem based on those facts.) A computer language consists of a standard set of symbols that may be typed by the user to command the computer to carry out various functions. Sometimes the computer language resembles English, whereas for some uses a kind of shorthand may be employed. Thus, users need to know what language is necessary for a particular computer. Business may use one kind of computer language, whereas engineering may use another, and different computer manufacturers make their machines for different languages.

A set of instructions telling a computer what to do is called a *computer program.* Systematically arranged sequences of the materials to be learned that are presented to humans are called *programmed instruction.* Programmed instruction, both as used in teaching machines and in programmed textbooks, has been generally better understood and more frequently available than is computer-assisted instruction. Relatively few computers have been available for instructional purposes. Instead, they have been used to compile statistics for experiments and other research, and to store and index quantities of facts and figures from which the computer can produce those desired in a matter of seconds. Sometimes this informaiton retrieval is a quite simple procedure for the human operator. He simply inserts the appropriate set of commands in the form of a program, and the machine goes into action, typing out the required information. If there is no standard set of commands already available, however, then the operator must write his own program. Because computers have not been mass produced, and their design has been changing so rapidly, the expense has been prohibitive to all but the most affluent users. Now, however, the two methods of instruction—programmed text materials and CAI (computer-assisted instruction)—employ the same kind of instructional materials.

Teachers are apt to think of computer-assisted instruction as a teaching activity only. But because there are several ways in which computers may assist in the instruction process, the term has been frequently broadened to include not only a tutorial function but also the case-study method, gaming (simulations), laboratory simulations, counseling, and library information retrieval.

Even a human tutor cannot adequately analyze the complexities involved in the human learner, who is never quite the same from day to day, or even moment to moment, and what serves as a reinforcer (reward) today may tomorrow be aversive (punishing). But computers, with their ability to store and sort through vast quantities of information, may serve as specialized libraries. Such storage, coupled with the increasing power to become adaptive to the needs of the user (learner), make CAI a force to be reckoned with in future teaching-learning designs. A computer may not only "learn" about a learner, that is, keep an accurate record of his answers, but it also may adjust its own functions according to those answers. And because his responses as fed into the computer are recorded, the computer is not vulnerable to the human error of forgetting.

To be adaptable to the needs of a student, any teaching device must be able to make decisions, not merely on an absolutely mechanical basis, providing information A when question 1 is asked and information B when question 2 comes up, but it must be capable of altering its reactions according to the responses of the learner. For example, it must be able to react to many different *patterns* of student responding, as well as to carry out simpler tasks. It must be able to suit its functioning to variations in human behavior. Future research in CAI is likely both to involve the development of computer processes that are similar to human learning processes and to improve the ability of the computer to respond to various input patterns, a task often called *pattern recognition*. Some progress in pattern recognition has been already made. Vossler (1962) designed a pattern-recognition program that makes it possible for the computer to "learn to recognize" such forms as printed and written letters, cartoon faces, photos, abstract shapes, and even some speech. One limiting factor, however, that will always apply to CAI is that adapting instruction to computer-assisting devices requires a compromise by the human learner and the computer—there are restrictions on how each can behave in interacting with the other. Attempts to make machines imitate human thinking have led to a better understanding of human mental processes, however, and the better human thinking is understood, the more likely it is that adaptive tutorial devices will assume some of the desirable characteristics of human tutors. Computers are also acquiring the ability to *present* or display patterns to their users, as well as to adapt to patterns that are fed into them. For example, voice patterns may be reproduced from a composite of sounds—a step in the direction of obtaining vocal answers to questions put to the machine.

COMPUTERS AND INDIVIDUALIZED INSTRUCTION

Brentwood School

One of the earliest and best known of the successful computer-assisted instruction installations is located in East Palo Alto, California. One hundred and fifty first graders and second graders engage in thirty-minute daily sessions, seated before a teaching machine. Each student faces two viewing screens, similar to those on television sets. When a child is ready, he puts on earphones, picks up an electronic pen, and touches his name with it when it appears on the screen on his right. He then matches pictures that appear on the left-hand screen with words that appear simultaneously on the right-hand one. He is given directions by the voice of his teacher coming in over the earphones, telling him, for example, to touch the correct word and to say it. If he touches the wrong one, he is asked to try again. In addition to the reinforcement provided by correct responding, the child is encouraged by the occasional appearance of his teacher's smiling face on the screen. If he continues to make errors, he may be given remedial instruction in an adjacent classroom. He continues with the lesson, however, as long as he progresses as expected. His next day's assignment will depend on his previous progress. The computer provides the teacher with complete records of all responses the child has made, as well as an analysis of the types of errors and their frequency. Currently, only reading and mathematics are thus taught, although plans include extending the math program to the third grade. One difficulty uncovered is that of reducing teacher conversation. Children become restless when the teacher talks too much and perform better if allowed to branch out into related topics, instead of sticking with assigned lessons. It also helps if they can engage in classroom discussions of points of interest in the computer-taught materials. Already, Brentwood's installation has demonstrated the advantage to be gained when feedback is immediate. In mathematics, for example, a child's incorrect way of solving problems is corrected as soon as he makes an error, without allowing it to be repeated perhaps on a whole page of problems.

CLASS (Computer-Based Laboratory for Automation in School Systems

Individual learning stations may also contain provisions for giving the student a very direct control over his rate of progress. In the CLASS system, described by Bushnell and Cogswell (1961), a student sits before a film viewer, which he controls. He moves the frames of a filmstrip into view according to his own ability to proceed. All items to be viewed have been carefully written, placed in what is expected to be an optimal sequence, and tested and revised, as is the case with a well-written programmed instruction unit. Some presentations require multiple-choice discrimination among five possible alternatives. A key is pressed, indicating the student's choice, and a light inside that key goes on, holding his answer for him, but not yet recording it as his answer. He may still change his selection until he presses the bar marked *enter*, when his choice enters the computer record, and he must go on to the next item. The computer checks his responses, and reports whether his answer is right or wrong by turning on a second light, located just above the key that gives the correct answer. It keeps a cumulative record of each student's performance, including the amount of time taken to make each response, the number of errors made, and the *pattern* of his errors. If his performance falls below a specified level, the pupil is branched to a special set of remedial items for the task on which he is failing. If he performs well on a few of the remedial items, he will then return to the basic series of items. If he does not, he may have to go through an entirely separate routine. If he never has to be given remedial aid, he may even be able to skip some material and to move on rapidly. But even if a student's progress seems to have been satisfactory, he must occasionally evaluate his own degree of improvement. This self-evaluation may reveal some confusion, and if it does, he will be taken to a remedial branch whose criterion level he had seemed already to have met. Auxiliary programs are provided for those who have required excessive remedial work. The auxiliary programs consist of a new series and may include not only a different training approach, but a change in learning media.

The teacher also has a display console, as well as a flexowriter, or teletypewriter device; a multiple-choice set of buttons, similar to those of the students; and a film viewer, which enables him to monitor what the students are viewing. When a student's error count becomes too great, or he takes too long in entering his responses, a light comes on on the teacher's console. He may then switch onto his viewing screen the same display being seen by the student and note the effects of the remedial track through the material to be learned. Later, he talks with the student, perhaps to amplify the topic, and devotes a full class discussion to it, if several students have had similar difficulty.

CLASS also provided a group mode of instruction, in which a television screen and a loudspeaker display information to all students. From the front of the room, the teacher can call up films or other displays. He can also stop the display when desired in order to prompt group discussion. Short filmstrips or sequences can be repeated at his wish, or a particular slide can be selected. His lecture can be interspersed with diagnostic questions, and a printout provided, so that individual or group responses may be seen. If the teacher wishes, a fully automatic mode of instruction can be used, without any teacher intervention. Up to six hundred thirty-five-millimeter slides are available on a random access basis—any slide can be chosen, no matter what its serial location, and it takes no longer than twelve seconds for it to appear.

CLASS can also be used for a system analysis of the entire school system. Such an analysis would seek to answer such questions as:

Who provides what information to whom?
What are the system requirements, i.e., reporting practices, tracking and advancement requirements, equipment utilization, etc.?
What parts of the total educational system are affected by different actions taken by other parts?

(Bushnell and Cogswell, 1961, p. 14)

Suppes (1968) pointed out that a computer can handle two hundred or more students, each at a different point in the curriculum. In a computer-based system, the necessities for effective teaching include:

1. Audio messages under computer control to the student.
2. A typewriter.
3. Graphic and pictorial displays under computer control.

Suppes also listed three levels of interaction between the student and the computer program:

1. Individualized drill-and-practice systems, to supplement the regular curriculum. A two hundred-terminal computer could handle as many as six thousand students on a daily basis.
2. Tutorial systems, responsible for both presenting concepts and developing skill in their uses.
3. Dialogue systems, aimed at permitting the student to conduct a genuine dialogue with the computer.

Synoetics

A computer is to some extent an adaptive machine when used in computer-assisted instruction. Humans and machines learn together, each modifying their responses according to the responses of the other. The Synoetics Laboratory, begun at the University of Wisconsin in 1964, now directed by John J. Lenahan, has as its objective the development of an intelligent system, a man-machine, closed-loop system in which human and computer learn together. An interdisciplinary staff, composed of engineers, computer scientists, psychologists, and educators, is attempting to carry out the design of a system whose components are adaptive to the mutual requirements of man and machine.

Grow

Sylvia Charp and Roger E. Wye (1968) are conducting Project GROW, in which students in the Germantown, Roosevelt, Overbrook, and Wanamaker Schools are learning via computer. Students may respond with either the typewriter keyboard or a light pen—an electronic pointer about the size of a ball-point pen. The central computer schedules the curriculum it offers, distributes materials, and evaluates student and curriculum performance. Any of the participating schools may also ask for additional curriculum presentations from the central computer. A computer unit located in each school, rather than in the computer center, stores on its tapes the performance of specific students, the amount of material that each student has used, the correct and incorrect responses of each, the time required for responses, and the unanticipated responses that are given. At the end of a school day, the computer center forwards to each school the schedule for the next day. Also, the material to be learned on the next day is transmitted to the units in each school so that it may be stored in the recorded memory devices of the local computer.

Printed reports consisting of running records of each student are produced on the teletypewriter located near the computer in each school, and/or on the high-speed printer located at the large central computer facility. Reports are furnished at the end of each instructional period, as well as at the end of each topic, so that a quick look may be taken at the progress of each student. This information is used by the teacher to determine whether a student's schedule ought to be modified. The teacher controls student access to the computer and makes up a student's schedule according to his progress. Ordinarily, eight students from each class work on the terminals (learning-station inputs), while eight others are receiving supplementary instruction from the teacher in conventional fashion.

To furnish the schools with programs is a complex undertaking, requiring the contributions of curriculum workers, coders, programmers, and clerical workers. Also, consultants, such as learning theory specialists, psychologists, and specialists in CAI, are available. Those interested in the research facilities afforded by the project hope to devise strategies on how best to utilize the new media. Questions of special interest include:

1. How much time should a student spend at a single CAI sitting?
2. Which subjects are best handled through CAI?
3. How can the computer be used to support the teacher most effectively?
4. To what extent should other media and media devices be combined with the basic CAI experience?
5. How much and what type of branching is needed?
6. To what extent should remediation and enrichment be used?
7. How do student attention span and motivation relate to CAI in general?
8. What type of response mode is most effective in different situations?

INTERNATIONAL COOPERATION IN CAI

EDUCOM (Educational Communications)

Many institutions of higher learning have allied themselves with an organization called *EDUCOM*. They are dedicated to the utilization of the emerging communications sciences in education. The interests of EDUCOM include library automation, information networks, and programmed instruction. (Membership is open to all accredited colleges and universities in the United States and Canada. For additional information, write to Dr. James G. Miller, Box 625, Ann Arbor, Michigan 48107.) EDUCOM issues bulletins ten times a year describing various research efforts and on-going computer-assisted instructional programs. For example, the March, 1966, issue describes "A Chatty Computer in Room B-3." The computer "speaks to the child," by typing out, "Hello. I hope we will be able to have a good conversation . . . I'm glad to meet you. . . ." (p. 3). The boy then goes on to take various tests, all constructed by his own classmates and fed into the computer. The children are able to feed them into the computer because they can speak to it via Computest, a natural language communication with the computer developed by John A. Starkweather. An advantage in permitting children to make tests is that each child is forced to consider a great many alternative answers that he is willing to consider correct, hence the child must study the material very closely. It also forces him to overcome ambiguity, to be more precise about his questions. (He must know enough to be able to ask relevant questions, of course.)

COMPUTER TRAINERS

Although this book does not discuss the training of computer programmers, it is of interest to note that efforts are being made to attack the problem of a shortage here. Many high schools now include some computer training in their offerings, but most do not. Colleges are beginning to teach more courses in computer use. But computers are still quite complex, difficult to construct, and very expensive, whether rented or bought. Time sharing, in which several or even many users have access to the same large computer almost simultaneously, has lowered costs appreciably. Kopstein and Seidel (1967) have analyzed and compared the economics of computer-administered instruction with traditionally administered instruction and although they must still say that traditional modes are less expensive, they are not pessimistic about future comparisons. "With the assumption that software costs and instructional programming costs can be very widely distributed and become negligibly small, the possibility of CAI at $0.11 per student hour becomes a probability" (p. 27).

However, until costs have actually been reduced substantially, many schools will be without either CAI or courses in computer programming. The Comspace Corporation (2372 Linden Boulevard, Brooklyn, New York) claims to have circumvented the high cost obstacle by developing a machine that acts as a computer trainer, but that is not actually a high-speed computer. It consists of six modules or units, which correspond to the six basic units found in most general purpose digital computers:

1. Core memory (simulated).
2. Program drum.
3. Input unit.
4. Arithmetic unit.
5. Control unit.
6. Output unit.

Lessons are provided describing the functions of each of the units, as well as teaching the operation of this computer simulator. Students learn to develop their own programs, read in information, sort data, transfer data from storage, and read out results, much in the same way they would in using a real computer. An additional advantage is claimed for the training offered in this way—each step is taken slowly, one at a time, with the student manually switching from one operation to the next. This switching would be carried out automatically at high speed in an actual computer, so the student would be unable to stop action to be able to see what happens as it happens.

TEACHER FUNCTIONS IN CAI

The discussion of computer-assisted instruction has not merely been reserved till the last because it is the last word. However, as Gage (1968) pointed out, at least two major problems of ordinary classroom teaching are clearly surmounted by computer-assisted instruction. The problem of *cognitive complexity*—of how the teacher can say just the right thing at the right time to develop a concept or to formulate a theory—can be solved by the working out and the programming in meticulous detail by experts of the necessary elements and relationships. The teacher's memory need no longer fail at a crucial moment concerning some detail, nor need he be at a loss to answer critical questions—the computer handles these matters with no strain. Furthermore, the computer's approaches to the handling of complex concepts can be improved with time, as responses to its presentations are recorded and analyzed. A second problem that is being approached ever more effectively by computers is the *individualization of instruction*, based on the special requirements and levels of pupils. The computer can act as a tutor on a one-to-one basis for a number of pupils almost at the same time. But there is no basis for the fear that teachers may become obsolete. Teachers will still need to use their own unique styles in explaining, in scheduling the computer sessions, in answering the unanticipated questions of pupils, and in assisting pupils to acquire various affective and social learnings.

Teachers will need to engage themselves in the new developments in teaching, whether they are computers or their successors or other innovative media. The computers, at the present state of the art, could easily become the means for state or federal decision making to take control of the schools. The uninterested teacher, who may nevertheless be subjected to the presence of a CAI installation, may find that he is contributing to the dehumanization of the educational process. Teachers may never need to be able to program a computer in the technical sense, but they will increasingly be called upon to control the remarkable powers of a computer in intelligent ways. The alert teacher will not merely sit back and allow the computer to take over. In addition to the functions mentioned in the previous paragraph, the teacher will notice the effects of sound, and its pacing, upon individual students. (Many can listen to and comprehend speech at a greatly increased rate of speed. Some can absorb compressed speech, in which many words of low utility to the sense of the sentence or paragraph are eliminated. Others require slower speeds with no word reduction.) Which work best, still pictures or animation? This may be a question of individual differences that the teacher must analyze. Which kinds of students ought to make what kinds of overt responses, and how long should responding persist for each? Teachers will note differences, using the computer as an aid in analysis. The computer will be used not just because it is available, but because it will become an indispensable tool. Although students generally like to learn via computer, and lower aptitude students are raised to higher levels (Coulson, 1962), they still like to intersperse short computer sessions with discussions and teacher interaction. The teacher using CAI will probably wish to experiment with the amount of remedial, review, drill and practice, tutorial, and interaction learning experiences that are best for each student. Without computer aid, such experimentation would be impossible.

There is probably more interest in the development of creativity in students than ever before. To many, an extremely systematic approach, as in programmed instruction and CAI, is antithetical to creative and original thinking. Bundy (1968) recommended that the extent to which creative thinking can be encouraged in a CAI environment should be a matter for research, implying that CAI does not obviate creative thinking—it provides additional possibilities and facilities for exploration. With adequate advising, a student may be given alternatives seldom open to him heretofore, so that he can follow his own needs and interests—the computer need not interpose artificial limitations.

Coulson (1968) wrote:

any successful application of these [various technological] developments is likely to require a more active coordination role at the state level, and much more cooperation within and among school districts than has commonly existed in most states in the past. (p. 6)

The high cost of some innovations is one reason for cooperative efforts, and the pervasiveness of the innovations, cutting across grade levels and activities, is another. A major cost factor lies in the development of instructional programs and coding them into the computer. Although the idea is futuristic, Rath (1968) posed the possibility that computers may be used in the writing of programmed books or CAI programs. If it ever becomes a reality, such a development would greatly decrease CAI cost.

REGIONAL EDUCATIONAL CENTERS

ERIC

Coulson's suggestion that educational technology will require increased coordination of local, state, and national groups has been paralleled by action on the part of the President's Science Advisory Committee. This committee established ERIC, the Educational Resources Information Center. Eighteen clearinghouses were set up to provide quick, comprehensive sources of information from research in the areas of:

Library and Adult and Continuing Education
    (Syracuse University).
Counseling and Personnel Services
    (University of Michigan, Ann Arbor).
The Disadvantaged
    (Yeshiva University, New York City).
Educational Administration
    (University of Oregon, Eugene).
Exceptional Children
    (National Education Association, Washington, D.C.).
Junior Colleges
    (UCLA, Los Angeles).
Linguistics and Uncommonly Taught Foreign Languages
    (A. Hood Roberts, 1717 Massachusetts Avenue, NW, Washington, D.C.)
Reading
    (Indiana University, Bloomington).
Rural Education and Small Schools
    (New Mexico State University, Las Cruces).

School Personnel
(City University of New York).
Science Education
(John Richardson, 1460 West Lane Avenue, Columbus, Ohio).
Educational Media and Technology
(Wilbur Schramm, Director, Institute for Communications Research, Stanford University).
Teaching of Foreign Languages
(Kenneth Mildenburger, Director, 62 Fifth Avenue, New York City).
Vocational and Technical Education
(The Ohio State University, Columbus).
Teaching English
(B. O'Donnell, Director, National Council of Teachers of English, Champaign, Illinois).
Library and Information Sciences
(University of Wisconsin, Madison).
Early Childhood Education
(University of Illinois, Urbana).

Unpublished conference papers, preliminary project reports, evaluation studies, and other documents of limited distribution are invited at ERIC, as well as the published research reports. In turn, organizations may receive regularly ERIC's notices of new reports.

Regional Laboratories

Laboratory centers have also been established with the stated aim of improving education in each area represented. Twenty of these laboratories are listed, and following its title the concerns and work of each of them is described.

1. Appalachia Educational Laboratory. Concerned, in general, with overcoming the effects of regional isolation, so that good education may be made accessible for every student.
   Charleston, West Virginia.

2. Center for Urban Education. Emphasis on the elementary level of urban education.
   Headquarters—New York City.

3. Central Atlantic Regional Education Laboratory. Main effort spent upon improving educational opportunities in early childhood.
   Alexandria, Virginia.

4. Central Midwestern Regional Educational Laboratory, Inc. Two primary areas: (a) curriculum and instructional systems; and (b) data systems. Saint Ann, Missouri.

5. Cooperative Educational Research Laboratory, Inc. Deals with the definition, development, field testing and dissemination of (a) a program to prepare leaders of teacher in-service education; and (b) a program for preparing evaluators. Chicago, Illinois.

6. Eastern Regional Institute for Education. Concerned with (a) design, development, and testing of prototype school systems; (b) evaluation of educational materials; and (c) design, development, and testing of new curricula. Syracuse, New York.

7. Education Development Center. Four major concerns: (a) curriculum development; (b) teacher training; (c) community educational development; and (d) instructional media. Boston, Massachusetts.

8. Far West Laboratory for Educational Research and Development. Two major areas: (a) teacher education (primary program); and (b) communications (secondary program). Berkeley, California.

9. Michigan-Ohio Regional Education Laboratory. Identifies major educational problems and develops a program for their solution. Encourages wider use of innovations. Detroit, Michigan.

10. Mid-continent Regional Educational Laboratory. Self-directed learning in pupils, as developed by teacher behaviors. Twofold effort: (a) preservice project in urban disadvantaged areas; and (b) in-service training in junior high school social studies. Kansas City, Missouri.

11. Northwest Regional Education Research Laboratory. Three main areas: (a) adoption of innovations; (b) education of the culturally different; and (3) improved education in small schools. Portland, Oregon.

12. Regional Education Laboratory for the Carolinas and Virginia. Concerned with (a) preparation of in-service teacher trainers; and (b) higher education, especially in developing institutions. Durham, North Carolina.

13. Research for Better Schools. Individualizing and humanizing education. Prescribed instruction programs including teacher training, technology, and evaluation.
Philadelphia, Pennsylvania.

14. Rocky Mountain Education Laboratory, Inc. Emphasis upon improving learning environment. Major areas of research: (a) individualization of instruction; (b) media; (c) preservice and inservice teacher education; and (d) affective behavior.
Denver, Colorado.

15. South Central Regional Educational Laboratory. Primarily concerned with compensatory education programs.
Little Rock, Arkansas.

16. Southeastern Educational Laboratory. Emphasis on providing motivations, processes, and improved instructional strategies to cope with educationally disadvantaged.
Atlanta, Georgia.

17. Southwest Educational Development Laboratory. Seeks solutions to problems created by interaction of cultures, via intercultural education.
Austin, Texas.

18. Southwestern Cooperative Educational Laboratory, Inc. Primarily concerned with reading, K–3, especially in intercultural approach with Spanish-

American, Indian, and Anglo cultures.
Albuquerque, New Mexico.

19. Southwest Regional Laboratory for Educational Research and Development. Educational engineering approach to development of improved instruction.
Los Angeles, California.

20. Upper Midwest Regional Educational Laboratory. Teacher competency improved through better articulation of preservice and in-service programs.
St. Paul, Minnesota.

Although the locations of the centers are given, the actual research is being carried out throughout widely scattered areas surrounding the centers. Only one of the laboratory efforts will be described in any detail, the Michigan-Ohio Regional Education Laboratory, whose center is in Detroit.

MOREL

A large-scale cooperative effort, recently attempted by MOREL, the Michigan-Ohio Regional Education Laboratory, has been described by Bright, in the September, 1966, *Phi Delta Kappan* as being dedicated to the following purpose:

> The primary purpose of the regional laboratory is to implement beneficial change in the schools in its territory. The laboratory will identify what it believes are the one or two major educational problems in a region and mount a program to solve the problems. To widen the use of innovations throughout a region the laboratory will, where necessary, utilize research components, demonstrations in local schools, dissemination activities, and so forth. (p. 4)

The statement, of course, includes the general purpose of all of the regional laboratories (often called *research and development centers*). Generally, the aim of MOREL is to develop methods of helping teachers improve classroom instruction, to evaluate those methods, and to make decisions about their effectiveness. What kinds of training designs are being used for this aim? The first consists of *simulations* in social skill training. Within this training design, teachers are learning concepts that describe teaching behavior, they are being provided with opportunities to practice the behavior patterns associated with each concept, and they are permitted to observe other teachers following these patterns. They then discuss with fellow teachers and others whether these patterns are suited to classroom teaching. The second design consists of practicing specified behavior patterns that have been discussed. Patterns are replicated, in microteaching, wherein intensive practice and feedback are furnished. Finally, each pattern is given feedback, which is made possible by the observational technique of *interaction analysis*. Teachers also study four *teaching models* and attempt to improve their own professional competence. Hilda Taba's model, based on ways to improve the thinking skills of children, built around content and how it is taught; Richard L. Turner's model, which analyzes teaching in terms of problem solving, with a focus on diagnostic decisions concerning learning difficulties; Ned Flanders's model, concerned with classroom management and variations in the amount of direct supervision given by the teacher; and the Robert S. Fox–Ronald Lippitt model, aimed at helping teachers analyze teaching difficulties by using the perceptions of all concerned to decide what kind of change is most likely to result in improvement—all are to be provided to teachers, so that each may select the one that has the greatest appeal.

Microteaching Training

Not every person can see himself as others see him, and some of those who can are unable or unwilling to modify their behaviors. Microteaching requires the participants to plan, to teach, to evaluate, and then to repeat the experiences over again, after they have viewed themselves in the mirror held up by fellow students and the others directing their training.

During the *planning phase*, which lasts five to ten minutes, a student plans how he is to teach a selected topic for five minutes. Next, he will *teach* a small group of three to five pupils for five minutes. During this time his performance is observed and recorded. Sometimes only audio tape is used, but video taping is advantageous. The observers, including specialists, analyze the major difficulties and weaknesses shown by the teacher, and during the *evaluation* phase, they select one factor and make suggestions for change. The student then reteaches to different pupils, attempting to improve his performance in that area of difficulty. The microteaching technique proceeds on the assumption that it is poor practice to try to correct many faults at a time. The teach-reteach sequence may be repeated several times, and each time, the student teacher is given a critique, and an opportunity to criticize his own efforts by viewing them as the video tape is played back. Finally, he plans longer lesson sequences with a team of fellow students, and each student teaches and is observed and evaluated by the group. Various methods of evaluation may be used, but one of the most effective methods uses a coding technique, called *interaction analysis*, to be discussed in the next section.

Simulated Social Skill Training

Only a small amount of what the teacher says is concerned with the pupil's ideas and feelings, or with the pupil himself, usually. Regardless of the nature of the content being taught, however, there are specifiable social skills that good teachers use effectively, but that poor teachers fail to exercise to any useful degree. It is MOREL's position that social skill training can be implemented by simulation. First, social skills can be divided into steps, which provide a carefully planned sequence. Second, the interactions that these steps require can be simulated, providing practice for each step. Feedback can then be given, so as to improve performance for each step.

Three classes of social skills are included in the training:

1. Question-asking ability.
2. Responding to pupil statements.
3. Complex teaching strategies.

A simulated social skills training session proceeds as a role-playing exercise, in which one member of the group acts out the specified pattern of behavior. Other members, called *foils*, react to the first one spontaneously. The remainder of the group attempts to analyze what has happened. The director coordinates the entire effort, giving verbal instructions and providing any necessary supplementations. Training groups may range from a membership of four to several hundred. The greater number requires facilities such as overhead projectors and microphones, so that the verbal instructions of the director may be aurally and visually reinforced. Six skills are criticized and subsequently trained:

1. Establishing set.
2. Achieving closure.
3. Recognizing attending behavior.

4. Controlling participation.
5. Building instructional alternatives.
6. Disciplining a class.

Microteaching is said to be useful in training, in supervision, in recording trainee progress, in research, and in prediction and selection. Some advantages are

1. Simplification of the complexities of teaching.
2. Greater control over practice.
3. Increased economy of operation.
4. The opening of new avenues for evaluating training.

Interaction Analysis

Interaction analysis (Flanders, 1967) facilitates the observation of teacher-pupil verbal interchanges, by using a time sampling technique and coding. Observers are trained in the method before they observe a teacher on their own. After this training, their observations, in coded form, are analyzed and placed in the form of suggestions, which will presumably aid the observed individual in modifying his behavior. If the teacher is using patterns of verbal communication that are not consistent with his intentions, he would profit from feedback that reveals their nature. If an in-service training program seeks to develop specified behaviors in teachers, interaction analysis might assist teachers and others in observing the progress made toward acquisition of the desired skills. And the technique can be used to evaluate microteaching efforts. The observer records a code number (1 to 10):

Teacher Talk

1. *Accepts and clarifies the feeling* of students.
2. *Praises or encourages student actions or behaviors.*
3. *Accepts or uses the ideas of students.*
4. *Initiates communication, by asking questions* about course content or procedures, expecting a student answer.

5. *Lectures.*

6. *Gives directions* or orders, which the student is expected to obey.

7. *Criticizes, or justifies his authority.*

Student Talk

8. *Students talk in response to the teacher.*

9. *Students initiate talk.*

10. *Silence or confusion.*

No category is necessarily better than any other. It is the patterning and frequency of categories that is important. By sampling about every three seconds, the observer will have made about four hundred entries in twenty minutes. From these data, a matrix may be drawn up, which will provide a number of possible analyses of verbal communication. A second matrix, after a teacher has evaluated his efforts, may indicate the degree of progress he has made in, for instance, acceptance of the student (or in whatever category he has chosen to emphasize or to change). However, care must be taken to note whether the difference may be due to a change in the kind of learning activity observed rather than in teacher change brought about by training. (The question has also been raised as to whether the behaviors sampled in interaction analysis are those that are most significant for improving teacher-pupil interaction.)

Teaching Models

To further their understanding of the teaching process and to develop suggestions for improvement, teachers in the MOREL project become acquainted with models. Each model is a representation of something, presented in such a way that problem solving is facilitated. It is hoped that the in-service training of participant teachers will be greatly facilitated by the use of the four models. For example, Taba's model can help a teacher in analyzing his own behavior. Turner's model can help him to diagnose the learning difficulties of pupils, and to solve the various problems in teaching. Using Flanders's model, a teacher may develop a strategy of teaching or classroom management, bolstered by a knowledge of interaction patterns in his classroom. The Fox–Lippitt model is expected to show how to analyze perceptual inputs and behavior outputs in a circular fashion, leading to greater understanding and more effective teacher direction.

Taba's Model

Taba's model on the logical processes of children includes ways in which teachers ought to act to assist in the development of thinking skills. It suggests a curriculum sequence focusing upon logical thinking, which utilizes three cognitive tasks:

1. Concept formation.
2. Generalizing and inferring through the interpretation of raw data.
3. The application of known principles and facts to explain and predict new phenomena.

In application, these tasks involve overt actions, covert thinking, and eliciting assistance provided by the teacher. MOREL uses Taba's model by determining what is occurring in the classroom, especially in the teacher's functioning; by developing explanations concerning teacher influence, comparing and analyzing the data observed; and by predicting and testing generalizations about the consequences of varying interaction patterns by experimenting with different teacher roles.

In teacher-pupil interaction, the first step in the sequence is called "drawing out the what's." Questions are asked that bring out the "who," "how," "when," and "where." Next, questions that probe for similarities, differences, changes, and "why's" are asked, to draw out explanations or comparisons. This step extends into an interpretation phase, going well beyond a mere consideration of the data on hand. The third step is aimed at stimulating discovery and establishing generalizations. The teacher probes for those generalizations or consequences that seem to follow from the discussion. He asks questions such as "What does this mean?" and "What will this mean?"

In the MOREL program for assisting teachers to become better teachers via in-service training, it is hoped that similar analyses and generalizations may be drawn about teacher's roles. Consistency between the ways in which pupils may analyze and draw generalizations and the ways in which guidelines for teachers may be provided would lead to teacher self-discovery of roles, and to parallels that teachers may readily recognize and use.

Turner's Model

Turner and Fattu have been primarily interested in developing tests that will determine how well teachers can diagnose the learning difficulties that pupils meet. How competent are teachers in their subject matters, and how well do they perceive the problems appropriate to different teaching situations? Turner first accepted the following as true:

(a) Teaching is a form of problem-solving behavior.
(b) The problem-solving skills of the teacher are acquired through training and experience.
(c) These problem-solving skills may be measured by teacher performance on simulated teaching tasks.
(d) The teaching-task performance of teachers is associated with teacher success.

(*MOREL*, 1967, p. 30)

Later, he modified this position statement by adding

(a) that teaching involves the performance of a body of work tasks the precise nature of which is contingent upon the setting in which teaching occurs;
(b) that both personal-social and problem-solving characteristics of teachers are relevant to performance on these tasks; and
(c) that the relationships between teacher problem-solving performance, the personal-social characteristics of the teacher, and teacher success are mediated by the school setting.

(*MOREL*, 1967, p. 30)

MOREL's report (1967) says that

Turner's approach in the MOREL program would provide a specialized emphasis on the competence of a teacher to perform teaching tasks which are in contrast with the more generalized, content-free orientation of Taba and the more social-skill orientations of the models of teaching. (p. 31)

The social-skill orientations mentioned are those of Flanders and of Fox and Lippitt.

A Model of Variation in Teacher Orientation (Flanders)

Flanders's model suggests three dimensions of classroom interaction. The *first dimension* is the viewpoint that learning goals, when first established, do not specify the tasks clearly for pupils. Thus, teachers need to devise means of making clear to pupils at least the first few steps for beginning the task, and to permit them to believe that they can meet the requirements; pupils also need to believe that the task is a desirable one, and to know roughly what product will emerge from its accomplishment. The *second dimension* concerns the teacher's own behavioral control, so that in the presence of unclear goals he asks more questions, gets pupils to ask more, and then integrates pupil thoughts and feelings into classroom discussions. As evidence of greater clarity of goals appears, he can begin to increase his expressions of opinions, be more directive, and ask pointed questions. The *third dimension* of this model is the shift in the form of the class: it is no longer a single large audience listening to a teacher, but becomes a number of small discussion groups or an even larger number of individuals, doing individual work—a shift that is reinforcing to the changes that brought it about. The authority position of the teacher has greatly subsided, and the learning-activities goal has increased in importance, while the ratio of teacher talk to pupil activity has been greatly reduced. (For further support of this concept, see Flanders [1965].)

The Fox-Lippitt Model

The Fox-Lippitt model is a model of circular process analysis, by which teachers may learn to develop their own *circular schemes,* using their own ideas and concepts. It is a useful model for combining theory and behavior in the classroom. It demands minimal direction, allowing teachers to select the problems and tasks that they themselves feel are of first importance, hence, they may draw their own diagrams for problem analysis. The diagram of such a circular process analysis as it appears in the MOREL report is reproduced in Figure 11.1.
This kind of diagram is useful for determining the points in the illustrated circular process at which change agents may be introduced for solving a problem at hand.

> For example, suppose a teacher is dissatisfied with the attitudes of pupils toward the teacher, at what logical point in the chain of circular events can one intervene with the best possible chance of altering attitudes? What kinds of intervention are possible? How does one choose among alternatives? and so on. (MOREL, p. 34)

Computer Applications in the Regional Educational Laboratory

The techniques of interaction analysis can be usefully applied to Taba's model in facilitating a detailed tabulation of teacher-pupil interactions. Interaction analysis has also been applied to microteaching, as one means

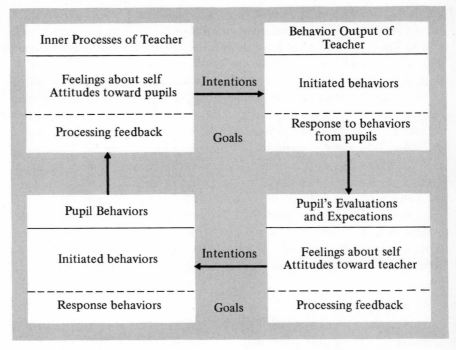

Inner Processes of Teacher		Behavior Output of Teacher
Feelings about self Attitudes toward pupils	Intentions →	Initiated behaviors
Processing feedback	Goals	Response to behaviors from pupils

Pupil Behaviors		Pupil's Evaluations and Expecations
Initiated behaviors	← Intentions	Feelings about self Attitudes toward teacher
Response behaviors	Goals	Processing feedback

Fig. 11.1. Diagram of One Possible Circular Process Analysis. (Reprinted with the permission of the publisher from Matthew Miles, Editor, *Innovation in Education* [New York: Teachers College Press], © 1964, Teachers College, Columbia University.)

of preparing the student teacher for a reteaching session. However, the manual coding of responses at three-second intervals, followed by a hand-drawn analysis and a matrix of response patterns can become time consuming and cumbersome. The value of this kind of feedback to the teacher and to teacher supervisors is greatly enhanced if it comes very soon after the teaching period has been completed. A computer, in the time-sharing mode, can be fed the responses via push buttons in several classrooms almost simultaneously, and the various teacher and pupil verbal communications will be analyzed and placed in matrices almost the instant the teaching session has ended. MOREL plans to utilize computer facilities to assist in analysis and feedback.

College Professors in Public Schools

The concept of the college professor as a scholarly gentleman in an ivory tower is rapidly changing. If regional efforts such as that of MOREL receive adequate financial support, it seems likely that professors of education will at least be given leaves of absence to enable them to work with laboratory staff on inservice training projects. The advantage of such a liaison is twofold: it will provide knowledge and skills to bolster the in-service training programs in the public schools, and it will utilize professorial abilities to develop new and different approaches to classroom instruction.

It is not merely fashionable to participate in team efforts to educate; the new forefronts of education make it very nearly imperative. As Trump insists, change is inevitable, and change is being thrust upon modern society at an accelerated rate. Education has struggled valiantly to catch up with the changes brought about by technology, but it needs to keep abreast of changes, or even to outstrip them, because education is the key to intelligent control. An economy is no longer acceptable that uses education to patch up deficiencies with efforts that look at the tools available to locate uses for them, rather than to cast about for the tools that are needed for a predesigned program.

THE PROFESSIONAL EVALUATOR

Not very long ago, a test was just a test, constructed primarily as an aid to teachers in assigning marks. Some teachers have felt that tests could also be used to help pupils evaluate their own efforts, but general use of evaluative instruments has been largely confined to the teacher side of the desk until recently. Now come the educational technologists who point out the importance of evaluation in shaping the curriculum design. The team involved in a system must coordinate its efforts within the new designs. The need for coordination is readily apparent when Reese's model is closely examined. Sorenson, in *Evaluation Comment* (1968), predicted that a new profession is emerging, that of the professional evaluator. Although there are difficulties that stand in the way of setting up absolute standards for the evaluation of either pupils or teachers, the professional evaluator will nevertheless be a valuable adjunct to education. His will not be a dictatorial role, but rather, he will help teachers and administrators to define their goals in terms of pupil performance. To avail themselves of his services, teachers will need to learn about writing behavioral objectives, basing them upon some kind of hierarchy of learning complexity, such as that found in Bloom's taxonomy. They will also need to learn to use more the sophisticated instruments invented by the evaluators, including criterion-referenced devices that measure *what* rather than *how much* (or how little) a person knows, in relation not to others in his class or group, but to the learning objectives. A second area of additional instruction for teachers will include teaching them systematic ways of discovering differences among pupils *that will require particular kinds of instruction*. Much is being said about the importance of recognition of individual differences, and it is admitted that provisions should be made for them, but too often little more is done than to establish groupings, or to provide some measure of self-pacing, or perhaps, to use textbooks of different levels of reading difficulty.

The analysis of individual differences, as taught by the professional evaluator, would include an examination of the interferences or blocks to learning, as well as the mere fact and amount of individual differences. He will seek answers to such questions as these:

1. How does the student arrive at his misconceptions and what are they?
2. What kinds of habits are holding up the learner's progress (such as failure to pay attention)?
3. What kinds of needs is he satisfying rather than learning (such as the need for group approval or the response to group pressures)?
4. Are there attitudes originating in class background and ethnic considerations, which are inhibiting learning?

Sorenson's point in connection with many of the subtle individual differences is that without sophisticated instruments for measuring and analyzing them, the teacher may assign causation where it does not belong. The professional evaluation, if available, however, could aid in the diagnostic function of the teacher.

Another important role of the professional evaluator would be to help teachers determine which instructional procedures are bringing about the most desirable returns. The research and development specialist is too often found outside the public school, publishing his ideas in the professional journals without interpreting them in terms of usefulness to teachers. The gap coud be bridged between the laboratory and the areas of application by the professional evaluator.

Another concept furnished by the emerging interest in technology and its teams of collaborators is that of learning for mastery. There is enough of the old in this new idea to elicit the comment, "So what else?" but enough of the new is here to merit pause for consideration. Bloom (1968) called attention to a source of wasted abilities: students who are below established cutoff lines of achievement. Teachers expect only a third of their students to learn adequately; another third will do fairly well; and a lower third will fail or just barely make it. But this manner of predicting outcomes, merely assigning letters or numbers that label *failure,* lowers aspirations (Beyers, 1958 and Child and Whiting, 1949), damages self-concepts and interpersonal relationships, and limits the goals of both teachers and students. Bloom opined that most students can master the appropriate subject matter, if a strategy can be developed for determining how individual differences can be related to the learning and teaching processes.

In addition to the immediate frustrations brought on by failing to achieve, today's student will be handicapped at an accelerated rate throughout life, because today's life patterns include learning that is continuous and necessary with a greater urgency than ever before. If success begets success and nurtures interest and sustained motivation, then it is especially important that pupils become successful—not merely in hedonistic pursuits and the ability to get along with others, but in developing adequate value systems in connection with the world of ideas and of self-development.

Bloom agreed with Carroll (1963) that all students can achieve mastery of a given task, if given sufficient time, but he added that there is, perhaps an upper 5 per cent who will not only achieve mastery of the given task, but achieve it at a higher level of complexity. Also, there may be 5 per cent or fewer who have special disabilities for a particular learning. For the 90 per cent remaining, the so-called A level of learning is within reach under appropriate conditions. Thus, *aptitude* for learning is a basic factor, but the degree to which the presentation, explanation, and *ordering of elements of the task to be learned approach optimum for a given learner is also* extremely important. *Ability to understand instruction* is not only a function of verbal ability and reading comprehension, but of modifications in instructions aimed at meeting the needs of individual students. Carroll also found that *perseverance*, or time willingly spent in learning, appears to be related to attitudes toward and interest in learning. Although the teaching situation is likely to exert little direct control over perseverance in learning, frequent feedback along with timely assistance may reduce the amount of perseverance necessary. Finally, *time* is the key to mastery, as far as Carroll is concerned. Although aptitude for learning may determine the individual rate of learning, most students can achieve mastery, given sufficient time. (And the amount of time needed will be affected by aptitude, verbal ability, the quality of instruction, and other assistance received.)

Bloom's Model for Mastery Training

On the basis of Carroll's work and studies carried out by Bloom and his associates, Bloom outlined a set of strategies for the achievement of mastery for 95 per cent of the students, excepting those with serious defects:

I. *Preconditions*
   a. Objectives are to be clearly defined.
   b. Content of instruction is to be made explicit.
II. *Operating Procedures*
   a. Regular instruction, using usual methods. (Until newer methods, based on diagnosis of individual needs can be widely implemented, it is thought best to use mastery training strategies in conjunction with regular instruction.)
   b. Supplementary instructional resources. Break up the course into smaller units (perhaps involving a week or two of learning activity). Analyze each unit into elements, ranging from specific terms or facts to more complex and abstract ideas such as concepts and principles, and then go on—to relatively complex processes, such as application of principles and analysis of complex theoretical statements. Use brief diagnostic-progress tests, for the purpose of: pacing learning; motivating students; focussing effort at appropriate times; ensuring mastery at each step; diagnosis of difficulties; prescription of additional aid. (Tests are to be graded only according to "mastery" or "nonmastery.")
   c. Alternative learning resources. Specific suggestions are given. Two or three students meet regularly for perhaps an hour per week to review results of their formative

evaluation tests—and to help each other overcome difficulties which are revealed.

Certain pages are reread.

Alternative pages are read and studied in alternative books.

Specific pages in workbooks or programs are read.

Selected audio-visual materials are used.

d. Outcomes.

Cognitive outcomes. When deficiencies are noted, they are compensated for by different strategies for mastery, with selection of strategy depending on individual need. Affective outcomes. Interest in the subject and increase in positive aspects of self-concept result from public and private recognition.

(Bloom, 1968)

Computer Aid

Classroom teachers and others may (rightly) object that such extreme concern for and attention to mastery for every pupil is an ideal that cannot be even approximated in the usual classroom. They fail to see the futility of trying to teach what they know will not be learned. Nor do they conceive of any other setting than "the usual classroom." They see these classrooms filled to overflowing with pupils showing an ever-widening range of aptitudes and interests, and they cannot conceive of rooms in which mastery is the constant and time the variable. However, the advent of the professional evaluator, along with the remarkable versatility of computer assistance, seems likely to usher in a great many heretofore impractical approaches to excellence in learning. If there are too many factors in individual learning styles, in aptitudes, values, backgrounds, aspiration levels, and frustration tolerance levels for one teacher to cope with, these inputs will be easily sorted and integrated into useful patterns by the computer. The professional evaluator will then make individual prescriptions, based on these patterns. Admittedly, the ability to note individual differences has outstripped the ability to prescribe for them, but the means for prescribing and strengthening are appearing. A by-product of rapid change has been the recognition that the nature of changes themselves often brings with it the means for dealing with change. McLuhan's insistence that the medium becomes at

least as important as the context; and Stufflebeam's utilization of evaluation, not merely as an after-the-fact assignment of worth, but rather
as applications from the outset of studied effects on decision making,
tend to raise educational sights and present new horizons. Ferster (1968),
along with Bloom, has insisted that the time consumed, rather than the
degree of mastery, should be used as a criterion of learning excellence.
Closer looks, broader interpretations, concerning what had been considered only peripheral attachments to the business of educating, are implementing automated devices, and are, in turn, being implemented by
them.

In-House Education

There is a rapidly growing trend, not only toward continuing (adult)
education, but toward the provision of education in-house, i.e., within
the building where one works and toward the use of visiting instructors
who hold seminars in business and industry on a package basis. For
example, the Industrial Education Institute in Boston conducts one-day
seminars on such subjects as "How to Prepare and Deliver Effective
Oral Presentations," somewhat along the lines suggested by Gilbert
Highet, but with an updated approach. Current audio-visual aids are
utilized, there are team presentations, and techniques of making speeches
are fitted into appropriate segments of the seminar. Literally hundreds
of companies have already participated in such seminars. Auto manufacturers not only utilize computers for their record keeping, but their
employees are instructed in the use of the computer by instructions
presented by that computer. The Philco-Ford system allows employees
at widely scattered points throughout the United States and abroad
to sit before the computer keyboards and obtain expert guidance without the immediate presence of experts.

Futuristic Ideas

With the continuing explosion of knowledge, and of persons needing
to acquire still more, the question of *what* is to be taught vies in importance with *how* it is to be taught. Kurland (1968) and Young (1967)
averred that there will be continuous education programs throughout
the day and year. The scheduling of the elements of those programs
will be determined by both the learner's needs and those of society. The
school may be like the public library, with each user entering with his
own requests, and each being accommodated, but with no two persons

being served in quite the same way. Age and grade divisions will have no meaning, and an adult and a child may sit down together to use the same medium for the same content. However, this librarylike learning center would not presume to meet all the user's demands—there would be other agencies.

As long as teachers are accepted merely as specialists in school subjects, the interrelationships among the different parts of a student's behavioral repertoire may not be recognized. As long as people place the emphasis on knowing, in order to teach, and upon teaching, rather than teaching for what end, then system designs and improvements in techniques of communication will not be in their proper perspective. As long as these blocks to progress remain, subject-matter "experts" will still show their arrogance by turning their backs on technological change (Kurland). In the future, students will not only learn according to their needs, they will seldom need the teacher who cannot manage learning resources. Grouping will be based on needs, so that sometimes one student will be learning with no adult present; sometimes one thousand students will be grouped with one adult; there may be a one-to-one, tutorial situation; and, occasionally, one student may confer with several adults. The dropout problem is likely to become a very minor one, because if a student does not learn well under a given program, he need not quit, but move to one better suited to his needs, interests, and abilities.

According to Young (1967), whatever the content of the new educational programs, they will be a part of a cybernetic, self-correcting system. The system will be comprised of component functions mentioned earlier in this book, and reviewed in general here as Young applies the system.

The system will

1. Assess the needs of the individual, making tentative decisions about his needs.
2. Create the environments and elements of the learner's program.
3. Evaluate the success of the system.
4. Redesign programs, to correct for the failures and move toward new learnings.

Komoski (1966) envisions a nationwide network of schools, using the products of technology, feeding back information as to product-performance, and being furnished with information about new product possibilities. It is difficult to imagine such a network in operation without the aid of a computer or whatever will supplant the computer as it now exists. Kurland has made fitting comment on the impact of technology on education:

> I believe that what we do *can* influence the outcome. The role of technology in education is now being *invented*. Decisions now being made will influence the way in which it will be introduced and used in education. If educators abdicate their roles in making these decisions, they will be made, but they will be made by industry people, by businessmen, by government people, and by others—they won't be made without the involvement of educators, but they can be. Or this process could be left to chance. I think it is absolutely vital and essential that the educators be involved. (1968, p. 15)

References

1. Allen, Dwight W., "A New Framework for In-service Education," *MOREL Annual Report*, Vol. II, September 1967.
2. Beyers, J. L., "An Investigation of the Goal Patterns of Academically Successful and Unsuccessful Children in a United States History Class," unpublished master's thesis. Madison, Wis., University of Wisconsin, 1958.
3. Bloom, Benjamin S., "Learning for Mastery," *Evaluation Comment*, May 1968, Vol. 1, No. 2.
4. Borko, Harold (ed.), *Computer Applications in the Behavioral Sciences.* Englewood Cliffs, N.J., Prentice-Hall, Inc., 1962.
5. Bright, R. L. (Interview), "The USOE and Research in Education," *P.D.K.*, September 1966, 2–5.
6. Bundy, Robert F., "Computer-Assisted Instruction—Where Are We?" *Phi Delta Kappan*, XLIX (April 1968), 424–429.
7. Bush, Robert N., and Dwight W. Allen, "Micro-Teaching: Controlled Practice in the Training of Teachers," *MOREL Annual Report*, Vol. II, September 1967.
8. Bushnell, Don, and John A. Cogswell, "A Computer-Based Laboratory for Automation in School Systems," SP-256. Santa Monica, Calif., System Development Corporation, March 2, 1961.
9. Carroll, John A., "A Model of School Learning," *Teachers College Record*, Vol. 64 (March 1963), 723–733.
10. Charp, Sylvia, and Roger E. Wye, "Philadelphia Tries Computer Assisted Instruction," *Educational Technology*, VIII (May 15, 1968), 13–15.

11. Child, I. L., and J. Whiting, "Determinants of Level of Aspiration: Evidence from Everyday Life," *J. Abn. Soc. Psychol.*, Vol. 44, 305–314.

12. *Computers in Higher Education.* Washington, D.C., U.S. Government Printing Office, Division of Public Documents.

13. Comspace Corporation, "The Craft of Computer Technology," a training course that provides both books and a simulated computer. Comspace Corporation, 2372 Linden Blvd., Brooklyn, N.Y.

14. Coulson, John E., et al., "Effects of Branching in a Computer Controlled Autoinstructional Device," *Journal of Applied Psychology*, Vol. 46 (December 1962), 389–392.

15. ———, "Technology and Educational Planning," *Educational Technology*, VIII (February 28, 1968), 3–7.

16. *EDUCOM*, Bulletin of the University Communications Council, Box 625, Ann Arbor, Mich. 48107.

17. *ENTELEK, Computer-Assisted Instruction Guide.* Newburyport, Mass., ENTELEK, Inc., 1968.

18. Ferster, C. B., and Mary C. Perrott, *Behavior Principles.* New York, Appleton-Century-Crofts, 1968.

19. Flanders, Ned, "Interaction Analysis and Inservice Training," *MOREL Annual Report*, Vol. II, September 1967.

20. ———, *Teacher Influence, Pupil Attitudes and Achievement*, U.S.O.E. Cooperative Research Monograph #12 (OE-25040), U.S. Government Printing Office, Washington, D.C., 1965.

21. Fox, Robert S., and Ronald Lippitt, "The Innovation of Classroom Mental Health Practices," *Innovation in Education*, Mathew B. Miles (ed.). New York, Bureau of Publications, Teachers College, Columbia University, 1964.

22. Gage, N. L., "An Analytical Approach to Research on Instructional Methods," *Phi Delta Kappan*, Vol. XLIX (June 1968), 601–606.

23. Gleason, Gerald T. "Computer-Assisted Instruction—Prospects and Problems," *Educational Technology*, VII (November 15, 1967), 1–6.

24. Hickey, Albert, *CAI: A Survey of the Literature.* Newburyport, Mass., ENTELEK, Inc., 1968.

25. Komoski, P. Kenneth, "Assessing Educational Technology," *Educational Technology*, VI (October 30, 1966), 1–6.

26. Kopstein, Felix F., and Robert J. Seidel, "Computer Administered Instruction Versus Traditionally Administered Instruction: Economics," Washington, D.C., Human Resources Research Office, The George Washington University, April 1967.

27. Kurland, Norman D., "The Impact of Technology on Education," *Educational Technology*, VIII (October 30, 1968), 12–15.

28. *MOREL Annual Report*, Vol. II, MOREL Program, September 1967. The Michigan-Ohio Regional Educational Laboratory, Detroit, Mich. 48201.

29. Rath, Gustave J., "Non-CAI Instruction Using Computers and Non-Instructional Uses of CAI Computers," *Educational Technology*, VIII (February 15, 1968), 11–13.

30. Scriven, Michael, "The Methodology of Evaluation," *Perspectives of*

Curriculum Evaluation, R. Stake (ed.). Chicago, Rand McNally & Company, 1967.

31. Skinner, B. F., *The Technology of Teaching*. New York, Appleton-Century-Crofts, 1968.

32. Sorenson, Garth, "A New Role in Education: The Evaluator," *Evaluation Comment*. Los Angeles, Calif., Center for the Study of Evaluation of Instructional Programs, U.C.L.A., January 1968.

33. Stufflebeam, D. L., "Evaluation as Enlightenment for Decision-Making." Columbus, Ohio, Evaluation Center, The Ohio State University, 1968.

34. Suppes, Patrick, "Computer Technology and the Future of Education," *Phi Delta Kappan*, XLIX (April 1968), 420–423.

35. ———, M. Jerman, and B. Brian, *Computer Assisted Instruction at Stanford: The 1965–66 Arithmetic Drill-and-Practice Program*. New York, Academic Press, 1968.

36. Taba, Hilda, *Teaching Strategies and Cognitive Functioning in Elementary School Children*, Cooperative Research Project No. 2404. San Francisco, San Francisco State College, February 1966.

37. ———, and J. L. Hills, *Teacher Handbook for Contra Costa Social Studies, Grades 1–6*. San Francisco, San Francisco State College, 1965.

38. Turner, Richard L., "Characteristics of the Beginning Teacher; and Differential Linkage with School System Types," *School Review*, Vol. 73 (Spring 1965), 48–58.

39. ———, and N. A. Fattu, *Skill in Teaching, a Reappraisal of the Concepts and Strategies in Teacher Effectiveness Research*, Bulletin of the School of Education. Bloomington, Ind., Indiana University, No. 3, May 1960.

40. Vossler, C., "Computer Simulations of a Perceptual Model for Sensory Pattern Recognition," *Proceedings of IFIP Congress of 1962*, Amsterdam, N. Holland Publishing Co., 1962.

41. Young, Milton A., "What Education Can Be Like in the Future," *Educational Technology*, VII (February 28, 1967), 1–10.

Index of Names

Subject Index

Time sampling (Flanders), 305, 306
Timing of instructional units (Searles), 137–139
Tradition in schools as motivational, 208
Transactional approach to teaching, 131
Transfer
  as application, in cognitive domain, 80
  interference with, 81
  and perturbed feedback, 233
  wholes, emphasis on (Putnam), 32
Translation, in cognitive domain, 80
Transliminal chamber (Rugg), 188
Transmission system to evoke creativity, 235
Tutorial method of communication, 205, 206
  appreciation of wholeness, 206

creation, 206
criticism, 206

Unity, in Froebel's method, 27

Values, changing (DeCarlo), 260, 261
Variables
  central, 6
  complex, in teaching functions, 70
  dependent, in teaching, 61
  independent, in teaching, 61

Work, satisfaction in, as motivational, 261